Stamps & Stories

The Encyclopedia of U.S. Stamps

Stamp quotations and other philatelic reference material reprinted from the Scott U.S. Specialized Catalogue, 1981 Edition and the Scott Standard Postage Stamp Catalogue, 1982 Edition.

Copyright © 1981 U.S. Postal Service
The Stamp numbering system, monetary value assigned to each stamp, and certain quotations contained herein are owned exclusively by Scott Publishing Co. © 1980, 1981. All rights thereto are reserved by Scott Publishing Co. under Pan American and Universal Copyright conventions and such materials are reproduced and used herein under license from Scott Publishing Co.

The designs of stamps and postal stationery issued since January 1, 1978, are the subject of individual copyrights by the United States Postal Service.

Library of Congress Catalogue
Card Number 81-52679

ISBN: 0-960-4756-1-3
Printed in the United States of America

United States Postal Service, Washington, D.C. 20260

Item No. 926

How to Use Stamps & Stories

Stamps & Stories is a color catalogue of postage stamps of the United States. This illustrated catalogue has been designed to put all the vital information you need in one, handy reference line.

Each line listing in Stamps & Stories contains the following information:

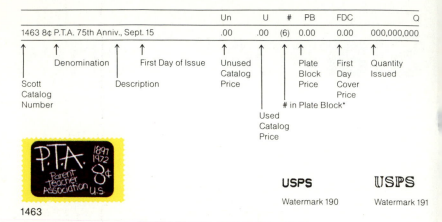

			Un	U	#	PB	FDC	Q
1463 8¢ P.T.A. 75th Anniv., Sept. 15			.00	.00	(6)	0.00	0.00	000,000,000

- ↑ Scott Catalog Number
- ↑ Denomination
- ↑ Description
- ↑ First Day of Issue
- ↑ Unused Catalog Price
- ↑ Used Catalog Price
- ↑ # in Plate Block*
- ↑ Plate Block Price
- ↑ First Day Cover Price
- ↑ Quantity Issued

USPS
Watermark 190

USPS
Watermark 191

1463

*All Plate Blocks are blocks of four unless otherwise indicated in parenthesis.

Stamps & Stories also lists philatelic details such as watermarks, perforations, and years of issue. These will aid you in identifying stamps of similar design. Watermarks (Wmk.) are designs incorporated in the paper on which certain stamps are printed. (Please refer to sample illustrations on this page for stamps marked as Watermark 190 or 191.) Perforations are the number of small holes in a two centimeter space on the edge of the stamp. A stamp which has 12 such holes is listed as Perf. 12 (perforated 12), while a stamp with no perforations is listed as Imperf. (imperforate). Coil stamps are perforated on two sides only, either horizontally or vertically. **When a perforation, year of issue, or watermark is mentioned, the description applies to all succeeding issues until a change is noted.**

Illustration Numbers. Some of the stamps catalogued in this book are not shown. The illustrations on such stamps are identified by a number in parenthesis. For example, in the listings which appear below, Scott No. 247 has the same illustration as Scott No. 246.

246	1 ¢ Franklin	0.00	0.00
247	1 ¢ blue Franklin (246)	00.00	.00

How to Order Stamps. When ordering stamps from a dealer, identify items wanted by country of issue, Scott No., and condition (unused or used).

Condition is an important factor of price. Prices are for stamps in fine condition. Off center, heavily cancelled, faded or stained stamps usually sell at large discounts. Values in italics indicate latest auction prices, infrequent sales, or fluctuating market values.

TABLE OF CONTENTS

INTRODUCTION TO STAMP COLLECTING

Philately, according to the dictionary, is the collecting or study of stamps. A philatelist is someone who does one or both of these. It's estimated that 20,000,000 people in the United States fit that category, pursuing what is said to be the world's most popular hobby. You begin your collection by saving the stamps from mail delivered to your home or you can go to your local post office and buy each new issue of stamp as it is released. You can trade with people who collect, join a stamp club, or buy from stamp dealers.

Whatever your collecting area, you will find that these colorful bits of paper capture the spirit and history of their place of origin. To look at them is to take a journey into the history of man and his accomplishments.

Philately is educational, inspiring, enjoyable and entertaining. Stamps and stamp collecting will provide you with a fun-filled way to use your leisure time.

How to Begin. There are many ways to collect. You can collect a specimen of each stamp issued by a country. You can expand on that and collect the various varieties of such stamps. Varieties are subtle differences in color and design or perhaps perforations. You can collect stamps "on cover"—that is the entire envelope containing the stamp, the postmark and the cancellation, showing how and where it went on its assignment to deliver the mail.

Topical collecting is very popular today. To form such a collection you should choose a subject or topic that interests you . . . sports, music, animals, ships, for example. If you have chosen one that is broad enough, you will find it quite easy to create a fascinating and personally meaningful collection. Many groups of specialized topical stamp collectors have prepared lists of stamp issues dealing with their subject, and these lists can easily be obtained to help you in starting.

Equipment. As with most hobbies, to enjoy them fully you must have the proper equipment. Stamp collecting is no exception. To get started, you should acquire an album to keep your stamps in, stamp hinges or stamp mounts to hold them in the album, and a pair of tongs so that they can be handled without damage. A magnifying glass helps to see important details.

Albums. Albums on the market are geared for every pocketbook, every taste, every specialty. Choose yours wisely and well. Make sure your album is well-illustrated on pages of good quality paper. Make sure the album is designed to do what you wish it to do. Albums with looseleaf pages are good because they allow for convenient expansion of your collection.

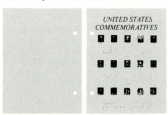

Types of Stamps. You may limit your collection to a simple type of stamp or to stamps of any kind. Stamp issues are normally divided into the following types:

Regular or Definitive Stamps. These are the stamps you'll find on most day-in, day-out mail. They are printed in huge quantities and are kept in use by the post office for sizable stretches of time—several years, usually. Definitives usually appear in a series, with values from 1 cent to higher values, say $5.00, with as many intermediate values as are needed for the postal rates then in effect.

Regular or Definitive

Commemorative Stamps. These are issued to honor an important event, person or special subject. They are usually larger than the definitives, more colorful and are circulated for a limited time. Often they depict famous people, but U.S. stamps never depict a living person.

Coil Stamps. These are stamps issued in rolls, so that each stamp has two straight edges and two perforated edges. Many collectors specialize in this type of stamp.

Coil

Commemorative

Air Mail Stamps. Air Mail stamps are no longer issued for postage within the U.S., Canada and Mexico. Some U.S. Air Mail stamps for use in sending mail overseas are still issued.

Postage Due Stamps. Postage due stamps are affixed to mail at the post office to indicate that the prepaid postage was not enough to carry the letter to its destination and more is to be paid for delivery.

Air Mail

Postage Due

Special Delivery Stamps. These stamps are sold to the sender at a premium price to secure extra-fast delivery for a letter or package.

Special Delivery

Mounts and Hinges. Mounts are special plastic envelopes that hold the stamp. Most mounts are pre-glued and can be placed into your album over the stamp illustration. Mounts should be used for never cancelled stamps to preserve their value. For less expensive stamps you can use very low cost stamp hinges. If you use hinges, fold back about one fourth of the hinge with the sticky side out. Moisten the folded-back part lightly and place it on the back of the stamp, centered at the top. Then, holding the hinged stamp with your tongs, moisten the bottom part and fasten the stamp in position on the album page.

Other Tools. As you progress, there are other tools you will want. The perforations found around the edges of a stamp can often be the sole means of determining the difference between two similar stamps. A gauge to measure the size and number of these perforations is, therefore, a very useful device. The gauge usually contains, as well, a millimeter measurement so that the dimensions of a stamp can be accurately determined.

A watermark detector is useful when the only way to distinguish between two stamps is by their watermarks. Watermarks can often be seen if the stamp is held up to a bright light. To see a watermark clearly and easily you must use a watermark detector. In its simplest form, this is a small black tray. The stamp is placed face down in the tray, a few drops of lighter fluid are poured over it and the watermark becomes visible. Be sure to air-dry the stamp before putting it back into your album and be careful of fire.

Catalogues. Even if you are a beginner, a catalogue is one of the most important adjuncts in forming a collection. The catalogue not only identifies a stamp and its major varieties by color and denomination, but also supplies such information as its date of issue, the method used to print it, and its perforation size and watermark, if any. It identifies the subject depicted on the stamp and often gives the reason for which it was issued. Added to all this, it provides the value of the stamp, both used and unused. The catalogue also contains descriptive identifying numbers for each stamp. These numbers are used by dealers and collectors as a shorthand way of identifying the stamp they wish to buy or sell. For U.S. stamps, Stamps & Stories is a wonderful catalogue that contains all the information needed to learn about and collect these items of American history.

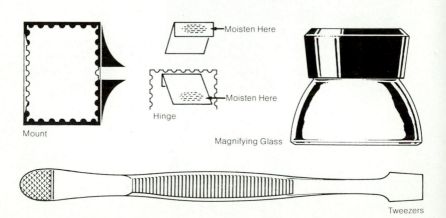

Moisten Here

Moisten Here

Hinge

Mount

Magnifying Glass

Tweezers

DEFINITION OF CATALOGUE PRICES

Stamp collectors use catalogue prices as a guide to help them in buying items for their collections or for the purpose of trading stamps with other collectors. The values for the stamps quoted in Stamps & Stories are taken from the latest issue of the catalogue used by most United States collectors. These price guides will help you to plan your stamp purchases or to evaluate the stamps that you may come across. However, there are a few things about catalogue prices that you must know so you will understand and use them correctly.

Catalogue values are simply guidelines to stamp values. Actual stamps may cost more or less than the values shown in the catalogue. As you may know, one reason for this is that stamp condition (see pp. 12-13) is very important in determining the value of any stamp. The catalogue gives a price for both unused (mint) stamps and for those that have been used or cancelled. In each case, the catalogue value is for a single stamp (except where prices of blocks or sheets of stamps are specifically noted).

Both the used and unused catalogue prices are for a stamp in **Fine Condition** and the catalogue price also assumes that the copy has been hinged. If you want a stamp with **Superb** centering and color that has never been hinged, it could cost several times the catalogue value. But, stamps in less than **Fine** condition or those that have been heavily hinged may be worth only a small percentage of catalogue value.

In the case of used stamps, the catalogue price is based on a light cancellation. Heavy cancellations lessen a stamp's value. Sometimes used stamps, however, are worth more than unused stamps. This frequently happens when the cancellation is of a special type or for a significant date. Of course, this could mean that the stamp is worth more **only** if it is still on the original envelope.

So, if you find old envelopes, be sure to have them evaluated before simply tearing off the stamp and discarding its "cover."

There are other important things that you should know about catalogue prices. One is that they are estimates of how much you should expect to pay for a copy of the stamp from a regular dealer. If you should wish to sell the same stamp to a dealer, he may offer you much less than the catalogue price. The dealer's quote will be based upon his own interest in owning your stamp: he may have a full supply of this stamp at the moment and he will only buy more at a very low price.

Another point about catalogue prices concerns very low priced stamps. Frequently the catalogue will show that a stamp is worth a small or "minimum" value, like $.03. This means that a stamp dealer cannot afford to sell you an individual stamp for less than this minimum amount. However, a packet of stamps made up of numerous inexpensive stamps is not necessarily worth the total of their individual catalogue values.

As a general rule you should try to collect only the best quality stamps. This practice will result in a hobby that can be enjoyable and rewarding for the rest of your life.

STAMP COLLECTOR'S TERMS

Terms to describe condition and color are only a part of the language of stamp collectors. Following is a glossary of basic philatelic terms that every stamp collector should know.

Approvals: Stamps sent to a collector for examination. Approvals must be bought or returned to the dealer within a specific time.

Bisect: Half of a stamp used to pay postage of half the face value of the original stamp. This variety must appear on its original cover with the cancellation or postmark covering the cut.

Block: An unsevered group of stamps at least two stamps wide and two stamps high.

Booklet Pane: A small pane of stamps especially printed and cut to be sold in booklets.

Cachet: A special handstamp or printed device on a cover to denote the special circumstances in which it was mailed.

Cancellation: A mark placed on a stamp by a postal authority to prevent its reuse.

Cancelled to Order (CTO): Stamps which are cancelled by the postal authorities without being sent through the mails. They are normally less desirable than stamps which have served their postal function.

Coils: Stamps issued in rolls for use in dispensers, affixing or vending machines.

Color Changeling: A stamp whose color has been changed, either accidentally or intentionally.

Commemoratives: Stamps which honor anniversaries, important people, or special events. Commemoratives are usually sold for a specific length of time.

Compound Perforations: A stamp with perforations of different sizes on different sides.

Condition: The state of a stamp in regard to centering, color, freshness, cancellation, and other related characteristics.

Cover: The entire wrapping or envelope in which a letter has been sent through the mail.

Cut Square: An envelope stamp cut out with a square margin.

Definitives: Regular issues of stamps as distinct from commemoratives.

Die: An engraving from which the plates for printing stamps can be made.

Errors: Stamps with accidental mistakes in color, paper, inscription, watermark, etc. Errors also include bicolored stamps with inverted centers.

Essays: Designs submitted in stamp form but not accepted for issuance.

First Day Cover: A cover bearing a new stamp and cancelled with the first day of use, usually at an officially designated location.

Flat Press Stamps: Stamps printed on a flat bed press, as distinguished from a rotary press.

Freaks: Stamps which show conspicuous deviations from the normal caused by shifted perforations, heavy inking, color shifts, or similar accidents during production. Not errors.

Grill: Parallel rows of small pyramids impressed or embossed on the stamp in order to break the fibers of the paper so that the cancellation ink will soak in and make washing for reuse impossible.

Gum: The adhesive on the back of a stamp.

Hinges: Small strips of paper gummed on one side and used by collectors to mount their stamps.

Imperforate: Stamps without perforations. They must be separated with scissors and are usually collected in pairs to prove their authenticity.

India Paper: A soft, thin, silky appearing wove paper usually used for proof impressions.

Inverted Center: A stamp with the center printed upside down in relation to the rest of the design.

Laid Paper: A paper showing alternate light and dark parallel lines when held to the light or immersed in benzine.

Locals: Stamps issued for use in restricted areas either by government or private carriers.

Margin: The border outside the printed design of a stamp, or the similar border of a pane of stamps.

Overprint: Any word, inscription, or device placed on a stamp to alter its use or locality, or to serve a special purpose.

Pair: Two unsevered stamps.

Pane: A portion of the original sheet as cut for sale at the post office.

Part-Perforate: A stamp which has perforations on one, two or three sides.

Pen Cancel: A cancellation supplied to the stamp with pen and ink.

Perforations: Line of small cuts or holes placed between two rows of stamps to facilitate separation.

Plate: The actual object from which the stamps are printed.

Plate Number Block: A block of stamps with sheet margin showing a plate number or numbers. Often it is known simply as a plate block.

Postal Stationery: Envelopes, postal cards, wrappers, etc. which had nonadhesive stamps embossed or printed on them.

Postmark: A mark struck upon envelopes, generally to indicate the name of the post office, date of mailing, etc.

Overprint

Imperforate Stamp

Precancel

Perforated

Coils. These stamps
are perforated on two
sides only.

Surcharge

Cut Square

Se-tenant

Precancels: Stamps with cancellations applied before the mailing of the article on which they prepay postage.

Proofs: Trial printing of a stamp made from the original die or the plate.

Provisionals: Stamps issued prior to the regular issues or to meet a temporary shortage of regular stamps.

Reissue: An official printing of a stamp, or stamps, that had been discontinued.

Remainders: Stocks of stamps on hand after the issue has been discontinued.

Reprints: Impressions from the original plates, blocks, or stones taken after the issuance of the stamps to post offices has ceased and their postal use has been voided.

Revenue Stamps: Stamps issued for use in collecting special taxes on documents, proprietary articles, products, etc.

Rotary Press Stamps: Stamps printed on a rotary type press from curved plates as compared to stamps printed from flat plates on a flat bed press. They will be slightly larger in one direction than flat press stamps.

Rouletting: Short consecutive cuts in the paper between rows of stamps to facilitate separation.

Se-tenant: An unsevered pair, strip or block of stamps which differ in value, design or surcharge.

Sheet: Complete unseparated group of stamps as originally printed.

Special Printing: Stamps of current design reissued, usually on a better grade of paper and in brilliant colors.

Stampless Cover: An envelope without stamps generally bearing a postmark and sometimes notations such as "Paid," "Paid 10," etc.

Straight Edge: The imperforate side of a stamp which is otherwise perforate.

Surcharge: An overprint which alters or restates the face value or denomination of the stamp to which it is applied.

Tied On: A stamp is "tied on" when the cancellation or postmark extends from the stamp to the envelope.

Topicals: Area of philately in which emphasis is on the subject portrayed on stamps rather than the stamps themselves.

Unused: A stamp with or without original gum which has no cancellation or other evidence of postal duty.

Used: A stamp which has done postal duty as evidenced by the cancellation.

Want List: A list of stamp numbers or philatelic items needed for a collection.

Watermark: A design or pattern incorporated into the paper during its manufacture.

Wove Paper: A paper of uniform texture throughout, showing no light or dark patterns when held to the light or immersed in benzine.

STAMP COLOR GUIDE

A slight difference in the color of a stamp can make it not only a different variety, but sometimes a thing of great rarity. The ability to recognize such color differences requires a practiced eye, but being able to ascertain a valuable shade is one of the real enjoyments of stamp collecting.

The stamp colors we produce here are not 100% accurate because printing processes such as the one used in Stamps & Stories use different kinds of ink and paper than the original stamps. As a result, the colors shown in the book are not exact reproductions.

In most catalogues the illustrations are only in black and white. The catalogue editors use many descriptive phrases to indicate the color of the stamps listed. Below we list some of the more popular names for the colors found on stamps along with some stamps that go with them.

Bright Blue

Blue

Dark Blue

Ultramarine

Purple

Violet

Carmine

Rose Lake

Peach Blossom

Red

Henna Brown

Brown

Bistre Brown

Sepia

Gray Brown

Dark Gray

Black

Light Green

Green

Olive

Light Olive Green

Blue Green

Yellow Gold

Orange

Deep Orange

Yellow-Black-Green

STAMP CONDITION

Condition, in the philatelic sense, means the state of a stamp— that is, whether it is a superb specimen, a mediocre specimen or a specimen that is below average. A stamp in fine condition is always more valuable than one that has been less well cared for.

When selecting a stamp to be placed in your collection, always make sure that it is the best you can obtain. Unused stamps should, if possible, be well-centered, fresh looking and have the original gum intact. Gum is the proper term for the adhesive applied to the back of the stamp. Remember, too, that unused stamps that have been hinged or with only part of the original gum are priced below a never hinged stamp with its original gum intact. Used stamps should be well-centered, lightly cancelled and never faded, dirty or stained. There should be no thinning of the paper. Thinning often occurs when stamps are improperly removed from envelopes or album pages and part of the stamp is removed as well.

Most dealers designate stamp condition by such term as "Superb," "Fine," and "Good." There are many gradations in the range from "Exceptionally Fine," "Very Fine," and "Very Good," through "Fair," "Poor," and "Spacefiller." However, for our purposes, "Superb," "Fine," and "Good" cover the ground for most newer collectors.

"Superb" means a stamp that is of the finest quality, has perfect centering, brilliant color and perfect gum. Used copies in this category also have perfect centering. They are fresh looking, are lightly cancelled, and are sound of body.

"Fine" means a stamp without flaws, average centering, gum with light hinge marks. Used copies in this category are not quite as fresh, cancels are heavier, and centering is average.

"Good" means stamps that are off-center, but fairly attractive and there may be minor defects such as disturbed gum, tiny thins, heavy hinge marks. Used copies, except for the gum, fall into this classification.

Stamps that fall below these standards should be ignored and are not worth acquiring. Of course, there are exceptions to these rules, but they do not come into the province of a new collector and will not be discussed here.

Superb

Fine

Good

Cancelled, Fine

Cancelled, Good

Lightly Cancelled

PRICE TRENDS OF
SELECTED STAMP ISSUES

As the price of goods and services continues to spiral, there is comfort in knowing that the value of your stamp collection is more than keeping pace. In many cases, stamp values outdistance most other investments, providing an invaluable safeguard against rising costs.

The graph gives you a good idea of how selected issues have increased over the past year. The stamp issues listed represent a broad range of stamps purchased by U.S. collectors. Also, the prices of classic U.S. issues have tended to hold up better than similar issues of other countries. Keep in mind, too, that many issues have out-performed those shown here, while still others have shown negligible increases. Overall, though, the trend in stamp values has been upward.

If you began your collection a few years ago, and have made wise choices since then, it is very possible that your stamps today may be worth several times the amount of your initial investment. And, of course, it's impossible to even put a price tag on the hours of enjoyment that stamp collecting provides.

Through the decade of the 1970s, stamp values more than held their own compared to a significant increase in our cost of living. If that performance continues during the 1980s, stamps will most certainly continue to be a fine investment value. In fact, the chart data shown here include only stamp types listed in Stamps & Stories. If other, higher value issues were included, stamp values would likely reflect an even greater increase.

It's important to remember two things. First, the primary purpose of stamp collecting is the enjoyment of the hobby, with value increases being an occasional benefit. Some stamps, in fact, do not increase in monetary value, yet are still fun to acquire and display. Secondly, the amount of gain indicated by stamp price comparisons in catalogues is overstated; catalogue prices are what you must pay to purchase a copy of the stamp. When you wish to sell your copy to another collector or a stamp dealer, you should expect to sacrifice anywhere between 10% and 50% of the current catalogue value.

The prices for these stamps have been taken from The Harris Postage Stamp Price Index, 1980-81 Edition (©1980 by H.E. Harris & Co., Inc.) and are reprinted by permission of the publisher. Prices refer to the market price for the issue in average condition in that year. Prices refer to uncancelled stamps.

Harris Postage Stamp Price Index

Scott #	Description	1950	1960	1970	1975	1980	%*
112	869 Pictorial	6.00	10.85	37.50	59.50	20.00	69.7
230	Columbian	.40	1.10	2.75	7.00	15.00	400.0
285	Trans-Mississippi	.60	1.65	4.50	8.50	2.50	82.4
294	Pan-American	.40	1.00	2.40	8.95	2.50	63.1
300	902 Regular	.14	.40	.70	1.40	8.00	471.4
40	915 Panama-Pacific	1.00	2.10	4.35	8.00	0.00	75.0
523	918 $2 Franklin	45.00	47.50	85.00	140.00	100.00	685.7
55	922 Regular	.02	.04	.05	.09	.25	77.8
910	Overrun Countries—Czechoslovakia	.10	.10	.12	.15	.35	33.3
1039	Liberty Issue		.08	.12	.15	.45	00.0
1178	Civil War 100th Anniversary Issue			.10	.20	.27	35.0
1229	6¢ Washington			.10	.16	1.30	12.5
1374	6¢ John Wesley Powell			.09	.14	.27	92.9
1460	1972 Olympic Games Issue				.12	.22	83.3
1529	10¢ Skylab II				.16	.30	87.5
C1	First Airmail	2.25	3.95	14.50	33.75	60.00	74.1
C4	Second Airmail	3.75	6.00	21.50	55.00	225.00	09.1
C13	Graf Zeppelin	14.50	22.75	90.00	225.00	075.00	77.8
E1	1885 Special Delivery	4.50	8.35	25.00	50.00	240.00	50.0
J1	Postage Due	.30	.60	1.50	2.75	6.00	481.8

*Refers to percentage increase between 1975 and 1980.

230

1039

1178

C1

C4

C13

E1

COMMEMORATIVE AND DEFINITIVE POSTAGE STAMPS

		Un	U
	Issues of 1847 to 1894 are Unwatermarked, Issue of 1847, Imperf.		
1	5¢ Benjamin		
	Franklin, July 1	5,500.00	875.00
2	10¢ George		
	Washington,		
	July 1	23,500.00	2,850.00
	Issue of 1875, Reproductions of 1 & 2		
3	5¢ Franklin	2,100.00	—
4	10¢ Washington	2,500.00	—

Reproductions. The letters R. W. H. & E. at the bottom of each stamp are less distinct on the reproductions than on the originals.

5¢. On the original the left side of the white shirt frill touches the oval on a level with the top of the "F" of "Five." On the reproduction it touches the oval about on a level with the top of the figure "5."

10¢. On the reproduction, line of coat at left points to right of "X" and line of coat at right points to center of "S" of CENTS. On the original, line of coat points to "T" of TEN and between "T" and "S" of CENTS.

On the reproduction the eyes have a sleepy look, the line of the mouth is straighter, and in the curl of hair near the left cheek is a strong black dot, while the original has only a faint one.

		Un	U
	Issue of 1851-56, Imperf.		
5	1¢ Franklin, type I	85,000.00	15,000.00
5A	1¢ Same, type Ib	9,000.00	2,500.00
	Nos. 6-9: Franklin (5)		
6	1¢ dark blue,		
	type Ia	11,000.00	3,500.00
7	1¢ blue, type II	450.00	85.00
8	1¢ blue, type III	4,000.00	1,150.00
8A	1¢ pale blue,		
	type IIIA	1,300.00	500.00
9	1¢ blue, type IV	285.00	75.00
10	3¢ orange brown Washington,		
	type I (11)	1,150.00	65.00
11	3¢ Washington, type I	100.00	7.00

		Un	U
12	5¢ Jefferson, type I	8,500.00	1,100.00
13	10¢ green Washington,		
	type I (15)	6,250.00	625.00
14	10¢ green, type II (15)	1,200.00	250.00
15	10¢ Washington, type III	1,250.00	260.00
16	10¢ green, type IV (15)	8,500.00	1,350.00
17	12¢ Washington	1,500.00	225.00

Bust of **5**

Detail of **6** Type Ia
Top ornaments and outer line partly cut away.
Lower scrollwork is complete.

1¢ Franklin Types I-IV of 1851-56

Bust of **5**

Detail of **5** Type I
Has curved, unbroken lines outside labels. Scrollwork is complete, forms little balls at bottom.

Detail of **5A** Type Ib
Lower scrollwork is incomplete, the little balls are not so clear.

1

2

3

4

5

11

12

15

17

Bust of **5**

→

Detail of **7** Type II
Lower scrollwork incomplete
(lacks little balls).
Side ornaments are complete.

←

Bust of **5**

↑

Detail of **8** Type III
Outer lines broken in the middle.
Side ornaments are complete.

Detail of **8A** Type IIIa
Outer lines broken top or bottom but
not both.

Bust of **5**

↑

↑

Detail of **9** Type IV
Outer lines recut top, bottom, or both.

Detail of **11**
THREE CENTS.
Type I. There is an outer frame line at top
and bottom.

Detail of **12**
FIVE CENTS.
Type I. There are projections on all four
sides.

THOMAS JEFFERSON

12

Thomas Jefferson began his career of public service early in life, and rather modestly at that. Paddling a canoe down the Rivanna, a gentle stream that flowed by his birthplace near Charlottesville, Virginia, the young Jefferson wondered whether the stream might be used to carry tobacco down to the James and on to the Tidewater ports. The stream would serve quite well, he decided, if only some large rocks were removed—and he proceeded to collect money from his neighbors to have the work done. If the neighbors were surprised to begin with, they were certainly pleased with the results: a navigable river, and easy access to the markets for their tobacco.

The son of the most prominent man in the county, it was only to be expected that Jefferson would find himself a member of the House of Burgesses at the age of 26. But it was on his own merits that he won the respect of his colleagues there. His reputation as a writer followed him to Philadelphia, to the Continental Congress, where he was asked to draft a declaration proclaiming that "these United Colonies are, and of right ought to be, free and independent states."

For 17 days in June of 1776, Jefferson worked at his writing box, sitting in an armchair at a dining table in his rented, second-floor suite. When he felt at last that every word was right, he submitted it to Congress for approval.

For three days, the delegates picked over his prose, making changes Jefferson called "depredations, mutilations." They took out his denunciations of the slave trade, but left intact his documenting of King George's abuses and usurpations. Finally, on July 4, the Declaration of Independence was adopted as it stands today.

Jefferson's reaction that day? He went out and bought his wife, Martha, seven pairs of gloves.

Thomas Jefferson drafting the Declaration of Independence, painting by N.C. Wyeth.

GEORGE WASHINGTON

If George Washington was "first in war, first in peace," he was first when it came to pomp and celebrations, as well. The inauguration of our first President was the event of the century.

The capital city in 1789 was New York, and by late April (the inauguration had been postponed to allow Congress time to assemble) its citizens were in a frenzy of anticipation. When Washington at last appeared, crossing the harbor on a ceremonial barge, they broke into wild cheers. As he stepped off and proceeded up Wall Street, they deluged him with flowers. They surrounded his elaborately designed, cream-colored coach as it wound its way to Federal Hall. And when he repeated the oath of office on a balcony of the Senate Chamber, they cried "Long live George Washington, President of the United States!" as cannons fired and bells pealed loud and long. Later—and for weeks to come—there would be fireworks and elegant balls.

New York society had "arrived"—and with it, suspicions among a few members of Congress that the rejected monarchy had infected the new republic. It would be a while before ceremonial pomp gave way to democratic circumstance.

Washington at the Delaware.

BENJAMIN FRANKLIN

Benjamin Franklin was above all a practical man. The great inventor founded the American Philosophical Society "for the promoting of useful knowledge." And his Poor Richard's Almanac *was full of practical adages like "early to bed and early to rise," which, according to Mark Twain, made the lives of millions of schoolboys miserable.*

112

It was with some embarrassment that Franklin spent four years experimenting with electricity, which he said possessed no earthly use. In a letter to a friend in 1749, Franklin professed he was "Chagrin'd a little that We have hitherto been able to discover Nothing in this Way of Use to Mankind."

Little did Franklin, who was so astute in so many other areas, realize that he was on the verge of a new science, one that would find more application than most discoveries in the history of mankind.

	Un	U
Issue of 1857-61, Perf. 15		
Nos. 18-24: Franklin (5)		
18 1¢ blue, type I	675.00	325.00
19 1¢ blue, type Ia	8,000.00	1,850.00
20 1¢ blue, type II	400.00	115.00
21 1¢ blue, type III	2,600.00	850.00
22 1¢ blue, type IIIa	500.00	165.00
23 1¢ blue, type IV	1,300.00	210.00
24 1¢ blue, type V	115.00	20.00

	Un	U
Nos. 25-26: Washington (11)		
25 3¢ rose, type I	600.00	27.50
26 3¢ dull red, type II	45.00	2.75
Nos. 27-29: Jefferson (12)		
27 5¢ brick red, type I	6,000.00	850.00
28 5¢ red brown, type I	1,350.00	225.00
28A 5¢ Indian red, type I	7,500.00	1,100.00
29 5¢ brown, type I	675.00	175.00

CIVIL WAR

One of the most unusual companies to form during the Civil War called itself the Bohemian Brigade. Its members took the field with Union Armies. None bore arms, but many risked their lives. The self-styled Bohemian Brigade was composed of 100 war correspondents for major Northern newspapers: the first war news reporters.

The Civil War was a turning point for American newspapers. No war had ever been so completely covered. James Gordon Bennett, publisher of the New York Herald, *employed 40 correspondents and spent over a half-million dollars on coverage.* New York Times *publisher Henry Jarvis Raymond assigned himself to the field, sending back eyewitness reports.*

The hand-in-hand problems of censorship and responsibility surfaced. Freedom of the press was threatened by not only military and government censors, but often by editorial irresponsibility.

And war brought firsts: the first press association (of the Confederate States); extensive use of the telegraph to transmit news; the invention of the "who, what, when, where and why" lead. And because the telegraph was so unreliable, newsmen began to send a summary paragraph—first! See Scott Nos. 63-73, 1178-1182.

10¢ Washington Types I-IV of 1855

Bust of **15** ↓   ↓

Detail of **13**
Type I. The "shells" at the lower corners are practically complete. The outer line below the label is very nearly complete. The outer lines are broken above the middle of the top label and the "X" in each upper corner.

Bust of **15** ↓

 ←

Detail of **14**
Type II. The design is complete at the top. The outer line at the bottom is broken in the middle. The shells are partly cut away.

 ←

Detail of **15**
Type III. The outer lines are broken above the top label and the "X" numerals. The outer line at the bottom and the shells are partly cut away, as in Type II.

Bust of **15** ↓

Detail of **16**
Type IV. The outer lines have been recut at top or bottom or both.
Types I, II, III and IV have complete ornaments at the sides of the stamps and three pearls at each outer edge of the bottom panel.

Bust of **5**

→

Detail of **24**
ONE CENT FRANKLIN
Type V. Similar to Type III of 1851-56 but with side ornaments partly cut away.

Bust of **11**

↑

Detail of **26**
THREE CENTS WASHINGTON
Type II. The outer frame line has been removed at top and bottom. The side frame lines were recut so as to be continuous from the top to the bottom of the plate.

↑

Detail of **30A**
FIVE CENTS JEFFERSON
Type II. The projections at top and bottom are partly cut away.

  ←

Detail of **35**
TEN CENTS WASHINGTON
(Two typical examples).
Type V. Side ornaments slightly cut away.
Outer lines complete except over right X.

		Un	U
	1857-61 continued		
30	5¢ orange brown		
	Jefferson, type II (30A)	650.00	775.00
30A	5¢ Jefferson, type II	375.00	130.00
	Nos. 31-35: Washington (15)		
31	10¢ green, type I	3,850.00	450.00
32	10¢ green, type II	1,100.00	125.00
33	10¢ green, type III	1,150.00	130.00
34	10¢ green, type IV	10,000.00	1,150.00
35	10¢ green, type V	165.00	50.00
36	12¢ black Washington		
	(17)	300.00	75.00
37	24¢ Washington	650.00	200.00
38	30¢ Franklin	775.00	285.00
39	90¢ Washington	1,400.00	2,750.00
	90¢ Same, with pen		
	cancel	—	800.00

Note: Beware of forged cancellations of No. 39. Genuine cancellations are rare.

1875: Government Reprints, Perf. 12, White Paper, Without Gum

		Un	U
40	1¢ bright blue Franklin (5)	500.00	—
41	3¢ scarlet Washington		
	(11)	2,750.00	—
42	5¢ orange brown		
	Jefferson (30A)	900.00	—
43	10¢ blue green		
	Washington (15)	2,250.00	—
44	12¢ greenish black		
	Washington (17)	2,350.00	—
45	24¢ blackish violet		
	Washington (37)	2,650.00	—
46	30¢ yel. org. Franklin		
	(38)	2,850.00	—
47	90¢ deep blue		
	Washington (39)	4,500.00	—

Issue of 1861, Perf. 12

Following the outbreak of the Civil War, the U.S. Government demonetized all previous issues.

		Un	U
55	1¢ Franklin	16,000.00	—
56	3¢ Washington	650.00	—
57	5¢ brown Jefferson	11,000.00	—
58	10¢ Washington	4,000.00	—
59	12¢ Washington	35,000.00	—

Issue of 1861

Detail of **55**

Detail of **57**

Issue of 1861-62

Detail of **63**
1¢. A dash has been added under the tip of the ornament at right of the numeral in upper left corner.

Detail of **67**
5¢. A leaflet has been added to the foliated ornaments at each corner.

Detail of **56**

Detail of **58**

		Un	U
	1861 continued		
60	24¢ dk. vio. Washington		
	(70)	4,750.00	—
61	30¢ red org. Franklin		
	(71)	*14,000.00*	—
62	90¢ dull blue		
	Washington (72)	*18,000.00*	—
62B	10¢ dark green		
	Washington (58)	4,000.00	450.00

Nos. 55-62 were not used for postage and do not exist in a cancelled state. The paper they were printed on is thin and semi-transparent, that of the following issues is more opaque.

	Issue of 1861-62, Perf. 12		
63	1¢ Franklin	100.00	17.50
64	3¢ Washington	3,000.00	250.00
65	3¢ rose Washington (64)	42.50	1.10
66	3¢ lake Washington (64)	*1,350.00*	—
67	5¢ Jefferson	3,600.00	325.00
68	10¢ Washington	190.00	18.50

Detail of **62**

Detail of **64**
3¢. Ornaments at corners have been enlarged and end in a small ball.

Detail of **68**
10¢. A heavy curved line has been cut below the stars and an outer line has been added to the ornaments above them.

		Un	U

1861-62 continued

69	12¢ Washington	400.00	33.50
70	24¢ Washington	450.00	33.50
71	30¢ Franklin	450.00	52.50
72	90¢ Washington	950.00	150.00

Issue of 1861-66, Perf. 12

73	2¢ Andrew Jackson		
	("Black Jack")	110.00	20.00
74	3¢ scarlet Washington		
	(64)	3,250.00	—
75	5¢ red brown Jefferson		
	(67)	1,100.00	175.00
76	5¢ brn. Jefferson (67)	225.00	40.00
77	15¢ Abraham Lincoln	425.00	57.50
78	24¢ lilac Washington (70)	200.00	30.00

No. 74 was not regularly issued.

Grills on U.S. Stamps

Between 1867 and 1870, postage stamps were embossed with grills to prevent people from re-using cancelled stamps. The pyramid-shaped grills absorbed cancellation ink, making it virtually impossible to remove a postmark chemically.

Issue of 1867, With Grills, Perf. 12

Grills A, B, C: Points Up

A. Grill Covers Entire Stamp

79	3¢ rose Washington		
	(64)	1,650.00	400.00
80	5¢ brn. Jefferson (67)	37,500.00	
81	30¢ org. Franklin (71)	—	32,500.00
	B. Grill about 18x15 mm.		
82	3¢ rose Washington (64)	—	35,000.00
	C. Grill about 13x16 mm.		
83	3¢ rose Washington (64)	1,250.00	275.00
	Grills, D, Z, E, F: Points Down		
	D. Grill about 12x14 mm.		
84	2¢ blk. Jackson (73)	2,150.00	650.00
85	3¢ rose Washington (64)	925.00	250.00
	Z. Grill about 11x14 mm.		
85A	1¢ bl. Franklin (63)	—	110,000.00
85B	2¢ blk. Jackson (73)	800.00	250.00
85C	3¢ rose Washington (64)	2,250.00	600.00
85D	10¢ green Washington		
	(68)	—	23,500.00
85E	12¢ black Washington		
	(69)	1,250.00	450.00

69

70

71

72

73

77

112

113

114

Detail of **69**
12¢. Ovals and scrolls have been added to the corners.

Detail of **72**
90¢. Parallel lines form an angle above the ribbon with "U. S. Postage"; between these lines a row of dashes has been added and a point of color to the apex of the lower pair.

GRILLS

In the mid-19th century, only the larger post offices were equipped with mechanical devices to cancel stamps. The postmasters of smaller offices generally relied on pens to mark the stamps with ink to make certain they could not be used again.

But the U.S. government began to worry that people could clean the stamps and re-use them. After all, only a little ink eradicator was needed to make the stamps look as good as new.

One of the devices developed to curb this practice was the "grill," a means of embossing stamps with a roller that was either pitted with small depressions or covered with small raised pyramids. The result: the grills that broke the fibres of the paper, causing the ink to be soaked up to such a degree that cleaning—and re-use— was impossible.

Grill

		Un	U
1867 continued			
85F	15¢ blk. Lincoln (77)	—	35,000.00
	E. Grill about 11x13 mm.		
86	1¢ blue Franklin (63)	525.00	165.00
87	2¢ black Jackson (73)	250.00	55.00
88	3¢ rose Washington (64)	185.00	8.50
89	10¢ grn. Washington (68)	925.00	125.00
90	12¢ blk. Washington (69)	1,000.00	130.00
91	15¢ black Lincoln (77)	2,000.00	300.00
	F. Grill about 9x13 mm.		
92	1¢ blue Franklin (63)	225.00	70.00
93	2¢ black Jackson (73)	110.00	22.50
94	3¢ red Washington (64)	75.00	2.50
95	5¢ brown Jefferson (67)	750.00	185.00
96	10¢ yellow green		
	Washington (68)	475.00	60.00
97	12¢ black Washington		
	(69)	525.00	70.00
98	15¢ black Lincoln (77)	550.00	75.00
99	24¢ gray lilac		
	Washington (70)	1,100.00	400.00
100	30¢ orange Franklin (71)	1,250.00	300.00
101	90¢ blue Washington		
	(72)	2,850.00	750.00
Reissues of 1875, Without Grill, Perf. 12			
102	1¢ blue Franklin (63)	475.00	650.00
103	2¢ black Jackson (73)	2,400.00	3,250.00
104	3¢ brown red		
	Washington (64)	2,750.00	3,500.00
105	5¢ brown Jefferson (67)	1,450.00	1,650.00
106	10¢ grn. Washington (68)	2,000.00	2,500.00
107	12¢ blk. Washington		
	(69)	2,850.00	3,350.00
108	15¢ black Lincoln (77)	2,850.00	3,500.00
109	24¢ deep violet		
	Washington (70)	3,100.00	4,000.00
110	30¢ brownish orange		
	Franklin (71)	3,850.00	5,000.00
111	90¢ blue Washington		
	(72)	5,000.00	7,500.00
Issue of 1869, With Grill Measuring 9½x9 mm., Perf. 12			
112	1¢ Franklin	225.00	55.00
113	2¢ Post Horse & Rider	160.00	25.00
114	3¢ Locomotive	125.00	5.00

S.S. ADRIATIC

In the 1840s, the New York merchant Edward K. Collins was determined to build steamships in America that would compete with the successful British Cunard line. With a small subsidy from Congress, Collins built a magnificent line of steamers, widely regarded as the strongest wooden ships ever built.

For years all went well. Then in 1855, the Arctic was rammed by a French ship and sank. The next year the Pacific set sail from Liverpool for New York and was never heard of again. Undaunted, Collins built another ship, the Adriatic, larger and faster than her sisters, the first ship to cost more than $1 million. But the Adriatic fared no better. She had barely made her initial crossing in 1857 when Congress withdrew its subsidies, putting Collins and the Adriatic out of business. See Scott No. 117.

The S.S. Adriatic leaving her pier, 1857.

POST RIDERS

The U.S. Mail played a crucial role in uniting the colonies, but it was a long time coming. Colonists had been petitioning for a mail service since 1638, but it wasn't until 1672 that the first step was taken toward connecting the colonies by post. In that year, Governor Lovelace of New York established a monthly postal route—the nation's first—between New York and Boston. The "stout and indefatigable" postman who covered this route through trackless forest was required to mark the trees on his journey for the benefit of future travelers.

113

18th Century Mail Carrier.

As post riders became more common, local committees sometimes helped to clear their paths. To prevent them from bogging down in mud and swamps, planks or logs were laid close together and lightly covered with earth. These "corduroy roads," however, were so rough that horses frequently were lamed and wagons jolted apart. Few but the intrepid post riders dared to travel them. See Scott No. 113.

EARLY LOCOMOTIVES

If you were asked to name two creatures that have contributed to the development of American railroads, cows and grasshoppers might not be at the top of the list. Yet both have left their mark on the modern locomotive.

114

In their early years, trains were forever colliding with cows that had wandered onto the tracks. When that happened, the engine often derailed, ending up in a ditch. The problem prompted Isaac Dripps, boss mechanic of the Camden & Amboy line, to devise a "cow-catcher," a low truck attached to the front end of the engine and equipped with pointed iron prongs. In its first foray, the device worked only too well: it impaled a big bull so firmly that block and tackle were required to detach the animal. Dripps modified his cowcatcher, substituting a heavy bar for the prongs. The device was the forerunner of the modern "pilot," a feature that sets American locomotives apart from those of almost all other countries.

Another locomotive innovation stemmed from a plague of grasshoppers which visited Pennsylvania in 1836. Billions of the insects overran the countryside, darkening skies and stripping the fields. Because of the insects, trains could not grip the tracks, so men with brooms preceded the engines, sweeping the hoppers from the rails. But more often than not, the insects were back by the time the next train came along. The railroads then tried attaching brooms to the front of the trains, but the brooms wore out too quickly. Finally, someone hit upon the idea of using sand. Stored in a box on top of the locomotive, the dry sand trickled down pipes running from the box to a point just in front of the engine. The system worked extremely well, and since then no American locomotive has been without a sandbox. See Scott No. 114.

The Rocket, 1829.

27

		Un	U
1869 continued			
115	6¢ Washington	775.00	85.00
116	10¢ Shield and Eagle	825.00	95.00
117	12¢ *S.S. Adriatic*	750.00	85.00
118	15¢ Columbus		
	Landing, type I	1,750.00	225.00
119	15¢ brown and blue		
	Columbus Landing,		
	type II (118)	850.00	115.00
119b	Center		
	inverted	*125,000.00*	16,000.00
120	24¢ Declaration of		
	Independence	2,500.00	500.00
120b	Center		
	inverted	*95,000.00*	16,000.00
121	30¢ Shield, Eagle		
	and Flags	2,250.00	250.00
121b	Flags inverted	*110,000.00*	45,000.00
122	90¢ Lincoln	6,750.00	1,150.00
Reissues of 1875, Without Grill, Hard White Paper, Perf. 12			
123	1¢ buff (112)	*300.00*	200.00
124	2¢ brown (113)	*375.00*	300.00
125	3¢ blue (114)	*2,750.00*	1,000.00
126	6¢ blue (115)	*825.00*	450.00
127	10¢ yellow (116)	*1,350.00*	900.00
128	12¢ green (117)	*1,450.00*	900.00
129	15¢ brown and blue		
	Columbus Landing,		
	type III (118)	*1,300.00*	500.00
130	24¢ grn. & vio. (120)	*1,250.00*	500.00
131	30¢ bl. & car. (121)	*1,650.00*	1,000.00
132	90¢ car. & blk. (122)	*5,000.00*	8,500.00
Reissues of 1880, Soft, Porous Paper, Perf. 12			
133	1¢ buff (112)	200.00	135.00
Issue of 1870-71, With Grill, White Wove Paper, Perf. 12			
134	1¢ Franklin	425.00	47.50
135	2¢ Jackson	275.00	30.00
136	3¢ Washington	225.00	7.50

AMERICA'S SYMBOL

The bald eagle has probably been endowed with more myth and mystique than any other wild animal. America's symbol has long been synonymous with bravery, ferocity and free-spiritedness.

Actually, the majestic bird is pretty much of a homebody. Eagles mate for life. Their nesting site is often used year after year, sometimes growing to a stupendous size. And, unlike other young birds, eaglets remain with their parents for many weeks.

Unfortunately, another word with which eagles have almost become synonymous is "extinction." Pollution, pesticides and bounties have nearly decimated the bald eagle population. In recent years, conservation groups have alerted the public to the eagle's plight, leading to stronger laws and protected roosting sites. But whether or not the great bird becomes a symbol of man's destructiveness remains to be seen. As ornithologist J. Hibbert Langille wrote of the eagle and man's encroachment of its habitat in 1892, "Look at him, and reflect on human imbecility." See Scott Nos. 116, 121.

Two representations of the American Eagle, 20th century stamp and 19th century lithograph.

1396

115

116

117

118

120

121

122

134

135

136

Detail of **118**
FIFTEEN CENTS.
Type I. Picture unframed.

Detail of **119.**
Type II. Picture framed.
Type III. Same as Type I but without fringe of brown shading lines around central vignette.

Issue of 1870-71: Printed by the National Bank Note Company.
Issued without secret marks (see Nos. 156-163).

Detail of **134**

Detail of **135**

Detail of **136**

		Un	U
1870-71 continued			
137	6¢ Lincoln	1,100.00	210.00
138	7¢ Edwin M. Stanton	925.00	200.00
139	10¢ Jefferson	1,350.00	350.00
140	12¢ Henry Clay	11,000.00	1,350.00
141	15¢ Daniel Webster	1,400.00	550.00
142	24¢ General Winfield		
	Scott	—	*10,500.00*

It is generally accepted as fact that the Continental Bank Note Co. printed and delivered a quantity of 24¢ stamps. They are impossible to distinguish from those printed by the National Bank Note Co.

143	30¢ Alexander		
	Hamilton	3,500.00	800.00
144	90¢ Commodore Perry	5,000.00	600.00
	Without Grill, White Wove Paper, Perf. 12		
145	1¢ ultra. Franklin (134)	120.00	5.50
146	2¢ red brn. Jackson		
	(135)	40.00	4.00
147	3¢ green Washington		
	(136)	85.00	.30
148	6¢ carmine Lincoln (137)	165.00	9.50
149	7¢ verm. Stanton (138)	300.00	40.00
150	10¢ brown Jefferson (139)	165.00	9.50
151	12¢ dull violet Clay (140)	450.00	40.00
152	15¢ bright orange Webster		
	(141)	425.00	40.00

Detail of **137**

Detail of **138**

Detail of **139**

Detail of **140**

Detail of **141**

137   138

139   140

141   142

143   144

EDWIN M. STANTON

Edwin M. Stanton, Abraham Lincoln's Secretary of War, was a fierce-looking man characterized in his time as the "black terrier." His violent temper and sharp tongue frequently made him a controversial figure, yet few doubted his honesty, energy and patriotism. Though he was, at first, a bitter opponent of Lincoln, the two came gradually to a mutual admiration and intimate association.

Stanton's claim to fame could lie with his successful law practice before the U.S. Supreme Court, or with his reorganization and "cleaning up" of the War Department, or with his peaceable disbandment of 800,000 soldiers at the end of the Civil War.

He may, on the other hand, be best remembered as the subject of the first article of impeachment against Andrew Johnson. When Johnson tried to force Stanton's removal from office, Stanton vowed that he would "continue in office until expelled by force." This disagreement constituted an issue against Johnson. However, when the impeachment charges against Johnson failed, Stanton resigned. See Scott Nos. 138, 149, 160.

HAMILTON THE FEDERALIST

The American Constitution—in 1787 a document in search of support—found no more eloquent defender than Alexander Hamilton. For he was the chief author—along with co-authors James Madison and John Jay—of The Federalist, a series of 85 essays that has become the chief historic commentary on this country's fundamental law.

1086

The three authors wrote under the name of "Publius," the hero who established a republican government in Rome after the fall of its last king. While Jay wrote mainly about foreign affairs and Madison about history, Hamilton himself undertook the task of exposing the weaknesses of the Articles of Confederation and of detailing the powers of the three branches of the new government: the Chief Executive, the Senate, and the Judiciary. The result was that the essays, though written as a tract for the times (originally to win over the people of New York to the cause of federalism), became a penetrating analysis of the Constitution, a document for the ages.

DANIEL WEBSTER

Daniel Webster knew the value of good public relations.

For 40 years, from 1812 to his death in 1852, he was more visible than almost any other American, playing a dominant national role as lawyer, orator, congressman, senator, secretary of state, leader of two major parties and perennial presidential candidate.

Undoubtedly he had what has come to be known as "charisma." But he also knew how to fashion his image. At a time when being an industrialist was a distinct liability for a presidential candidate, Webster carefully cultivated an image as "the great farmer." He liked to be interviewed while standing in a bed of onions or feeding his prized ram Goliath at his ancestral farm in New Hampshire. And he saw to it that he was painted in his hunting jacket, and that stories of his skill with rod and gun circulated to the press.

Some of his appeal stemmed from his physical appearance. He had a massive chest, furrowed brows and a head so large that it was said to be to common brows "what the great dome of St. Peters is to the small cupolas at its side." The Webster head measured 25 inches around (compared with 23 for Henry Clay) and, at his death, was found to weigh 63¾ ounces (compared with an average weight of 50 ounces).

But despite his dramatic appearance, his oratorical style and his reputation as "defender of the Constitution," Webster was denied an opportunity to play the biggest political role of all: the President of the United States.

		Un	U
1870-71 continued			
153	24¢ purple W. Scott (142)	475.00	60.00
154	30¢ black Hamilton (143)	850.00	80.00
155	90¢ carmine Perry (144)	1,000.00	125.00
Issue of 1873, Without Grill, Perf. 12, White Wove Paper, Thin to Thick			
156	1¢ Franklin	40.00	1.75
157	2¢ Jackson	115.00	5.50
158	3¢ Washington	35.00	.10
159	6¢ Lincoln	150.00	6.50
160	7¢ Stanton	350.00	45.00
161	10¢ Jefferson	160.00	7.50
162	12¢ Clay	500.00	45.00
163	15¢ Webster	450.00	40.00
165	30¢ Hamilton (143)	450.00	40.00
166	90¢ Perry (144)	1,000.00	135.00

The Hon. Daniel Webster's reception on Boston Common.

56

157

58

159

60

161

62

163

79

1873: Printed by the Continental Bank Note Co.

Designs of the 1870-71 Issue with secret marks on the values from 1¢ to 15¢ as described and illustrated below.

Detail of **159**

6¢. The first four vertical lines of the shading in the lower part of the left ribbon have been strengthened

Detail of **160**

7¢. Two small semi-circles are drawn around the ends of the lines which outline the ball in the lower right hand corner.

Detail of **161**

10¢. There is a small semi-circle in the scroll, at the right end of the upper label.

Detail of **162**

12¢. The balls of the figure "2" are crescent shaped.

Detail of **163**

15¢. In the lower part of the triangle in the upper left corner two lines have been made heavier forming a "V". This mark can be found on some of the Continental and American (1879) printings, but not all stamps show it.

Secret marks were added to the dies of the 24¢, 30¢ and 90¢ but new plates were not made from them. The various printings of these stamps can be distinguished only by the shades and paper.

		Un	U
Issue of 1875, Special Printing, Hard, White Wove Paper, Without Gum			
167	1¢ ultra. Franklin (156)	*5,000.00*	—
168	2¢ dark brown		
	Jackson (157)	*5,000.00*	—
169	3¢ blue green		
	Washington (158)	*8,500.00*	—
170	6¢ dull rose Lincoln		
	(159)	*6,750.00*	—
171	7¢ reddish vermilion		
	Stanton (160)	*1,600.00*	—
172	10¢ pale brown		
	Jefferson (161)	*5,750.00*	—
173	12¢ dark violet Clay		
	(162)	*2,000.00*	—
174	15¢ bright orange		
	Webster (163)	*6,250.00*	—
175	24¢ dull purple		
	W. Scott (142)	*1,500.00*	—
176	30¢ greenish black		
	Hamilton (143)	*5,750.00*	—
177	90¢ violet car. Perry		
	(144)	*5,750.00*	—

Although perforated, these stamps were usually cut apart with scissors. As a result, the perforations are often much mutilated and the design is frequently damaged.

		Un	U
	Yellowish Wove Paper		
178	2¢ vermilion Jackson		
	(157), June 21	125.00	3.25
179	5¢ Zachary Taylor,		
	June 21	135.00	6.50

Special Printing, Hard, White Wove Paper, Without Gum

		Un	U
180	2¢ carmine verm.		
	Jackson (157)	*16,500.00*	—
181	5¢ bright blue Taylor		
	(179)	*30,000.00*	—

Issue of 1879. Printed by the American Bank Note Company. Soft, Porous Paper Varying from Thin to Thick.

		Un	U
182	1¢ dark ultramarine		
	Franklin (156)	90.00	1.00
183	2¢ vermilion Jackson		
	(157)	50.00	1.00

		Un	U
1879 continued			
184	3¢ green Washington		
	(158)	37.50	.08
185	5¢ blue Taylor (179)	150.00	5.75
186	6¢ pink Lincoln (159)	400.00	9.00
187	10¢ brown Jefferson (139)		
	(no secret mark)	575.00	10.00
188	10¢ brown Jefferson (161)		
	(with secret mark)	375.00	12.00
189	15¢ red orange		
	Webster (163)	150.00	13.50
190	30¢ full black Hamilton		
	(143)	425.00	18.50
191	30¢ carmine Perry (144)	950.00	120.00
Issue of 1880, Special Printing, Soft, Porous Paper, Without Gum			
192	1¢ dark ultramarine		
	Franklin (156)	*7,750.00*	—
193	2¢ black brown		
	Jackson (157)	*4,250.00*	—
194	3¢ blue green		
	Washington (158)	*11,000.00*	—
195	6¢ dull rose Lincoln		
	(159)	*8,000.00*	—
196	7¢ scarlet vermilion		
	Stanton (160)	*2,000.00*	—
197	10¢ deep brown		
	Jefferson (161)	*6,750.00*	—
198	12¢ blackish purple		
	Clay (162)	*4,000.00*	—
199	15¢ orange Webster		
	(163)	*6,500.00*	—
200	24¢ dark violet		
	W. Scott (142)	*2,000.00*	—
201	30¢ greenish black		
	Hamilton (143)	*6,000.00*	—
202	90¢ dull car. Perry (144)	*6,000.00*	—
203	2¢ scarlet vermilion		
	Jackson (157)	*15,000.00*	—
204	5¢ deep blue Taylor		
	(179)	*25,000.00*	—

WINFIELD SCOTT

When the Civil War began, the Union was almost totally
unprepared to fight it. The North had almost no army, few
good weapons, and an archaic system of military command.

To head the army, President Lincoln turned to Winfield
Scott. A veteran of two wars, General Scott was the most
experienced soldier in the country. Unfortunately, he was
also old, frail, and physically incapable of commanding
troops in the field. "If I could only mount a horse," he would say wistfully, "but
I am past that."

786

The general worked hard, sometimes putting in 17-hour days. But this war
required more complex strategies and larger masses of troops than Scott could
handle. His men complained about his plodding ways, nicknaming him "Old Fuss
and Feathers." He was too tired to run an army, and he and Lincoln both knew it.
In October of 1861, Lincoln regretfully asked Scott to step down, and the general
was retired with every honor the President and Congress could bestow. See Scott
Nos. 142, 153, 175, 200, 786.

EARLY NAVAL WARFARE

Rumors of impending peace were at hand when John Barry put to sea in the
Continental frigate Alliance in March 1783, accompanied by the 20-gun
Duc de Lauzun.

Early one morning Barry sighted three British frigates. The Alliance could out-
run them, but Barry wouldn't abandon the slower Lauzun. As the gap narrowed,
Barry sighted a 50-gun French ship on the horizon. Thinking help was at hand,
Barry attacked the closest British vessel – alone. As the French two-decker stood
by, the Alliance battled the British ship, leaving it a battered wreck. The French
captain later told an angry Barry that he thought the Alliance had already been
captured and didn't want to be lured into a trap.

Barry dropped anchor on March 20. Three days later he heard the momentous
news: the British had ended hostilities. John Barry and the Alliance had fought
the Continental Navy's final battle.

			Un	U
	Issue of 1882			
205	5¢ Garfield, Apr. 10		85.00	3.50
	Special Printing. Soft, Porous Paper, Without Gum			
205C	5¢ gray brown (205)		*16,500.00*	—
	Issue of 1881-82, Designs of 1873 Re-engraved.			
206	1¢ Franklin		30.00	.50
207	3¢ Washington		35.00	.08
208	6¢ Lincoln		235.00	40.00
209	10¢ Jefferson		67.50	2.00
	Issue of 1883			
210	2¢ Washington, Oct. 1		28.50	.08
211	4¢ Jackson, Oct. 1		135.00	7.00
	Special Printing. Soft, Porous Paper.			
211B	2¢ pale red brown			
	Washington (210)		675.00	—
211D	4¢ deep blue green			
	Jackson (211) no gum		*13,000.00*	—

			Un	U
	Issue of 1887			
212	1¢ Franklin		50.00	.60
213	2¢ green Washington			
	(210)		20.00	.05
214	3¢ vermilion			
	Washington (207)		42.50	30.00
	Issue of 1888, Perf. 12			
215	4¢ carmine Jackson			
	(211)		135.00	10.00
216	5¢ indigo Garfield (205)		115.00	6.00
217	30¢ orange brown			
	Hamilton (143)		375.00	70.00
218	90¢ purple Perry (144)		725.00	120.00
	Issue of 1890-93, Perf. 12			
219	1¢ Franklin		20.00	.10
219D	2¢ Washington		125.00	.45
220	2¢ carmine (219D)		16.50	.05

MATTHEW C. PERRY

Matthew Calbraith Perry never became quite as famous as his brother, Oliver Hazard ("We have met the enemy and they are ours") Perry. Nevertheless, he is an important figure in his own right, sometimes called the "Father of the Steam Navy." For it was Perry who commanded an experimental "steam battery" in New York harbor in the 1830s. And it was his experience as commander of the Fulton, *the first naval steamer, that led to the organization of naval service in steam, culminating in the building of the* Mississippi, *second only to the* Constitution *among historic ships-of-war.*

Perry was, in fact, a man of many accomplishments. He organized the first apprentice system of the U.S. Navy, led a squadron sent to Africa to help suppress the slave trade, and negotiated a major treaty between the U.S. and Japan in 1854.

205

206

207

208

209

210

211

212

219

219D

Detail of **206**
1¢. Upper vertical lines have been deepened, creating a solid effect in parts of background. Upper arabesques have lines of shading.

Detail of **207**
3¢. Shading at sides of central oval is half its previous width. A short horizontal dash has been cut below the "TS" of "CENTS".

Detail of **208**
6¢. Has three vertical lines instead of four between the edge of the panel and the outside of the stamp.

Detail of **209**
10¢. Has four vertical lines instead of five between left side of oval and edge of the shield. Horizontal lines in lower part of background have been strengthened.

	Un	U
1890-93 continued		
221 3¢ Jackson	60.00	3.25
222 4¢ Lincoln	60.00	1.50
223 5¢ Ulysses S. Grant	60.00	1.50
224 6¢ Garfield	60.00	11.50
225 8¢ William T. Sherman	45.00	8.50
226 10¢ Webster	120.00	1.50
227 15¢ Clay	175.00	15.00
228 30¢ Jefferson	275.00	18.50
229 90¢ Perry	425.00	80.00

WILLIAM T. SHERMAN

It was not fighting a hard war, but negotiating a soft peace that landed Union General Sherman in political hot water at the end of the Civil War. Like President Lincoln, Sherman wanted not revenge, but a quick, lenient peace. The day after Sherman captured Raleigh, Lincoln was assassinated. In good faith, Sherman granted defeated Confederates milder terms than Lincoln had intended—terms that Washington officials repudiated. Peace was renegotiated and Sherman's honor survived —unlike some of his personal friendships that perished in this fray. See Scott Nos. 225, 257, 272, 787.

221

222

223

224

225

226

227

228

229

PAN AMERICAN EXPOSITION

When is a stamp not a stamp? Why, when, it's an essay, a sample of an unaccepted stamp design.

294a   295a

Take, for example, the case of the 1901 Pan American 4-cent stamp with inverted center (Scott No. 296 a). Unlike most inverts, two sheets of these (400 stamps) were deliberately printed as errors by the Bureau of Engraving and Printing. Some were distributed "by courtesy" to various persons of influence, others retained by the Post Office Department and eventually included in the Government stamp collection. But none were sold "as evidence of prepayment of postage"—that is, as actual stamps.

The inverts came, though, from a series of perfectly normal, usable stamps, an issue commemorating the Pan American Exposition held in Buffalo, New York, from May through October, 1901. The Exposition was a salute to the engineering achievements of the turn of the century—the most modern means of transportation and communication developed up to that time. The stamps, accordingly, showed subjects such as a steamer on the Great Lakes; a railway train speeding along at 60 miles per hour; an electric automobile; the world's largest single-span steel bridge, at Niagara Falls (which, incidentally, collapsed in 1938); the canal locks at Sault Ste. Marie; and an ocean cruiser of the Spanish-American War.

The commemorative stamps were issued in denominations of 1, 2, 4, 5, 8, and 10 cents. Besides the deliberate error on the 4-cent stamp, there were two quite genuine errors in the series. The most valuable is the 2-cent stamp with an inverted railway train, the 20th Century Limited. Fewer than 200 of these are known to exist, and they are now worth many thousands of dollars each. Somewhat less valuable is the 1-cent stamp with inverted lake steamer, of which there were about 1,000 printed.

Even without the errors, the Pan American Exposition stamps are themselves worth remembering. Not only were they the first bi-color stamps since 1869, they were also the first stamps issued in the 20th century. See Scott Nos. 294-299.

		Un	U	#	PB	FDC	Q
	Columbian Exposition Issue, 1893, Perf. 12						
230	1¢ Columbus Sights Land	30.00	.25	(6)	600.00	1,800.00	449,195,550
231	2¢ Landing of Columbus	27.50	.06	(6)	550.00	1,450.00	1,464,588,750
232	3¢ The Santa Maria	70.00	14.00	(6)	950.00	5,000.00	11,501,250
233	4¢ Fleet of Columbus ultramarine	100.00	5.50	(6)	1,250.00	5,000.00	19,181,550
233a	4¢ blue (error) (233)	6,500.00	2,500.00				
234	5¢ Columbus Seeking Aid	110.00	7.00	(6)	1,650.00	5,000.00	35,248,250
235	6¢ Columbus at Barcelona	100.00	17.50	(6)	1,500.00	5,750.00	4,707,550
236	8¢ Columbus Restored to Favor	70.00	7.50	(6)	1,000.00	5,750.00	10,656,550
237	10¢ Columbus Presenting Indians	160.00	6.00	(6)	3,250.00	6,500.00	16,516,950
238	15¢ Columbus Announcing His Discovery	290.00	55.00	(6)	5,250.00		1,576,950
239	30¢ Columbus at La Rabida	400.00	80.00	(6)	7,500.00		617,250
240	50¢ Recall of Columbus	500.00	125.00	(6)	11,000.00		243,750
241	$1 Isabella Pledging Her Jewels	1,500.00	575.00	(6)	21,000.00		55,050
242	$2 Columbus in Chains	1,650.00	500.00	(6)	22,500.00	12,000.00	45,550
243	$3 Columbus Describing His Third Voyage	3,200.00	900.00	(6)	50,000.00		27,650
244	$4 Isabella and Columbus	4,250.00	1,300.00	(6)	90,000.00		26,350
245	$5 Portrait of Columbus	4,500.00	1,450.00	(6)	95,000.00		27,350

COLUMBUS SAW THE LIGHT

Could Columbus, one of the world's most skillful mariners, have been mistaken about sighting land?

Columbus saw a light from the Santa Maria *at 10 p.m. on October 11, 1492. He called his companions, and together they watched the distant light rise and fall. Columbus claimed the light was land.*

Four hours later, at 2 a.m., land was sighted in the moonlight by a sailor aboard the Pinta: *it was Watling Island in the Bahamas, the first landfall in the newly discovered continent. But the small, low-lying island the sailor sighted by moonlight at a distance of six miles could hardly have been seen by Columbus four hours earlier—and 35 to 45 miles farther away.*

Science offers a modern clue to this centuries-old mystery. Small fireworms living among the Bahamas' coral reefs swim to the surface in groups to spawn. There the females shed intensely phosphorescent eggs in several "flashes." They spawn every month—after the sun sets and before the moon rises. No doubt, this is what Columbus saw. See Scott Nos. 230-245.

Columbus takes leave of Isabella and Ferdinand.

230

231

232

233

234

235

236

237

238

239

240

241

242

243

244

245

246

251

253

254

255

256

257

258

259

260

261

262

263

282 C

283

Watermark 191

JOHN MARSHALL

The adage "clothes make the man" was constantly overruled by the fourth Chief Justice of the Supreme Court. John Marshall's carelessness of dress was noteworthy from his days as a Revolutionary War captain, Virginia lawyer, diplomatic envoy and Secretary of State. Even his 1801 appointment as Chief Justice by outgoing President John Adams didn't improve Marshall's fashion sense—or dampen his sense of humor. For example, he once accepted a tip to deliver a turkey for a shopper who had no idea that Marshall was officially Chief Justice of the Supreme Court.

Considered by many to be America's greatest Chief Justice, Marshall raised the fledgling court to its position as one of the three great branches of government. It was under his tenure that the new Constitution, the supreme law of the land, began to be defined. During his 35 years on the bench, Marshall was the father of many major legal principles that govern us even today. See Scott No. 263.

Bureau Issues

Starting in 1894, the Bureau of Engraving and Printing at Washington has produced all U.S. postage stamps except Nos. 909-921 (Overrun Countries), 1335 (Eakins painting), 1355 (Disney), 1410-1413 (Anti-Pollution), 1414-1418 (Christmas, 1970),1789 (John Paul Jones), 1804 (Benjamin Banneker), 1825 (Veterans Administration) and 1833 (American Education).

Issue of 1894, Perf. 12, Unwmkd.

		Un	U	#	PB
246	1¢ Franklin	21.00	3.00	(6)	275.00
247	1¢ blue Franklin (246)	47.50	1.75	(6)	550.00
248	2¢ Washington, type I	17.50	2.00	(6)	185.00
	Nos. 249-252: Washington (248)				
249	2¢ carmine lake, type I	110.00	1.35	(6)	1,000.00
250	2¢ carmine, type I	21.00	.20	(6)	275.00
251	2¢ carmine, type II	165.00	2.50	(6)	2,200.00
252	2¢ carmine, type III	85.00	3.00	(6)	1,000.00
253	3¢ Jackson	75.00	6.25	(6)	800.00
254	4¢ Lincoln	85.00	2.00	(6)	950.00
255	5¢ Grant	55.00	3.50	(6)	650.00
256	6¢ Garfield	120.00	12.50	(6)	1,250.00
257	8¢ Sherman	90.00	10.00	(6)	800.00
258	10¢ Webster	175.00	6.00	(6)	2,200.00
259	15¢ Clay	265.00	45.00	(6)	3,500.00
260	50¢ Jefferson	375.00	75.00	(6)	6,000.00
261	$1 Commodore Perry, type I	975.00	200.00	(6)	*13,000.00*
261A	$1 black Perry, type II (261)	1,750.00	400.00	(6)	*20,000.00*
262	$2 James Madison	2,350.00	525.00	(6)	35,000.00
263	$5 John Marshall	3,750.00	950.00	(6)	12,000.00

2¢ Washington
Types I-III of 1894

Triangle of **248-250**
Type I. Horizontal lines of uniform thickness run across the triangle.

Triangle of **251**
Type II. Horizontal lines cross the triangle, but are thinner within than without.

Triangle of **252**
Type III. The horizontal lines do not cross the double frame lines of the triangle.

$1 Perry
Types of 1894

 ←

Detail of **261**
Type I. The circles enclosing $1 are broken.

 ←

Detail of **261A**
Type II. The circles enclosing $1 are complete.

 ←

Detail of **282C**
TEN CENTS
Type I. The tips of the foliate ornaments do not impinge on the white curved line below "TEN CENTS."

 ←

Detail of **283**
Type II. The tips of the ornaments break the curved line below the "E" of "TEN" and the "T" of "CENTS."

		Un	U	#	PB	FDC		Q
	Issue of 1895, Perf. 12, Wmkd. 191							
264	1¢ blue Franklin (264)	6.00	.06	(6)	150.00			
	Nos. 265-267: Washington (248)							
265	2¢ carmine, type I	22.50	.65	(6)	325.00			
266	2¢ carmine, type II	27.50	2.75	(6)	400.00			
267	2¢ carmine, type III	4.50	.05	(6)	125.00			
268	3¢ purple Jackson (253)	32.50	1.00	(6)	575.00			
269	4¢ dk. brown Lincoln (254)	32.50	1.10	(6)	600.00			
270	5¢ chocolate Grant (255)	27.50	1.60	(6)	600.00			
271	6¢ dull brn. Garfield (256)	67.50	3.50	(6)	900.00			
272	8¢ vio. brn. Sherman (257)	28.50	1.00	(6)	600.00			
273	10¢ dk. green Webster (258)	57.50	1.20	(6)	1,100.00			
274	15¢ dark blue Clay (259)	185.00	7.00	(6)	3,000.00			
275	50¢ orange Jefferson (260)	285.00	20.00	(6)	5,000.00			
276	$1 black Perry, type I (261)	650.00	60.00	(6)	*10,000.00*			
276A	$1 blk. Perry, type II (261)	1,450.00	110.00	(6)	*18,500.00*			
277	$2 brt. blue Madison (262)	975.00	250.00	(6)	*17,500.00*			
278	$5 dk. grn. Marshall (263)	2,000.00	375.00	(6)	*50,000.00*			
	Issue of 1898, Perf. 12							
279	1¢ dp. green Franklin (246)	9.00	.06	(6)	160.00			
279B	2¢ red Washington, type III (248)	8.50	.05	(6)	150.00			
279Be	Booklet pane of 6	375.00	*200.00*					
280	4¢ rose brn. Lincoln (254)	30.00	.70	(6)	550.00			
281	5¢ dark blue Grant (255)	32.50	.50	(6)	650.00			
282	6¢ lake Garfield (256)	45.00	2.00	(6)	900.00			
282C	10¢ Webster, type I	140.00	2.00	(6)	2,500.00			
283	10¢ Webster, type II	95.00	1.75	(6)	1,500.00			
284	15¢ olive green Clay (259)	105.00	5.75	(6)	2,000.00			

JAMES MADISON

James Madison, fourth President of the United States and Secretary of State under Thomas Jefferson, presents an oddly contradictory figure to those who would study him. Known today as "Father of the Constitution," major architect of the Bill of Rights, and co-author of The Federalist, *earlier historians viewed him as "Jefferson's errand boy."*

Perhaps that view stemmed in part from "Jemmy" Madison's small stature. Standing only 5'4" and weighing less than 100 pounds, he was described by Washington Irving as "a withered little apple-john."

Nevertheless, Madison was the first—and only—President to face enemy fire while in office. It happened in the controversial War of 1812, which Madison himself had declared. When the British invaded Washington, he personally took command of an artillery battery, in a vain attempt to help defend the city. But the hopelessness of the situation soon became clear, and Madison moved off quickly, out of the line of fire. See Scott Nos. 266, 277, 312, 479.

BUFFALO

Once near extinction, the American buffalo (bison) has made such a successful comeback that it is finding its way to America's dinner tables.

1392

More and more farmers are turning to buffalo ranching to satisfy a growing consumer yen for buffalo steak. Just why such a demand exists is a mystery. Fans claim bison meat is tastier than beef; others contend it is dry, tough and gamey.

Buffalo are popular with ranchers because they gain weight faster than cattle, are more disease-resistant, can survive winter blizzards, and will eat weeds that cattle won't touch. Buffalo ranching does have its shortcomings, however. The animals are cantankerous, inclined to stampede, and able to climb high fences. As one rancher remarked, "You don't tell them where to go, you ask them."

Whatever their gastronomic or commercial merits, one fact seems clear: the buffalo is back to stay. See Scott Nos. 287, 1392.

WESTERN PROSPECTORS

Even as the great California gold rush of 1849 was getting under way, prospectors were striking out for new territories, panning new streams and searching for rumored "lost mines" all over the American West. Leading mules, pushing hand-carts, or driving prairie schooner wagons, they rushed to follow any lead.

No rush was wilder than the one to Pike's Peak in 1859. Spurred by glowing newspaper accounts of the "new El Dorado," thousands of gold seekers set off, bearing the famous slogan, "Pike's Peak or Bust." Once there, however, they found they had been "humbugged" by exaggerated reports, and there was little gold to be panned. Sadly they returned home with a new slogan: "Busted, by God." Only those with the capital and equipment for more intense mining in the quartz lodes upstream would see the major gold strikes yet to come. See Scott No. 291.

Old timers, Spriggs, Lamb and Dillon washing and panning gold, Rockerville, Dakota, 1889.

	Un	U	#	PB	FDC	Q
Trans-Mississippi Exposition Issue, June 17, Perf. 12						
285	1¢ Marquette on the Mississippi	32.50	5.50		325.00	*4,000.00*	70,993,400
286	2¢ Farming in the West	30.00	1.50		300.00	3,500.00	159,720,800
287	4¢ Indian Hunting Buffalo	180.00	20.00		1,750.00		4,924,500
288	5¢ Frémont on the Rocky Mts.	150.00	17.50		1,650.00	*4,750.00*	7,694,180
289	8¢ Troops Guarding Train	210.00	35.00		2,500.00	*7,500.00*	2,927,200
290	10¢ Hardships of Emigration	225.00	20.00		3,000.00		4,629,760
291	50¢ Western Mining Prospector	900.00	1.50		*17,500.00*	9,000.00	530,400
292	$1 Western Cattle in Storm	2,150.00	575.00		*35,000.00*		56,900
293	$2 Mississippi River Bridge						
	at St. Louis	3,350.00	800.00		*90,000.00*		56,200
Pan-American Exposition Issue, 1901, May 1, Wmkd. 191						
294	1¢ Great Lakes Steamer	25.00	4.50		92.50	*3,000.00*	91,401,500
294a	Center inverted	*11,000.00*	*2,500.00*				
295	2¢ An Early Locomotive	25.00	1.00		92.50	*2,500.00*	209,759,700
295a	Center inverted	*50,000.00*	*10,000.00*				
296	4¢ Closed Coach Automobile	135.00	16.50		525.00	*3,750.00*	5,737,100
296a	Center inverted	*14,000.00*					
297	5¢ Bridge at Niagara Falls	140.00	17.50		550.00	*4,250.00*	7,201,300
298	8¢ Sault Ste. Marie Canal Locks	200.00	65.00		750.00		4,921,700
299	10¢ American Line Steamship	285.00	30.00		1,075.00		5,043,700

NIAGARA FALLS

"Yours till Niagara Falls," the saying goes. But will Niagara keep falling forever? Not likely.

Niagara Falls, now one of the most spectacular natural wonders of North America, was probably formed about 12,000 years ago, when the last great ice sheet melted from the region. The melting ice caused Lake Erie to overflow, forming the Niagara River. The river ran northward over a high cliff where, over the centuries, it gradually cut out the falls.

But the pounding, swirling waters continue to wear away the underlying rocks, moving the falls upstream toward Lake Erie at the rate of one to three inches a year. In 1969, U.S. Army engineers built a dam to stop the flow of water temporarily, and a board of American and Canadian experts studied the rock ledge to see if further erosion could be prevented. Their conclusion: the cost would be too high. So Niagara continues to fall—for the time being—while it slowly works its way back to its origins.

See Scott No. 297.

285   286   287

288   289   290

291   292   293

294   294a   295   295a

296   296a   297

298   299

300   301   302   303   304

305   306   307   308   309   310

311   312   313   319

323   324   325   326

		Un	U	#	PB	FDC	Q
	Regular Issue of 1902-03, Perf. 12, Wmkd. 191						
300	1¢ Franklin, 1903	10.00	.05	(6)	175.00	*2,500.00*	
300b	Booklet pane of 6	*550.00*	*250.00*				
301	2¢ Washington, 1903	12.50	.05	(6)	200.00	3,500.00	
301c	Booklet pane of 6	*475.00*	*250.00*				
302	3¢ Jackson, 1903	65.00	2.50	(6)	950.00	*2,500.00*	
303	4¢ Grant, 1903	65.00	.90	(6)	950.00	*2,500.00*	
304	5¢ Lincoln, 1903	70.00	.85	(6)	1,000.00	*2,750.00*	
305	6¢ Garfield, 1903	75.00	2.00	(6)	1,100.00	*2,750.00*	
306	8¢ Martha Washington, 1902	40.00	2.00	(6)	825.00	*3,000.00*	
307	10¢ Webster, 1903	80.00	1.50	(6)	1,300.00	*3,000.00*	
308	13¢ Benjamin Harrison, 1902	40.00	8.50	(6)	675.00		
309	15¢ Clay, 1903	200.00	5.50	(6)	3,750.00		
310	50¢ Jefferson, 1903	625.00	25.00	(6)	8,000.00		
311	$1 David G. Farragut, 1903	1,050.00	50.00	(6)	*15,000.00*		
312	$2 Madison, 1903	1,350.00	175.00	(6)	*22,500.00*		
313	$5 Marshall, 1903	3,000.00	625.00	(6)	*60,000.00*		
	For listings of 312 and 313 with Perf. 10, see Nos. 479 and 480.						
	Issues of 1906-08, Imperf.						
314	1¢ blue green Franklin (300),-06	37.50	21.00	(6)	300.00		
314A	4¢ brown Grant (303), 1908	*15,000.00*	*7,500.00*				
315	5¢ blue Lincoln (304), 1908	900.00	325.00	(6)	5,500.00		
	No. 314A was issued imperforate, but all copies were privately perforated with large oblong perforations at the sides. (Schermack type III).						
	Coil Stamps, Perf. 12 Horizontally						
316	1¢ blue green pair						
	Franklin (300), 1908	*20,000.00*					
317	5¢ blue pair Lincoln (304),-08	*4,000.00*					
	Perf. 12 Vertically						
318	1¢ blue green pair Franklin						
	(300), 1908	*3,250.00*					
	Issue of 1903, Perf. 12, Shield-shaped Background						
319	2¢ Washington, Nov. 12	7.00	.04	(6)	120.00		
319g	Booklet pane of 6	120.00	*20.00*				
	Issue of 1906, Nos. 320-322: Washington (319), Imperf.						
320	2¢ carmine, Oct 2	32.50	20.00	(6)	325.00		
	Issue of 1908, Coil Stamps, Perf. 12, Horizontally						
321	2¢ carmine pair	*35,000.00*					
	Perf. 12 Vertically						
322	2¢ carmine pair	4,250.00					
	Issue of 1904, Perf. 12, Louisiana Purchase Exposition Issue, Apr. 30						
323	1¢ Robert R. Livingston	32.50	4.50		125.00	*3,000.00*	79,779,200
324	2¢ Thomas Jefferson	30.00	1.50		115.00	*2,750.00*	192,732,400
325	3¢ James Monroe	100.00	30.00		395.00	*3,500.00*	4,542,600
326	5¢ William McKinley	130.00	20.00		525.00	*4,000.00*	6,926,700

		Un	U	#	PB	FDC	Q
	1904 continued						
327	10¢ Map of Louisiana Purchase	300.00	30.00		1,200.00	*6,250.00*	4,011,200
	Issue of 1907, Perf. 12, Jamestown Exposition Issue						
328	1¢ Captain John Smith	27.50	5.50	(6)	350.00	*2,000.00*	77,728,794
329	2¢ Founding of Jamestown	32.50	3.25	(6)	475.00	*2,000.00*	149,497,994
330	5¢ Pocahontas	150.00	30.00	(6)	3,250.00		7,980,594
	Regular Issues of 1908-09, Perf. 12, Wmkd. 191						
331	1¢ Franklin, 1908	8.00	.05	(6)	80.00	*900.00*	
331a	Booklet pane of 6	150.00	*35.00*				
332	2¢ Washington, 1908	7.50	.05	(6)	65.00	*900.00*	
332a	Booklet pane of 6	120.00	*35.00*				
333	3¢ Washington, type I, 1908	25.00	3.00	(6)	300.00		
	Nos. 334-342: Washington (333)						
334	4¢ orange brown, 1908	27.50	1.00	(6)	350.00		
335	5¢ blue, 1908	37.50	2.00	(6)	500.00	*1,500.00*	
336	6¢ red orange, 1908	47.50	4.50	(6)	700.00	*1,500.00*	
337	8¢ olive green, 1908	32.50	2.50	(6)	475.00	*1,500.00*	
338	10¢ yellow, 1909	65.00	1.50	(6)	850.00	*1,850.00*	
339	13¢ blue green, 1909	35.00	20.00	(6)	500.00	*2,000.00*	
340	15¢ pale ultramarine, 1909	57.50	5.75	(6)	650.00	*2,250.00*	
341	50¢ violet, 1909	325.00	12.50	(6)	*6,500.00*		
342	$1 violet brown, 1909	475.00	75.00	(6)	*8,500.00*		
	Imperf.						
343	1¢ green Franklin (331), 1908	11.00	3.50	(6)	100.00	*950.00*	
344	2¢ car. Washington (332), 1908	15.00	2.50	(6)	175.00		
	Nos. 345-347: Washington (333)						
345	3¢ deep violet, type I, 1909	30.00	13.50	(6)	300.00		
346	4¢ orange brown, 1909	55.00	20.00	(6)	500.00		
347	5¢ blue, 1909	85.00	35.00	(6)	850.00		
	Coil Stamps of 1908-10						
	Nos. 350-351, 354-356: Washington (333), Perf. 12 Horizontally						
348	1¢ green Franklin (331), 1908	22.50	12.00				
349	2¢ car. Washington (332), 1909	45.00	5.00				
350	4¢ orange brown, 1910	100.00	50.00				
351	5¢ blue, 1909	120.00	65.00				
	1909, Perf. 12 Vertically						
352	1¢ green Franklin (331), 1909	50.00	15.00			*950.00*	
353	2¢ car. Washington (332), 1909	45.00	5.50				
354	4¢ orange brown, 1909	120.00	37.50				
355	5¢ blue, 1909	130.00	55.00				
356	10¢ yellow, 1909	1,200.00	325.00				
	Issues of 1909, Bluish Paper, Perf. 12						
	Nos. 359-366: Washington (333)						
357	1¢ green Franklin (331)	100.00	80.00	(6)	1,100.00		
358	2¢ car. Washington (332)	95.00	60.00	(6)	1,100.00		

327

328

329

330

331

332

333

334

335

336

337

338

342

		Un	U	#	PB	FDC	Q
	1909 continued						
359	3¢ deep violet, type I	1,350.00	850.00	(6)	*13,000.00*		
360	4¢ orange brown	*13,500.00*					
361	5¢ blue	3,250.00	4,000.00	(6)	*30,000.00*		
362	6¢ red orange	875.00	500.00	(6)	*9,500.00*		
363	8¢ olive green	*13,500.00*		(6)			
364	10¢ yellow	900.00	575.00	(6)	*10,000.00*		
365	13¢ blue green	2,000.00	950.00	(6)	*15,000.00*		
366	15¢ pale ultramarine	850.00	500.00	(6)	*8,500.00*		
	Lincoln Memorial Issue, Feb. 12						
367	2¢ Lincoln, Perf. 12	9.50	2.75	(6)	225.00	*425.00*	148,387,191
368	2¢ Lincoln, Imperf.	60.00	30.00	(6)	550.00	*1,850.00*	1,273,900
369	2¢ Lincoln, Perf. 12, Bluish Paper	325.00	175.00	(6)	*4,250.00*		637,000
	Alaska-Yukon Exposition Issue						
370	2¢ William Seward, Perf. 12	14.00	2.25	(6)	365.00	*2,000.00*	152,887,311
371	2¢ William Seward, Imperf.	75.00	35.00	(6)	625.00	*2,500.00*	525,400
	Hudson-Fulton Celebration Issue, Sep. 25						
372	2¢ Half Moon and Clermont, Perf. 12	17.50	4.00	(6)	425.00	*900.00*	72,634,631
373	2¢ Half Moon and Clermont, Imperf.	100.00	35.00	(6)	700.00	*2,250.00*	216,480
	Issues of 1910-13, Perf. 12, Wmkd. 190						
	Nos. 376-382: Washington (333)						
374	1¢ green Franklin (331), 1910	7.50	.06	(6)	85.00		
374a	Booklet pane of 6	135.00	*30.00*				
375	2¢ car. Washington (332), 1910	6.75	.03	(6)	75.00		
375a	Booklet pane of 6	110.00	*25.00*				
376	3¢ deep violet, type I, 1911	15.00	1.50	(6)	155.00		
377	4¢ brown, 1911	20.00	.50	(6)	200.00		
378	5¢ blue, 1911	20.00	.50	(6)	250.00		
379	6¢ red orange, 1911	37.50	.75	(6)	500.00		
380	8¢ olive green, 1911	115.00	11.50	(6)	1,250.00		
381	10¢ yellow, 1911	105.00	4.00	(6)	1,250.00		
382	15¢ pale ultramarine, 1911	275.00	13.50	(6)	2,250.00		
	Imperf.						
383	1¢ green Franklin (331), 1911	5.00	3.00	(6)	90.00		
384	2¢ car. Washington (332), 1911	7.00	1.50	(6)	225.00		
	Coil Stamps, Perf. 12 Horizontally						
385	1¢ green Franklin (331), 1910	25.00	10.00				
386	2¢ car. Washington (332), 1910	37.50	9.00				
	Perf. 12 Vertically						
387	1¢ green Franklin (331), 1910	75.00	20.00				
388	2¢ car. Washington (332), 1910	550.00	70.00				
389	3¢ dp. vio. Washington, type I (333), 1911	*12,000.00*	*3,750.00*				
	Perf. 8½ Horizontally						
390	1¢ green Franklin (331), 1910	5.00	2.50				

367 368 370 371

372 373

LINCOLN MEMORIAL

Although everyone agreed that there should be a memorial to President Abraham Lincoln, few agreed on the site that was chosen for it.

The Commission of Fine Arts had considered many locations, but ended up choosing Potomac Park, an isolated swamp. The selection was vigorously attacked. One Congressman said that "Old Abe" would shiver and shake himself to pieces with ague and malaria if placed in the desolate swamp. The Commission replied, "In judging a site of a memorial to endure throughout the ages we must regard not what the location was . . . but what it can be made for all time to come."

The Commission's vision turned out to be sharper than that of the Congressman. The location of the Lincoln Memorial is regarded today as one of the most beautiful in the nation's Capitol. Flanked by a reflecting pool and rows of elm trees, the Memorial is dominated by the imposing 19-foot statue of the former President. It is a fitting site for the inscription: "In this Temple, as in the hearts of the people for whom he saved the Union, the memory of Abraham Lincoln is enshrined forever." See Scott Nos. 367-369.

397

398

399

400

405

406

414

420

BUILDING THE PANAMA CANAL

"Tell them I am going to make the dirt fly on the isthmus." That was President Theodore Roosevelt's answer to those who criticized this country's plans to build the Panama Canal.

Their criticism, though, had good cause. First, the French had failed miserably in their attempt to dig a canal—a fiasco compounded of poor engineering, bankruptcy, bribery and fraud. Then, the U.S. itself had acted less than honorably in supporting Panama's secession from Colombia, primarily to assure a prompt and favorable treaty.

Even then, it took a while for any real progress to be made. To be sure, digging began immediately—but with no plan in hand. Several commissions and chief engineers came and went. Finally, even Roosevelt became disgusted, and turned to the Army engineers.

Colonel George Washington Goethals took command of the project in 1907, and at last the dirt began to fly. Fifty-six thousand men set to work in the tropical heat, digging enough dirt and rock each month to fill the Empire State Building two and three times over. When the canal, with its massive locks, dams and lakes, was at last finished in 1914, it was indeed "the greatest engineering feat of the ages."
See Scott Nos. 397-398.

		Un	U	#	PB	FDC	Q
	1910-13 continued						
391	2¢ car. Washington (332), 1910	45.00	7.00				
	Perf. 8½ Vertically, Nos. 394-396: Washington (333)						
392	1¢ green Franklin (331), 1910	22.50	14.00				
393	2¢ car. Washington (332), 1910	50.00	4.50				
394	3¢ deep violet, type I, 1911	60.00	25.00			1,250.00	
395	4¢ brown, 1912	60.00	25.00				
396	5¢ blue, 1913	60.00	25.00				
	Panama Pacific Exposition Issue, 1913, Perf. 12						
397	1¢ Balboa	22.50	1.75	(6)	225.00	3,000.00	167,398,463
398	2¢ Locks, Panama Canal	25.00	.50	(6)	450.00	3,000.00	251,856,543
399	5¢ Golden Gate	115.00	11.00	(6)	3,000.00		14,544,363
400	10¢ Discovery						
	of San Francisco Bay	225.00	23.50	(6)	4,000.00	5,250.00	8,484,182
400A	10¢ orange (400)	325.00	18.50	(6)	12,000.00		
	1914-15, Perf. 10						
401	1¢ green Balboa (397), 1914	37.50	6.00	(6)	500.00	1,250.00	167,398,463
402	2¢ carmine Canal Locks (398),-15	125.00	1.50	(6)	2,350.00		251,856,543
403	5¢ blue Golden Gate (399),-15	275.00	17.50	(6)	5,500.00	3,000.00	14,544,363
404	10¢ orange Discovery of						
	San Francisco Bay (400), 1915	1,850.00	72.50	(6)	20,000.00		8,484,182
	Issues of 1912-14						
	Nos. 405-413: Washington (333), Perf. 12						
405	1¢ green, 1912	8.00	.06	(6)	110.00	1,300.00	
405b	Booklet pane of 6	65.00	7.50				
406	2¢ carmine, type I, 1912	7.00	.03	(6)	125.00	950.00	
406a	Booklet pane of 6	70.00	17.50				
407	7¢ black, 1914	100.00	7.00	(6)	1,200.00	1,250.00	
408	1¢ green, Imperf., 1912	1.50	.60	(6)	55.00	850.00	
409	2¢ carmine, type I, Imperf., 1912	1.65	.60	(6)	60.00	850.00	
	Coil Stamps, Perf. 8½ Horizontally						
410	1¢ green, 1912	7.00	3.00				
411	2¢ carmine, type I, 1912	8.50	3.00				
	Perf. 8½ Vertically						
412	1¢ green, 1912	25.00	4.50				
413	2¢ carmine, type I, 1912	45.00	.50			1,000.00	
	Perf. 12, Nos. 415-421: Franklin (414)						
414	8¢ Franklin, 1912	35.00	1.25	(6)	475.00	1,400.00	
415	9¢ salmon red, 1914	45.00	13.50	(6)	625.00	1,050.00	
416	10¢ orange yellow, 1912	35.00	.20	(6)	525.00	1,400.00	
417	12¢ claret brown, 1914	30.00	4.00	(6)	375.00	1,300.00	
418	15¢ gray, 1912	70.00	3.00	(6)	750.00	1,750.00	
419	20¢ ultramarine, 1914	175.00	14.00	(6)	1,850.00	1,850.00	
420	30¢ orange red, 1914	130.00	14.00	(6)	1,750.00	2,000.00	

		Un	U	#	PB	FDC	Q
	1912-14 continued						
421	50¢ violet, 1914	575.00	14.00	(6)	7,000.00		
	Nos. 422-423: Franklin (414), Perf. 12						
422	50¢ violet, Feb. 12, 1912	300.00	14.00	(6)	4,750.00		
423	$1 violet brown, Feb. 12, 1912						
	Wmkd. 191	600.00	70.00	(6)	8,500.00		
	Issues of 1914-15, Perf. 10, Wmkd. 190						
	Nos. 424-430: Washington (333)						
424	1¢ green, 1914	3.00	.06	(6)	60.00		
424d	Booklet pane of 6	4.00	.75				
425	2¢ rose red, type I, 1914	2.75	.04	(6)	45.00		
425e	Booklet pane of 6	15.00	*3.00*				
426	3¢ deep violet, type I, 1914	12.50	1.25	(6)	120.00		
427	4¢ brown, 1914	30.00	.40	(6)	400.00		
428	5¢ blue, 1914	27.50	.40	(6)	300.00		
429	6¢ red orange, 1914	35.00	1.00	(6)	300.00		
430	7¢ black, 1914	90.00	4.25	(6)	900.00		
	Nos. 431-440: Franklin (414)						
431	8¢ pale olive green, 1914	35.00	1.50	(6)	350.00		
432	9¢ salmon red, 1914	47.50	7.50	(6)	475.00		
433	10¢ orange yellow, 1914	45.00	.25	(6)	500.00		
434	11¢ dark green, 1915	20.00	5.50	(6)	175.00		
435	12¢ claret brown, 1914	21.50	3.75	(6)	200.00		
437	15¢ gray, 1914	135.00	6.25	(6)	675.00		
438	20¢ ultramarine, 1914	250.00	3.50	(6)	2,750.00		
439	30¢ orange red, 1914	325.00	11.00	(6)	4,250.00		
440	50¢ violet, 1914	825.00	15.00	(6)	8,500.00		
	Coil Stamps, Perf. 10, 1914						
441	1¢ green	1.00	.75				
442	2¢ carmine, type I	10.00	6.50				
443	1¢ green	22.50	4.50				
444	2¢ carmine, type I	37.50	1.00				
445	3¢ violet, type I	250.00	100.00				
446	4¢ brown	150.00	32.50				
447	5¢ blue	55.00	17.50				
	Coil Stamps, Washington (333), 1915-16, Perf. 10 Horizontally						
448	1¢ green, 1915	7.00	2.75				
449	2¢ red, type I, 1915	1,400.00	120.00				
450	2¢ carmine, type III, 1916	12.00	2.50				
	1914-16, Perf. 10 Vertically						
452	1¢ green, 1914	9.00	1.50				
453	2¢ red, type I, 1914	135.00	3.75				
454	2¢ carmine, type II, 1915	150.00	12.00				
455	2¢ carmine, type III, 1915	12.50	.85				

		Un	U	#	PB	FDC	Q
	1914-16 continued						
456	3¢ violet, type I, 1916	300.00	75.00				
457	4¢ brown	35.00	15.00				
458	5¢ blue	35.00	15.00				
	Issue of 1914 Washington (333), Imperf., Coil						
459	2¢ carmine, type I, June 30	550.00	*600.00*				
	Issues of 1915, Perf. 10, Wmkd. 191						
460	$1 violet black Franklin						
	(414), Feb. 8	900.00	85.00	(6)	9,000.00		
	Perf. 11						
461	2¢ pale carmine red, type I.						
	Washington (333), June 17	85.00	65.00	(6)	850.00		
	Privately perforated copies of No. 409 have been made to resemble No. 461.						
	From 1916 all postage stamps except Nos. 519 and 832b are on unwatermarked paper.						
	Issues of 1916-17, Perf. 10						
	Nos. 462-469: Washington (333)						
462	1¢ green, 1916	8.00	.30	(6)	135.00		
462a	Booklet pane of 6	*12.00*	*1.00*				
463	2¢ carmine, type I, 1916	5.00	.10	(6)	100.00		
463a	Booklet pane of 6	*75.00*	*15.00*				
464	3¢ violet, type I, 1916	85.00	11.00	(6)	1,100.00		
465	4¢ orange brown, 1916	50.00	1.50	(6)	750.00		
466	5¢ blue, 1916	80.00	1.40	(6)	950.00		
467	5¢ car. (error in plate of 2¢), 1917	975.00	525.00				
468	6¢ red orange, 1916	95.00	5.50	(6)	900.00		
469	7¢ black, 1916	115.00	10.00	(6)	1,250.00		

DISCOVERY OF SAN FRANCISCO BAY

It was the famous ship the Golden Hinde, *bearing the company of Sir Francis Drake, that first brought Europeans to the vicinity of San Francisco Bay in 1579. Near Point Reyes they came ashore, where the Indians, awed by the strange white visitors, brought gifts of feathers and tobacco and placed a crown on Drake's head.*

400

But close as they were—perhaps a few miles north of the Golden Gate—Sir Francis and his men never set eyes on the huge landlocked anchorage now known as San Francisco Bay. That was for others, though precisely who *first set eyes on the Bay remains a subject of debate.*

Some say it was the shipwrecked Cermeno, *in 1595. Others, that it was a small band of soldiers led by Sergeant Jose Francisco Ortega, sent up the coast by Don Gaspar de Portola in 1769. Most today give credit to Portola's young lieutenant, Pedro Fages, who led a second expedition in 1772. But whatever the truth, it was Drake who opened that part of the North American continent and paved the way for all who would follow. See Scott No. 400.*

		Un	U	#	PB	FDC	Q
	1916-17 continued Nos. 470-478: Franklin (414)						
470	8¢ olive green, 1916	50.00	5.00	(6)	525.00		
471	9¢ salmon red, 1916	52.50	13.50	(6)	600.00		
472	10¢ orange yellow, 1916	110.00	1.00	(6)	1,350.00		
473	11¢ dark green, 1916	27.50	13.50	(6)	275.00		
474	12¢ claret brown, 1916	42.50	4.25	(6)	500.00		
475	15¢ gray, 1916	165.00	10.00	(6)	2,000.00		
476	20¢ light ultramarine, 1916	275.00	11.00	(6)	2,750.00		
476A	30¢ orange red, 1916	—	—	(6)			
477	50¢ light violet, 1917	1,400.00	67.50	(6)	17,500.00		
478	$1 violet black, 1916	900.00	15.00	(6)	9,000.00		
	Issues of 1917, Perf. 10, Mar. 22						
479	$2 dark blue Madison (312), 1917	675.00	35.00	(6)	6,250.00		
480	$5 light green Marshall (313), 1917	575.00	37.50	(6)	4,750.00		
	Issues of 1916-17, Washington (333), Imperf.						
481	1¢ green, 1916	1.25	.75	(6)	17.50	925.00	
482	2¢ carmine, type I, 1916	1.65	1.50	(6)	37.50		
482A	2¢ carmine, type Ia, 1916	—	5,500.00				
483	3¢ violet, type I, 1917	20.00	8.50	(6)	210.00		
484	3¢ violet, type II, 1917	14.00	4.00	(6)	150.00		
485	5¢ car. (error in plate of 2¢),-17	15,000.00					
	Coil Stamps, Washington (333), 1916-19, Perf. 10 Horizontally						
486	1¢ green, 1918	1.00	.15			575.00	
487	2¢ carmine, type II, 1919	20.00	2.50				
488	2¢ carmine, type III, 1917	4.00	1.50				
489	3¢ violet, type I, 1917	6.00	1.00				
	1916-22, Perf. 10 Vertically						
490	1¢ green, 1916	.75	.15				
491	2¢ carmine, type II, 1916	1,450.00	185.00				
492	2¢ carmine, type III, 1916	11.00	.15				
493	3¢ violet, type I, 1917	30.00	2.50				
494	3¢ violet, type II, 1918	15.00	.60				
495	4¢ orange brown, 1917	15.00	3.50				
496	5¢ blue, 1919	5.00	.60				
497	10¢ orange yellow Franklin						
	(414), 1922	28.50	8.50			1,100.00	
	Issues of 1917-19, Perf. 11						
	Nos. 498-507: Washington (333)						
498	1¢ green, 1917	.25	.04	(6)	16.50	950.00	
498e	Booklet pane of 6	1.75	.35				
498f	Booklet pane of 30	600.00					
499	2¢ rose, type I, 1917	.25	.03	(6)	12.50	950.00	
499e	Booklet pane of 6	2.00	.50				
499f	Booklet pane of 30	7,500.00					

		Un	U	#	PB	FDC	Q
	1917-19 continued						
500	2¢ deep rose, type Ia, 1917	300.00	110.00	(6)	2,500.00		
501	3¢ light violet, type I, 1917	15.00	.08	(6)	150.00	*950.00*	
501b	Booklet pane of 6	75.00	*15.00*				
502	3¢ dark violet, type II, 1917	18.50	.25	(6)	200.00		
502b	Booklet pane of 6, 1918	50.00	*10.00*				
503	4¢ brown, 1917	14.50	.20	(6)	160.00	*950.00*	
504	5¢ blue, 1917	11.50	.08	(6)	135.00	*1,000.00*	
505	5¢ rose (error in plate of 2¢),-17	650.00	400.00				
506	6¢ red orange, 1917	17.50	.30	(6)	200.00	*1,000.00*	
507	7¢ black, 1917	32.50	1.00	(6)	350.00	*1,100.00*	
	Nos. 508-518: Franklin (414)						
508	8¢ olive bistre, 1917	14.00	.70	(6)	225.00	*1,100.00*	
509	9¢ salmon red, 1917	21.00	2.25	(6)	250.00	*1,100.00*	
510	10¢ orange yellow, 1917	24.00	.05	(6)	325.00	*1,200.00*	
511	11¢ light green, 1917	10.50	3.25	(6)	135.00	*1,200.00*	
512	12¢ claret brown, 1917	11.00	.45	(6)	130.00	*1,200.00*	
513	13¢ apple green, 1919	14.00	6.00	(6)	150.00		
514	15¢ gray, 1917	62.50	.90	(6)	800.00	*1,200.00*	
515	20¢ light ultramarine, 1917	70.00	.30	(6)	800.00	*1,450.00*	
516	30¢ orange red, 1917	65.00	.85	(6)	700.00	*1,600.00*	
517	50¢ red violet, 1917	125.00	.65	(6)	1,750.00	*2,000.00*	
518	$1 violet brown, 1917	110.00	1.50	(6)	1,650.00	*4,000.00*	
	Issue of 1917, Perf. 11, Wmkd. 191						
519	2¢ carmine Washington						
	(332), Oct. 10	200.00	160.00	(6)	2,000.00		
	Privately perforated copies of No. 344 have been made to resemble No. 519.						
	Issues of 1918, Unwmkd., Perf. 11						
523	$2 orange red and black						
	Franklin (547), Aug. 19	1,850.00	175.00	(8)	*28,500.00*		
524	$5 deep green and black						
	Franklin (547), Aug. 19	725.00	25.00	(8)	12,000.00	*8,000.00*	
	Issues of 1918-20, Washington (333)						
	Perf. II						
525	1¢ gray green, 1918	2.25	.60	(6)	32.50	*725.00*	
526	2¢ carmine, type IV, 1920	30.00	3.00	(6)	250.00	*750.00*	
527	2¢ carmine, type V, 1920	18.50	1.00	(6)	150.00		
528	2¢ carmine, type Va, 1920	9.00	.15	(6)	75.00		
528A	2¢ carmine, type VI, 1920	50.00	.75	(6)	375.00		
528B	2¢ carmine, type VII, 1920	20.00	.12	(6)	175.00		
529	3¢ violet, type III, 1918	2.25	.10	(6)	60.00	*550.00*	
530	3¢ purple, type IV, 1918	.70	.06	(6)	15.00	*550.00*	
	Imperf.						
531	1¢ green, 1919	11.00	8.00	(6)	120.00	*600.00*	

		Un	U	#	PB	FDC	Q
	1918-20 continued						
532	2¢ car. rose, type IV, 1919	40.00	25.00	(6)	425.00	*700.00*	
533	2¢ carmine, type V, 1919	325.00	70.00	(6)	2,500.00		
534	2¢ carmine, type Va, 1919	15.00	9.00	(6)	140.00		
534A	2¢ carmine, type VI, 1919	45.00	25.00	(6)	500.00		
534B	2¢ carmine, type VII, 1919	1,900.00	425.00	(6)	*14,500.00*		
535	3¢ violet, type IV, 1918	11.00	6.50	(6)	90.00	*700.00*	
	Issues of 1919						
	Perf. 12½						
536	1¢ gray green Washington						
	(333), Aug. 15	15.00	11.00	(6)	175.00	*550.00*	
	Perf. 11						
537	3¢ Allied Victory, Mar. 3	15.00	4.25	(6)	200.00	*625.00*	99,585,200
	The Armistice of Nov. 11, 1918, ended World War I on a note of triumph for the Allies.						
	Nos. 538-546: Washington (333), 1919, Perf. 11x10						
538	1¢ green	10.00	9.00		90.00	*600.00*	
539	2¢ carmine rose, type II	2,250.00	550.00		*14,000.00*		
540	2¢ carmine rose, type III	10.00	9.00		95.00		
541	3¢ violet, type II	37.50	32.50		475.00	*725.00*	
	1920, Perf. 10x11						
542	1¢ green, May 26	7.50	.75	(6)	120.00	*475.00*	
	1921, Perf. 10						
543	1¢ green	.50	.06		20.00		
	1921, Perf. 11						
544	1¢ green, 19x22½mm	*6,500.00*	*1,500.00*				
545	1¢ green, 19½—20mm x 22mm	165.00	90.00		1,000.00		
546	2¢ carmine rose, type III	110.00	70.00		750.00		
	Issues of 1920, Perf. 11						
547	$2 Franklin	625.00	35.00	(8)	13,500.00		
	Pilgrims 300th Anniv. Issue, Dec. 21						
548	1¢ Mayflower	8.50	3.00	(6)	95.00	*600.00*	137,978,207
549	2¢ Pilgrims Landing	12.50	2.25	(6)	125.00	*525.00*	196,037,327
550	5¢ Signing of Compact	77.50	18.50	(6)	1,000.00		11,321,607
	Issues of 1922-25, Perf. 11						
551	½¢ Nathan Hale, 1925	.15	.05	(6)	8.50	*21.00*	
552	1¢ Franklin (19x22mm), 1923	2.75	.07	(6)	32.50	*35.00*	
552a	Booklet pane of 6	5.50	.50				
553	1½¢ Harding, 1925	4.50	.15	(6)	50.00	*35.00*	
554	2¢ Washington, 1923	2.00	.03	(6)	35.00	*45.00*	
554c	Booklet pane of 6	7.00	*1.00*				
555	3¢ Lincoln, 1923	25.00	1.00	(6)	265.00	*37.50*	
556	4¢ Martha Washington, 1923	22.50	.20	(6)	275.00	*47.00*	
557	5¢ Theodore Roosevelt, 1922	22.50	.06	(6)	285.00	*110.00*	
558	6¢ Garfield, 1922	45.00	.75	(6)	700.00	*175.00*	

537   547

548   549   550

551   552   553   554   555

556   557   558

559

560

561

562

563

564

565

566

567

568

569

		Un	U	#	PB	FDC	Q
	1922-25 continued						
559	7¢ McKinley, 1923	10.00	.60	(6)	85.00	*110.00*	
560	8¢ Grant, 1923	57.50	.75	(6)	1100.00	*100.00*	
561	9¢ Jefferson, 1923	18.50	1.00	(6)	225.00	*100.00*	
562	10¢ Monroe, 1923	23.50	.10	(6)	425.00	*110.00*	
563	11¢ Rutherford B. Hayes, 1922	2.50	.25	(6)	60.00	*500.00*	
564	12¢ Grover Cleveland, 1923	9.00	.08	(6)	95.00	*140.00*	
565	14¢ American Indian, 1923	7.50	.85	(6)	80.00	*300.00*	
566	15¢ Statue of Liberty, 1922	28.50	.06	(6)	285.00	*325.00*	
567	20¢ Golden Gate, 1923	32.50	.10	(6)	300.00	*350.00*	
568	25¢ Niagara Falls, 1922	30.00	.50	(6)	300.00	*550.00*	
569	30¢ Buffalo, 1923	42.50	.35	(6)	600.00	*650.00*	

STATUE OF LIBERTY

The Statue of Liberty is a great lady in every sense of the word.

Her vital statistics alone tell an impressive story: she stands 305 feet tall, from pedestal base to torch, and weighs 225 tons. She boasts a 42-foot right hand, an eight-foot index finger, and a 13-inch fingernail. Her head measures 17 feet from chin to cranium, with a four-foot nose and a three-foot-wide mouth.

With those statistics, the construction of the great statue posed a monumental task. French sculptor Frederick Bartholdi built a nine-foot "working model," then worked up to a full-scale plaster model. When all the pieces were finally put together in 1884, the statue had to be dismantled for shipment to New York City. There it was painstakingly reassembled over a massive iron framework designed by Gustave Eiffel (whose tower came later).

But it is not the size of the statue or the undertaking that accounts for Liberty's appeal. The colossal monument—a gift from the people of France to the people of America—has come to symbolize not only the continuing friendship of the two nations, but also the ideals of human liberty and freedom upon which this country was founded. See Scott No. 566.

Toes and torch prior to construction, Bedloe's Island.

		Un	U	#	PB	FDC	Q
	1922-25 continued						
570	50¢ Arlington Amphitheater, 1922	100.00	.12	(6)	1,500.00	*800.00*	
571	$1 Lincoln Memorial, 1923	90.00	.45	(6)	750.00	*4,000.00*	
572	$2 U.S. Capitol, 1923	275.00	8.50	(6)	2,500.00	*8,500.00*	
573	$5 Head of Freedom,						
	Capitol Dome, 1923	575.00	14.50	(8)	9,250.00	*14,000.00*	
	Issues of 1923-25, Imperf.						
575	1¢ green Franklin (552), 1923	12.00	3.50	(6)	150.00		
576	1½¢ yellow brown Harding (553),-25	3.00	1.75	(6)	55.00	*45.00*	
577	2¢ carmine Washington (554)	3.50	2.00	(6)	50.00		
	For listings of other perforated stamps of issues 551-573 see:						
	Nos. 578 and 579	Perf. 11x10					
	Nos. 581 to 591	Perf. 10					
	Nos. 594 and 595	Perf. 11					
	Nos. 622 and 623	Perf. 11					
	Nos. 632 to 642, 653, 692 to 696	Perf. 11x10½					
	Nos. 697 to 701	Perf. 10½x11					
	Perf. 11x10						
578	1¢ green Franklin (552)	80.00	60.00		750.00		
579	2¢ carmine Washington (554)	57.50	45.00		425.00		
	Issues of 1923-26, Perf. 10						
581	1¢ green Franklin (552), 1923	6.00	.65		75.00	*1,800.00*	
582	1½¢ brown Harding (553), 1925	5.00	.60		45.00	*45.00*	
583	2¢ carmine Washington (554), 1924	2.50	.05		30.00	*50.00*	
583a	Booklet pane of 6	75.00	*25.00*				
584	3¢ violet Lincoln (555), 1925	32.50	1.75		300.00	*55.00*	
585	4¢ yellow brown						
	M. Washington (556)	18.50	.40		185.00	*55.00*	
586	5¢ blue T. Roosevelt (557), 1925	18.50	.25		175.00	*55.00*	
587	6¢ red orange Garfield (558), 1925	8.00	.40		75.00	*70.00*	
588	7¢ black McKinley (559), 1926	11.50	5.00		110.00	*65.00*	
589	8¢ olive green Grant (560), 1926	35.00	3.00		300.00	*70.00*	
590	9¢ rose Jefferson (561), 1926	5.00	2.25		45.00	*75.00*	
591	10¢ orange Monroe (562), 1925	70.00	.06		675.00	*95.00*	
	Perf. 11						
594	1¢ green Franklin,						
	19¾x22¼mm (552)	7,000.00	1,750.00				
595	2¢ carmine Washington,						
	19¾x22¼mm (554)	200.00	125.00		1,600.00		
596	1¢ green Franklin,						
	19¼x22¾mm (552)		12,000.00				
	Coil Stamps 1923-29, Perf. 10 Verically						
597	1¢ green Franklin (552), 1923	.25	.06			*400.00*	
598	1½¢ brown Harding (553), 1925	.75	.08			*50.00*	

570   571   572   573

610   611

U.S. CAPITOL

"Make no little plans. They have no magic to stir men's blood. . . . Remember that our sons and grandsons are going to do things that will stagger us. Let your watchword be order and your beacon beauty."

Pierre Charles L'Enfant wrote these words to the planners of the Capitol Building, and, from the results, it would seem they were taken to heart. For the Capitol is considered one of the architectural masterpieces of the world, its great mass and fine balance giving it a sense of unity and strength, of grace and grandeur.

Atop the dome of the Capitol stands the Statue of Freedom—ironically, cast in bronze by slaves around 1860. The statue's base bears the legend E Pluribus Unum, "One out of Many." The words are not only the nation's motto, but a fitting description of the building itself, for while it appears to be a coherent whole, it was in fact built in pieces and patches, and bears the stamp of many hands and minds.

Over the years, the Capitol has seen lives begin, continue and end. A visiting mother gave birth there in 1880. Two homeless men lived in its rooms undetected for years. And scores of Union and Confederate soldiers died in the rotunda when it was turned into an emergency hospital during the Civil War. See Scott No. 572.

Night view of the Capitol in Washington, DC, 1934.

INVERTED AIRMAIL

The year was 1918. It was a "first" for the mails: the first experimental airmail service, between Washington, D.C., and New York. The stamp itself was a triple "first": the world's first definitive airmail stamp, the first showing an airplane, the first airmail stamp to be printed in two colors, red and blue. In the world of philately, that itself was an event. It would soon become a greater one.

C3a

On the morning of May 14, stamp collector William Robey withdrew some money from his savings account and went to the Post Office in downtown Washington to buy a sheet of the new stamps—100 of them for $24. There were only a few left, and they were badly centered, but the clerk said he was expecting a new batch around lunchtime.

Robey returned at noon, and the same clerk handed him a sheet of stamps. Then, as Robey later said, "my heart stood still." His collector's eye had seen 100 borders, right-side-up, and 100 airplanes . . . upside down!

Thrilled, Robey showed his find to the clerk and later to his co-workers, then he went out to look for more of the inverted stamps. His search was in vain, and by the time he returned to his office two postal inspectors were waiting for him. They offered him a sheet of "good" stamps in exchange for the "mistakes," but Robey wisely refused.

Over the next week, Robey made the rounds of Washington and New York stamp dealers. The first offered him $500, but it was the final offer of $15,000 that Robey finally accepted.

Today, the whereabouts of only 81 of the 100 stamps is known. A single copy of the famous 24-cent Inverted Airmail is valued at $130,000! See Scott No. C3a.

PHILATELY'S "BLUE BOY"

When Mr. Hough proposed marriage to Jannett Brown by mail in 1847, he may well have believed it to be the most important letter he'd ever written. He could scarcely have known how important the envelope in which he sent it would be, more than a century later, to stamp collectors around the world.

Recently, the cover of Mr. Hough's love letter, bearing the 5-cent "Blue Alexandria" stamp, was sold in Geneva for $1 million, the highest price ever paid for a philatelic item.

The stamp is part of a "provisional" issue, the rarest kind of stamp in American philately. Provisional stamps were created and issued by local postmasters before the U.S. government began to issue its own stamps on July 1, 1847. The "Blue Alexandria," also known affectionately as the "Blue Boy," by Postmaster Daniel Bryan of Alexandria, Virginia, is considered the greatest postmaster provisional.

7

		Un	U	#	PB	FDC	Q
	Coil Stamps 1923-29 continued						
599	2¢ carmine Washington, type I (554), 1929	.30	.04			650.00	
599A	2¢ carmine Washington, type II (554), 1929	165.00	9.00				
600	3¢ violet Lincoln (555)	9.00	.08			70.00	
601	4¢ yellow brown M. Washington (556), 1923	4.00	.40			60.00	
602	5¢ dark blue Theodore Roosevelt (557), 1924	1.50	.18			75.00	
603	10¢ orange Monroe (562), 1924	3.50	.06			95.00	
	Coil Stamps 1923-25 Perf. 10 Horizontally						
604	1¢ yellow green Franklin (552), 1924	.25	.08			82.50	
605	1½¢ yellow brown Harding (553), 1925	.30	.18			50.00	
606	2¢ carmine Washington (554), 1923	.30	.10			80.00	
	Harding Memorial Issue, 1923, Flat Plate Printing (19¼x22¼mm)						
610	2¢ Harding, Perf. 11, Sept. 1	1.00	.10	(6)	42.50	45.00	1,459,487,085
611	2¢ Harding Imperf., Nov. 15	23.50	5.50	(6)	210.00	90.00	770,000
	Rotary Press Printing (19¼x22¾mm)						
612	2¢ black, Perf. 10 (610), Sept. 12	32.50	2.00		450.00	110.00	99,950,300
613	2¢ black Perf. 11 (610)		11,500.00				

THEODORE ROOSEVELT

Teddy Roosevelt a "victim?" It's hard now to imagine the "bully" President, big game hunter and hero of San Juan Hill as a ninety-pound weakling. But Roosevelt's physical strength and stamina did not come naturally—they were the result of a conscious decision and years of perserverance.

As a child, Roosevelt greatly admired men who were fearless, who could hold their own in the world. He wanted to be like them, but was plagued by poor eyesight and asthma. The former was corrected by thick glasses; the latter took more determination.

At the age of fourteen, because of an asthma attack, Teddy was put on a stage coach and sent to Moosehead Lake. On the way out he met a couple of mischievous boys about his own age. Roosevelt later described the encounter in his autobiography: "They found that I was a foreordained and pre- destined victim, and industriously proceeded to make life miserable for me. The worst feature was that when I finally tried to fight them I discov- ered that either one singly could . . . handle me with easy contempt . . . I made up my mind that I must try to learn so that I would not again be put in such a helpless position." And indeed, he never again was. See Scott Nos. 557, 586, 663, 856, 1023, 1039.

		Un	U	#	PB	FDC	Q
Huguenot-Walloon 300th Anniv. Issue, 1924, May 1							
614	1¢ Ship *New Netherland*	7.50	5.00	(6)	75.00	45.00	51,378,023
615	2¢ Landing at Fort Orange	12.50	3.50	(6)	140.00	55.00	77,753,423
616	5¢ Huguenot Monument, Florida	65.00	22.50	(6)	625.00	110.00	5,659,023
In the seventeenth century Dutch Walloons and French Huguenots fled to America to escape religious persecution. The Walloons founded Albany, New York.							
Lexington-Concord Issue, 1925, Apr. 4							
617	1¢ Washington at Cambridge	8.50	5.25	(6)	75.00	45.00	15,615,000
618	2¢ Birth of Liberty	13.50	7.50	(6)	165.00	55.00	26,596,600
619	5¢ Statue of Minute Man	62.50	20.00	(6)	525.00	90.00	5,348,800
Norse-American Issue, 1925, May 18							
620	2¢ Sloop *Restaurationen*	13.00	5.00	(8)	425.00	35.00	9,104,983
621	5¢ Viking Ship	45.00	22.50	(8)	1,350.00	70.00	1,900,983
In 1825, the first Norwegian immigrants arrived in New York City on the sloop *Restaurationen*							
Issues of 1925-26							
622	13¢ Benjamin Harrison, 1926	28.50	.65	(6)	225.00	30.00	
623	17¢ Woodrow Wilson, 1925	32.00	.30	(6)	235.00	27.50	
Issues of 1926							
627	2¢ Independence,						
	150th Anniv., May 10	5.25	.60	(6)	90.00	17.50	307,731,900
628	5¢ Ericsson Memorial, May 29	13.00	5.50	(6)	145.00	30.00	20,280,500
John Ericsson designed and built the Union warship *Monitor*.							
629	2¢ Battle of White Plains, Oct. 18	3.25	2.50	(6)	90.00	6.50	40,639,485

THE MONITOR

When John Ericsson first submitted his design for an armored warship to the Navy Department in 1861, it was met with disdain. "Take it home and worship it," said Commander Davis. "It will not be idolatry. It is in the image of nothing in the heaven above, or the earth beneath, or the waters under the earth."

Fortunately for the Union, wiser heads prevailed, and the armor-plated raft— called by some a "tin can on a shingle"—made the transition from Ericsson's imagination to reality in just a hundred days. The fast-revolving, mechanized iron gun turret that sat on her deck—patented by Theodore Timby—was like nothing ever seen before. "It was the cannon in the rotary turret," Ericsson later wrote, "that tore the fetters from millions of slaves." The Confederate Merrimac could only fight it to a draw. It took a hurricane, off the Carolina coast on the last day of 1862, to bring the Monitor down to the bottom with all hands.
See Scott No. 628.

614

615

616

617

618

619

620

621

622

623

627

628

629

631

633

643

644

645

646

648

649

650

MOLLY PITCHER

During the American Revolution, many women joined their husbands in camp. Mary Hays, wife of a New Jersey barber, was no exception. Like other camp followers, she made herself useful by doing washing, cooking and nursing for the soldiers. But unlike the others, she also made herself a name in history.

The Battle of Monmouth was fought on June 28, 1778, an extremely hot day. Mary Hays accompanied the soldiers to battle and spent the day carrying pitchers of water from a nearby spring to the parched and tired troops. When her husband was wounded, Mary even loaded his cannon for the rest of the battle, contributing to the American victory.

Her pitcher-carrying activities earned Mary Hays the nickname "Molly Pitcher"—and a permanent place in American history. See Scott No. 646.

At the Battle of Monmouth, June 28, 1778.

		Un	U	#	PB	FDC	Ω
	International Philatelic Exhibition Issue, Oct. 18, Souvenir Sheet						
630	2¢ car. rose, sheet of 25 with						
	selvage inscription (629)	750.00	500.00			1,000.00	107,398*
	Imperf.						
631	1½¢ Harding, Aug. 27,						
	18½—19mmx22mm	2.00	1.75		90.00	35.00	
	Issues of 1926-27, Perf. 11x10½						
632	1¢ green Franklin (552), 1927	.15	.03		3.50	50.00	
632a	Booklet pane of 6, 1927	2.50	.25				
633	1½¢ Harding, 1927	2.25	.08		100.00	50.00	
634	2¢ carmine Washington,						
	type I (554), 1956	.15	.03		1.20	55.00	
634d	Booklet pane of 6, 1927	1.00	.15				
634A	2¢ carmine Washington,						
	type II (554), 1926	425.00	10.00		2,500.00		
635	3¢ violet Lincoln (555), 1957	.65	.04		7.50	47.50	
636	4¢ yellow brown						
	M. Washington (556), 1927	6.00	.08		125.00	50.00	
637	5¢ dark blue T. Roosevelt (557),-27	5.75	.03		30.00	50.00	
638	6¢ red orange Garfield (558), 1927	5.75	.03		30.00	60.00	
639	7¢ black McKinley (559), 1927	5.75	.08		32.50	65.00	
640	8¢ olive green, Grant (560), 1927	5.75	.05		35.00	65.00	
641	9¢ orange red Jefferson (561), 1927	5.70	.05		35.00	85.00	
642	10¢ orange Monroe (562), 1927	8.50	.03		50.00	90.00	
	Issues of 1927, Perf. 11						
643	2¢ Vermont 150th Anniversary,						
	Aug. 3	2.00	1.25	(6)	80.00	6.00	39,974,900
	150th Anniversary of the Battle of Bennington.						
644	2¢ Burgoyne Campaign, Aug. 3	6.00	3.75	(6)	90.00	20.00	25,628,450
	Commemorating the Battles of Bennington, Oriskany, Fort Stanwix and Saratoga.						
	Issues of 1928						
645	2¢ Valley Forge, May 26	1.30	.65	(6)	65.00	5.00	101,330,328
	Perf. 11x10½						
646	2¢ Battle of Monmouth, Oct. 20	1.85	1.75		80.00	16.00	9,779,896
	Memorial to Revolutionary heroine Molly Pitcher who fired a cannon for the rebels at the Battle of Monmouth, N.J., in 1778.						
647	2¢ carmine (648)	8.50	6.00		265.00	20.00	5,519,897
648	5¢ Hawaii 150th Anniv., Aug. 13	25.00	21.50		525.00	40.00	1,459,897
	A salute to the Hawaiian Islands on the 150th anniversary of their discovery by Captain Cook in 1778.						
	Aeronautics Conference Issue, Dec. 12, Perf. 11						
649	2¢ Wright Airplane	2.00	1.40	(6)	27.50	10.00	51,342,273
650	5¢ Globe and Airplane	10.00	5.00	(6)	135.00	15.00	10,319,700
	The International Civil Aeronautics Conference, held in 1928, coincided with the 25th anniversary of the flight of the Wright Brothers.						

*Sheet of 25

EDISON'S LIGHT

Outwardly, Thomas Alva Edison gave little sign of the technological genius lurking within. People saw the inventor as a typical countryman come to town, wide-eyed and wondering. A New

945

York reporter wrote, "His manner is modest and retiring, and exhibits a total lack of egotism or self-assurance."

But although Edison was modest, he did not lack self-confidence or persistence. In response to a question about the nature of genius, he said, "Well, about 99 percent of it is a knowledge of the things that will not work. The other one percent may be genius, but the only way that I know to accomplish anything is everlastingly to keep working with patient observation."

Edison spent years looking for a substance that would give off light without burning up. He tested thousands before he found one that would work: carbon. It took more than a decade of persistence, but in 1879 Edison gave the world its first electric light.
See Scott No. 654.

Edison and Dr. Irving Langmuir discussing the vacuum tube at the General Electric Research Laboratory.

651

654

656 (Coil Pair)

657   669

	Un	U	#	PB	FDC	Q
Issues of 1929						
651 2¢ George Rogers Clark, Feb. 25	.95	.80	(6)	18.50	6.00	16,684,674
Perf. 11x10½						
653 ½¢ olive brown Nathan Hale (551)	.05	.04		1.00	25.00	
Electric Light Jubilee Issue, Perf. 11						
654 2¢ Edison's First Lamp, June 5	1.20	1.00	(6)	55.00	10.00	31,679,200
Perf. 11x10½						
655 2¢ carmine rose (654), June 11	.90	.25		85.00	65.00	210,119,474
Coil Stamp, Perf. 10 Vertically						
656 2¢ carmine rose (654), June 11	25.00	1.75			85.00	133,530,000
Thomas A. Edison invented the first practical incandescent electric light bulb on Oct. 21, 1879.						
Perf. 11						
657 2¢ Sullivan Expedition, June 17	.85	.90	(6)	50.00	3.50	51,451,880
In 1779, General Sullivan led a daring Revolutionary War raid against the Iroquois in New York State.						
Regular Issue of 1926-27						
Perf. 11x10½, 658-668 Overprinted Kansas						
658 1¢ green Franklin (552)	2.50	1.65		32.50	25.00	13,390,000
659 1½¢ brown Harding (553)	4.00	3.00		50.00	25.00	8,240,000
660 2¢ carmine Washington (554)	3.50	.65		50.00	25.00	87,410,000
661 3¢ violet Lincoln (555)	20.00	12.00		185.00	27.50	2,540,000
662 4¢ yellow brown						
M. Washington (556)	21.50	7.50		185.00	27.50	2,290,000
663 5¢ deep blue T. Roosevelt (557)	15.00	9.00		170.00	30.00	2,700,000
664 6¢ red orange Garfield (558)	32.50	15.00		475.00	40.00	1,450,000
665 7¢ black McKinley (559)	33.50	21.00		425.00	40.00	1,320,000
666 8¢ olive green Grant (560)	95.00	67.50		750.00	75.00	1,530,000
667 9¢ light rose Jefferson (561)	17.50	10.00		200.00	65.00	1,130,000
668 10¢ orange yellow Monroe (562)	27.50	9.50		350.00	70.00	2,860,000
669-679 Overprinted Nebraska						
669 1¢ green Franklin (552)	2.50	1.75		32.50	25.00	8,220,000
670 1½¢ brown Harding (553)	3.25	2.25		45.00	25.00	8,990,000
671 2¢ carmine Washington (554)	1.75	.85		35.00	25.00	73,220,000
672 3¢ violet Lincoln (555)	16.00	8.75		200.00	30.00	2,110,000
673 4¢ yellow brown						
M. Washington (556)	20.00	11.00		210.00	35.00	1,600,000
674 5¢ deep blue T. Roosevelt (557)	19.00	12.50		225.00	35.00	1,860,000
675 6¢ red orange Garfield (558)	42.50	19.00		525.00	55.00	980,000
676 7¢ black McKinley (559)	22.50	14.00		225.00	55.00	850,000
677 8¢ olive green Grant (560)	33.50	22.00		325.00	60.00	1,480,000
678 9¢ light rose Jefferson (561)	37.50	23.00		450.00	60.00	530,000
679 10¢ orange yellow Monroe (562)	115.00	17.50		900.00	70.00	1,890,000

Warning: Excellent forgeries of the Kansas and Nebraska overprints exist.

		Un	U	#	PB	FDC	Q
	1926-27 continued						
	Perf. 11						
680	2¢ Battle of Fallen Timbers,						
	Sept. 14	1.40	1.10	(6)	60.00	2.75	29,338,274
	A memorial to General "Mad" Anthony Wayne (1745-1796), who fought in the Revolution.						
681	2¢ Ohio River Canal, Oct. 19	.90	.75	(6)	45.00	2.75	32,680,900
	Issues of 1930						
682	2¢ Mass. Bay Colony, Apr. 8	.80	.50	(6)	65.00	2.75	74,000,774
683	2¢ Carolina-Charleston, Apr. 10	1.75	1.60	(6)	100.00	3.00	25,215,574
	260th anniversary of the Carolina Province and 250th anniversary of the city of Charleston, S.C.						
	Perf. 11x10½						
684	1½¢ Warren G. Harding	.20	.05	(6)	1.50	3.50	
685	4¢ William H. Taft	.40	.06	(6)	10.00	7.00	
	Coil Stamps, Perf. 10 Vertically						
686	1½¢ brown Harding (684)	.70	.07			6.00	
687	4¢ brown Taft (685)	1.65	.40			25.00	
	Perf. 11						
688	2¢ Braddock's Field, July 9	1.75	1.60	(6)	75.00	4.25	25,609,470
	The Battle of Braddock's Field, fought near Ft. Duquesne, Pennsylvania in the French and Indian War, was a crushing defeat for the English.						
689	2¢ Von Steuben, Sept. 17	.90	.75	(6)	45.00	4.25	66,487,000
	200th anniversary of the birth of the Prussian general (1730-1794), who helped train the Continental Army.						
	Issues of 1931						
690	2¢ Pulaski, Jan. 16	.30	.18	(6)	32.50	3.25	96,559,400
	Perf. 11x10½						
692	11¢ light blue Hayes (563)	5.00	.10		25.00	80.00	
693	12¢ brown violet Cleveland (564)	8.00	.06		40.00	80.00	
694	13¢ yellow green Harrison (622)	3.75	.10		25.00	85.00	
695	14¢ dark blue Indian (565)	6.00	.30		30.00	85.00	
696	15¢ gray Statue of Liberty (566)	15.00	.06		70.00	90.00	
	Perf. 10½x11						
697	17¢ black Wilson (623)	7.00	.20		45.00	1,650.00	
698	20¢ car. rose Golden Gate (567)	17.50	.05		90.00	130.00	
699	25¢ blue green Niagara						
	Falls (568)	15.00	.08		75.00	1,650.00	
700	30¢ brown Buffalo (569)	28.50	.07		145.00	225.00	
701	50¢ lilac Amphitheater (570)	95.00	.07		475.00	300.00	
	Perf. 11						
702	2¢ Red Cross, May 21	.15	.12		2.50	2.00	99,074,600
	The American Red Cross was founded by Clara Barton in 1881.						
703	2¢ Yorktown, Oct. 12	.40	.35		4.00	3.00	25,006,400

680

681

682

683

684

685

688

689

690

702

703

MAD ANTHONY WAYNE

Of all the adjectives that could have been appended to Anthony Wayne's name, "mad" was probably the least appropriate. Nonetheless, the Revolutionary War general lives through history as "Mad Anthony."

The designation came from a character known as Jemy the Rover, Wayne's principal spy during the Valley Forge campaign. Shortly before Yorktown, Jemy appeared in camp after a long, and not entirely sober, absence. His unruly behavior irked General Wayne, who ordered 29 lashes in the guardhouse, a fairly moderate sentence during Revolutionary War times. Aggrieved by his beloved general's rebuke, Jemy exclaimed, "Then Anthony is mad, stark mad." He repeated the remark again and again, "Mad Anthony Wayne! Mad Anthony Wayne." The name stuck. And the general—who should have been known for his courage, his sober judgment and his long string of victories—has carried through history a nickname that marks him as something he was not. See Scott No. 680.

704

705

706

707

708

709

710

711

712

713

714

715

716

717

		Un	U	#	PB	FDC	Q
	Issues of 1932. Perf. 11x10½, Washington Bicentennial Issue, Jan. 1						
704	½¢ Portrait by Charles W. Peale	.08	.05		4.50	4.00	87,969,700
705	1¢ Bust by Jean Antoine Houdon	.13	.04		5.50	4.50	1,265,555,100
706	1½¢ Portrait by Charles W. Peale	.40	.06		25.00	4.50	304,926,800
707	2¢ Portrait by Gilbert Stuart	.10	.03		1.75	4.50	4,222,198,300
708	3¢ Portrait by Charles W. Peale	.60	.06		22.50	5.00	456,198,500
709	4¢ Portrait by Charles P. Polk	.30	.06		7.00	5.00	151,201,300
710	5¢ Portrait by Charles W. Peale	2.25	.08		25.00	5.50	170,565,100
711	6¢ Portrait by John Trumbull	5.50	.06		90.00	6.00	111,739,400
712	7¢ Portrait by John Trumbull	.40	.12		8.50	6.00	83,257,400
713	8¢ Portrait by Charles B.J.F.						
	Saint Memin	5.75	.70		115.00	6.00	96,506,100
714	9¢ Portrait by W. Williams	4.50	.25		75.00	7.00	75,709,200
715	10¢ Portrait by Gilbert Stuart	17.50	.10		200.00	8.50	147,216,000
	Perf. 11						
716	2¢ Olympic Games, Jan. 25	.35	.20	(6)	20.00	4.00	51,102,800
	The Olympic Winter Games of 1932 were held at Lake Placid in New York.						
	Perf. 11x10½						
717	2¢ Arbor Day, Apr. 22	.18	.08		12.50	2.00	100,869,300

WINTER OLYMPICS OF 1932

Americans captured most of the gold medals at the 1932 winter games in Lake Placid, New York. But none equalled the accomplishment of Eddie Eagan, member of America's four-man bobsled team.

Eagan had won the Olympic light-heavyweight boxing championship in 1920. But until Lake Placid, he had never even been on a bobsled, a treacherous sport described by one reporter as "a modern version of an ancient form of suicide."

Eagan recalled his first run down the 80-degree bank: "It took only about two minutes to make that run, but to me it seemed like an eon. I remember the snow-covered ground flashing by like a motion picture out of focus. Speeding only a few inches from the ground without any sense of security, I hung on to the straps. My hands seemed to be slipping, but still I clung."

Shaken, but safe, Eagan completed the run. And a few weeks later, his style polished by continuous practice, he accepted his second gold medal in twelve years. His summer-winter Olympic feat has never been matched. See Scott No. 716.

		Un	U	#	PB	FDC	Q
	10th Olympic Games Issue, June 15						
718	3¢ Runner at Starting Mark	1.10	.06		32.50	4.75	168,885,300
719	5¢ Myron's Discobolus	1.60	.30		45.00	6.00	52,376,100
720	3¢ Washington, June 16	.15	.03		1.50	7.00	
720b	Booklet pane of 6	22.50	5.00				
	Coil Stamps, Perf. 10 Vertically						
721	3¢ deep violet (720), June 24	2.50	.08			15.00	
	Perf. 10 Horizontally						
722	3¢ deep violet (720), Oct 12	1.85	.45			15.00	
	Perf. 10 Vertically						
723	6¢ red orange Garfield						
	(558), Aug. 18	10.00	.25			15.00	
	Perf. 11						
724	3¢ William Penn, Oct. 24	.30	.25	(6)	22.50	2.00	49,949,000
725	3¢ Daniel Webster, Oct. 24	.50	.35	(6)	40.00	2.00	49,538,500
	Issues of 1933						
726	3¢ Georgia 200th Anniv., Feb. 12	.35	.25	(6)	27.50	2.00	61,719,200
	Perf. 10½x11						
727	3¢ Peace of 1783, Apr. 19	.15	.10		7.00	2.25	73,382,400
	Century of Progress Issue, May 25						
728	1¢ Restoration of Ft. Dearborn	.12	.06		3.00	1.85	348,266,800
729	3¢ Fed. Building at Chicago 1933	.18	.04		4.00	1.75	480,239,300
	American Philatelic Society Issue, Souvenir Sheets, Aug. 25, Without Gum, Imperf.						
730	1¢ deep yellow green						
	sheet of 25 (728)	65.00	50.00			125.00	456,704*
730a	Single stamp	1.00	.50			2.50	11,417,600
731	3¢ deep violet, sheet of 25 (729)	60.00	40.00			125.00	441,172*
731a	Single stamp	.85	.50			2.50	11,029,300
	Perf. 10½x11						
732	3¢ NRA, Aug. 15	.14	.03		2.00	2.00	1,978,707,300
	Perf. 11						
733	3¢ Byrd's Antarctic Expedition,						
	Oct. 9	.95	.80	(6)	30.00	6.00	5,735,944

*Sheet of 25

718

719

720

723

724

725

726

727

728

729

732

733

NATIONAL RECOVERY ACT

If you sighted a blue eagle in 1933, chances are it wasn't a hallucination but a symbol of the National Recovery Act. Passed in 1933, the NRA was part of Franklin Roosevelt's New Deal, an attempt to stimulate recovery from the Great Depression.

At the heart of the act was a system of codes of "fair competition" covering each major industry, along with maximum hours, minimum wages and the right to collective bargaining.

The NRA met an early death, however, with the "sick chicken" case of 1935. Four brothers had been found guilty of selling diseased fowl in violation of the NRA's poultry code. Their lawyers appealed to the Supreme Court, which ruled against the NRA on two counts. First, they said, Congress had no right to delegate its lawmaking powers to the President; second, they called poultry marketing a local activity, not subject to federal regulation.

It was a death blow for the NRA. As one man wrote, "A few sick chickens had murdered the mighty Blue Eagle." See Scott No. 732.

The NRA eagle, symbol of America's recovery from the Great Depression.

734

736

737

739

740

741

742

743

744

745

746

747

748

749

	Un	U	#	PB	FDC	Q
1933 continued						
734	5¢ Tadeusz Kosciuszko, Oct. 13	.85	.40	(6)	65.00	5.25	45,137,700
Issues of 1934, National Stamp Exhibition Issue, Souvenir Sheet,						
Feb. 10, Without Gum, Imperf.						
735	3¢ dk. blue sheet of 6 (733)	40.00	30.00			55.00	811,404*
735a	Single stamp	3.25	2.50			6.00	4,868,424
	Perf. 11						
736	3¢ Maryland 300th Anniversary,						
	Mar. 23	.20	.15	(6)	15.00	1.25	46,258,300
Mothers of America Issue, May 2, Perf. 11x10½						
737	3¢ Whistler's Mother	.15	.06		1.75	1.25	193,239,100
	Perf. 11						
738	3¢ deep violet (737)	.20	.18	(6)	7.25	1.75	15,432,200
739	3¢ Wisconsin 300th Anniversary,						
	July 7	.20	.12	(6)	7.00	1.50	64,525,400
National Parks Issue						
740	1¢ El Capitan, Yosemite, Calif.	.10	.06	(6)	1.50	1.75	84,896,350
741	2¢ Grand Canyon, Arizona	.15	.06	(6)	2.00	1.75	74,400,200
742	3¢ Mt. Rainier and Mirror Lake,						
	Washington	.20	.06	(6)	3.50	1.75	95,089,000
743	4¢ Mesa Verde, Colorado	.55	.50	(6)	12.00	2.25	19,178,650
744	5¢ Old Faithful, Yellowstone,						
	Wyoming	1.30	.90	(6)	14.50	2.25	30,980,100
745	6¢ Crater Lake, Oregon	1.85	1.25	(6)	30.00	3.00	16,923,350
746	7¢ Great Head, Acadia Park,						
	Maine	1.30	1.00	(6)	17.50	3.00	15,988,250
747	8¢ Great White Throne,						
	Zion Park, Utah	2.85	2.50	(6)	35.00	3.25	15,288,700
748	9¢ Mt Rockwell and Two Medicine						
	Lake, Glacier National Park,						
	Montana	3.00	.90	(6)	27.50	3.50	17,472,600
749	10¢ Great Smoky Mountains,						
	North Carolina	5.00	1.35	(6)	57.50	6.50	18,874,300
American Philatelic Society Issue, Souvenir Sheet, Imperf.						
750	3¢ deep violet sheet of six						
	(742), Aug. 28	60.00	35.00			60.00	511,391*
750a	Single stamp	5.25	4.50			6.00	3,068,346

*Sheet of 6

		Un	U	#	PB	FDC	Q
	1934 continued						
	Trans-Mississippi Philatelic Issue						
751	1¢ green sheet of six (740), Oct. 10	25.00	15.00			37.50	793,551*
751a	Single stamp	2.50	1.75			3.75	4,761,306
	Special Printing (Nos. 752 to 771 inclusive), Issued March 15, 1935, Without Gum						
	Issues of 1935, Perf. 10½x11						
752	3¢ violet Peace of 1783 (727)						
	Issued in sheets of 400, Mar. 15	.20	.15		17.50	10.00	3,274,556
	Perf. 11						
753	3¢ dk. blue Byrd's Antarctic						
	Expedition (733)	.60	.60	(6)	25.00	11.00	2,040,760
	Imperf.						
754	3¢ dp. vio. Whistler's Mother (737)	1.00	.60	(6)	45.00	11.00	2,389,288
755	3¢ deep violet Wisconsin						
	300th Anniversary (739)	1.00	.60	(6)	45.00	11.00	2,294,948
756	1¢ green Yosemite (740)	.30	.15	(6)	7.50	11.00	3,217,636
757	2¢ red Grand Canyon (741)	.40	.25	(6)	9.50	11.00	2,746,640
758	3¢ dp. vio. Mt. Rainier (742)	.75	.55	(6)	27.50	12.00	2,168,088
759	4¢ brown Mesa Verde (743)	2.00	1.25	(6)	35.00	12.00	1,822,684
760	5¢ blue Yellowstone (744)	2.50	1.75	(6)	40.00	12.00	1,724,576
761	6¢ dk. blue Crater Lake (745)	3.50	2.25	(6)	55.00	12.50	1,647,696
762	7¢ black Acadia (746)	2.75	2.00	(6)	50.00	12.50	1,682,948
763	8¢ sage green Zion (747)	3.25	2.25	(6)	75.00	13.00	1,638,644
764	9¢ red orange Glacier Nat'l Park						
	(748)	3.25	2.25	(6)	75.00	14.00	1,625,224
765	10¢ gray black Smoky Mts. (749)	6.00	5.00	(6)	92.50	15.00	1,644,900
766	1¢ yellow green (728)	65.00	50.00				98,712**
	Pane of 25 from sheet of 225 (9 panes)						
766a	Single stamp	1.00	.50			10.00	2,467,800
767	3¢ violet (729)	60.00	40.00				85,914**
	Pane of 25 from sheet of 225 (9 panes)						
767a	Single stamp	.85	.50			10.00	2,147,850
768	3¢ dark blue (733)	40.00	25.00	–			267,200*
	Pane of 6 from sheet of 150 (25 panes)						
768a	Single stamp	3.25	2.75			12.00	1,603,200
769	1¢ green (740)	15.00	12.00				279,960*
	Pane of 6 from sheet of 120 (20 panes)						
769a	Single stamp	1.75	1.50			7.00	1,679,760
770	3¢ deep violet (742)	37.50	25.00				215,920*
	Pane of 6 from sheet of 120 (20 panes)						
770a	Single stamp	3.75	3.00			8.75	1,295,520

*Pane of 6
**Pane of 25

GLACIER NATIONAL PARK

Travel west across Montana's big-sky country, to where the rolling, shadeless plains abruptly end, and you come upon the backbone of the continent, the Rocky Mountains at their most rugged and spectacular: Glacier National Park.

Here even the inexperienced eye can read the history of the land: how, eons ago, the earth's crust rose, the seas drained off and the up-thrust rocks grew into mountains;

748

how Ice Age snow formed rivers of ice called glaciers; how the glaciers, flowing almost imperceptibly but surely, carved out the U-shaped valleys and amphitheaters that would later hold lakes of cobalt blue.

The park today holds remnants of perhaps 60 glaciers. They are not the huge ice rivers of Alaska, but they cling still to the mountain slopes and crevices. Each year, however, they recede slightly. Barring changes in climate, they will be gone in a mere thousand years. See Scott No. 764.

MOUNT RAINIER

As mountains go, Mount Rainier is a relative youngster. Geologists estimate that the fiery mountain's existence goes back only a few hundred thousand years, making it a fairly recent addition to the landscape of the state of Washington.

What the mountain lacks in age it has made up in activity. Its "growing pains" have consisted of periodic eruptions, which have shaken the ground and darkened the sky as molten rock and clouds of ash were violently ejected into the air. And volcanic gases rising from the bottom of the crater have melted passageways through the ice, producing the highest known caves in the world. (These "steam caves" give credence to early Indian legends describing a "fiery lake of steaming water.")

In recent years the volcanic giant has been dormant. It may recreate the violent scenes of its past, but geologic advances should provide an early warning system should Mount Rainier awake. See Scott No. 758.

		Un	U	#	PB	FDC	Q
	1935 continued						
771	16¢ dark blue Seal of U.S. (CE2),						
	issued in sheets of 200	4.75	3.50	(6)	150.00	22.50	1,370,560
	Perf. 11x10½						
772	3¢ Connecticut 300th Anniv.,						
	Apr. 26	.12	.06		2.00	7.00	70,726,800
773	3¢ California-Pacific Exposition,						
	May 29	.12	.06		2.00	7.00	100,839,600
	The 1935 Exposition was held in San Diego.						
	Perf. 11						
774	3¢ Boulder Dam, Sep. 30	.12	.06	(6)	2.50	9.00	73,610,650
	Perf. 11x10½						
775	3¢ Michigan 100th Anniv., Nov. 1	.12	.06		2.00	7.00	75,823,900
	Issues of 1936						
776	3¢ Texas 100th Anniv., Mar. 2	.12	.06		2.00	7.00	124,324,500
	Perf. 10½x11						
777	3¢ Rhode Island 300th Anniv.,						
	May 4	.12	.06		2.00	7.00	67,127,650
	Third International Philatelic Exhibition Issue, Souvenir Sheet, Imperf.						
778	Violet, sheet of 4 different stamps						
	(772, 733, 775 and 776), May 9	4.25	3.00			13.50	2,809,039*
	Perf. 11x10½						
782	3¢ Arkansas 100th Anniv., June 15	.12	.06		2.00	7.00	72,992,650
783	3¢ Oregon Territory, July 14	.12	.06		2.00	7.00	74,407,450
784	3¢ Susan B. Anthony, Aug. 26	.10	.05		.75	9.00	269,522,200

*Sheet of 4

SUSAN B. ANTHONY

In 1872, Susan B. Anthony marched into a polling place, demanding to be registered and cast her ballot for President, becoming the first woman to vote in this country.

But the ballot was never counted. Instead, police arrested the defiant Anthony and fined her $100 for having the audacity to exercise a right that was reserved only for men.

Anthony spent her life barnstorming the country, demanding suffrage for women. But she never lived to see her crusade become reality. Two days before her death in 1906, she held up her hand and measured a tiny space on one finger. "I have been striving for more than 60 years for a little bit of justice no bigger than that," she said. "And yet, I must die without obtaining it. Oh, it seems so cruel."

But Susan Anthony's cause carried on after her death, and, in 1920, the 19th Amendment to the Constitution gave women the right to vote.
See Scott No. 784.

772

773

774

775

776

777

782

783

784

785

786

787

788

789

790

791

792

793

794

		Un	U	#	PB	FDC	Q
	Issues of 1936-37						
	Army Issue						
785	1¢ George Washington						
	and Nathanael Greene, 1936	.10	.06		1.00	5.00	105,196,150
786	2¢ Andrew Jackson and						
	Winfield Scott, 1937	.15	.06		1.10	5.00	93,848,500
787	3¢ Generals Sherman,						
	Grant and Sheridan, 1937	.20	.08		1.50	5.00	87,741,150
788	4¢ Generals Robert E. Lee						
	and "Stonewall" Jackson, 1937	.65	.15		13.00	5.00	35,794,150
789	5¢ U.S. Military Academy,						
	West Point, 1937	.90	.15		15.00	6.00	36,839,250
	Navy Issue						
790	1¢ John Paul Jones						
	and John Barry, 1936	.10	.06		1.00	5.00	104,773,450
791	2¢ Stephen Decatur						
	and Thomas MacDonough, 1937	.15	.06		1.10	5.00	92,054,550
792	3¢ Admirals David G. Farragut						
	and David D. Porter, 1937	.20	.08		1.50	5.00	93,291,650
793	4¢ Admirals William T. Sampson,						
	George Dewey and Winfield						
	S. Schley, 1937	.65	.15		13.00	5.00	34,552,950
794	5¢ Seal of U.S. Naval Academy						
	and Naval Cadets, 1937	.90	.15		15.00	6.00	36,819,050

NATHANAEL GREENE

The military career of Nathanael Greene began late and with little promise. In 1774, at the age of 32, he helped raise a militia company in Rhode Island called the Kentish Guards—but because of a stiff knee, he was disqualified as an officer and had to join his own company as a private.

Nevertheless, he came to be a great hero of the American Revolution, mastermind of Washington's campaigns and the general's first choice to be his own successor.

In 1780, Greene was given command of the Southern Army, charged with salvaging the situation in the South. He conducted several successful campaigns against the British, forcing them to retreat to the three coastal bases and finally to Yorktown. Greene returned home in triumph, and became known as "the man who saved the South." See Scott No. 785.

		Un	U	#	PB	FDC	Q
	Issues of 1937						
795	3¢ Northwest Ordinance						
	150th Anniversary, July 13	.12	.06		2.00	7.00	84,825,250
	Perf. 11						
796	5¢ Virginia Dare, Aug. 18	.40	.25	(6)	11.50	7.50	25,040,400
	Society of Philatelic Americans, Souvenir Sheet, Imperf.						
797	10¢ blue green (749), Aug. 26	1.50	.60			6.50	5,277,445
	Perf. 11x10½						
798	3¢ Constitution 150th Anniv.,						
	Sept. 17	.15	.07		1.65	7.00	99,882,300
	Issued on the 150th anniversary of the signing of the Constitution, Sept. 17, 1787.						
	Territorial Issues, Perf. 10½x11						
799	3¢ Hawaii, Oct. 18	.15	.07		2.00	7.50	78,454,450
	Perf. 11x10½						
800	3¢ Alaska, Nov. 12	.15	.07		2.00	7.50	77,004,200
801	3¢ Puerto Rico, Nov. 25	.15	.07		1.75	7.50	81,292,450
802	3¢ Virgin Islands, Dec. 15	.15	.07		2.00	7.50	76,474,550

VIRGINIA DARE

On May 8, 1587, three small ships set sail from Plymouth, England, for the New World. On board were 91 men, 17 women and 9 boys. They had intended to settle on Chesapeake Bay, but on July 22 the pilot of the expedition set them down instead on Roanoke Island in Virginia (later North Carolina).

Three weeks later a baby girl was born to Eleanor White, daughter of John White, governor of the new colony; and Ananias Dare, a tiler and bricklayer. The infant was christened Virginia because, as her grandfather recorded, "this child was the first Christian borne in Virginia."

Unfortunately, this record of the first child born to English parents in the New World is also the last trace we have of Virginia Dare. The infant was a member of the "Lost Colony," which disappeared from Roanoke Island sometime before 1590, and whose fate remains a mystery today. See Scott No. 796.

The baptism of Virginia Dare.

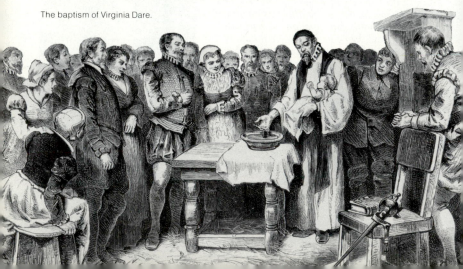

795

796

798

799

800

801

802

803   804   805   806

807   808   809   810   811   812

813   814   815   816   817

818   819   820   821   822   823

824   825   826

827   828   829   830   831   832

		Un	U	#	PB	FDC	Q
	Presidential Issue, 1938*						
803	½¢ Benjamin Franklin	.05	.03		.50	1.10	
804	1¢ George Washington	.06	.03		.30	1.25	
804b	Booklet pane of 6	1.75	.20				
805	1½¢ Martha Washington	.06	.03		.35	1.25	
806	2¢ John Adams	.06	.03		.35	1.50	
806b	Booklet pane of 6	4.25	.50				
807	3¢ Thomas Jefferson	.10	.03		.50	1.50	
807a	Booklet pane of 6	8.50	.50				
808	4¢ James Madison	.35	.04		2.00	1.50	
809	4½¢ White House	.20	.06		2.00	2.00	
810	5¢ James Monroe	.35	.03		2.00	2.00	
811	6¢ John Q. Adams	.35	.03		2.00	2.00	
812	7¢ Andrew Jackson	.40	.05		2.25	2.25	
813	8¢ Martin Van Buren	.45	.04		2.50	2.25	
814	9¢ William H. Harrison	.50	.04		2.50	2.40	
815	10¢ John Tyler	.40	.03		2.25	2.50	
816	11¢ James K. Polk	.90	.08		4.50	2.50	
817	12¢ Zachary Taylor	1.25	.06		6.25	2.65	
818	13¢ Millard Filmore	1.20	.08		6.00	2.65	
819	14¢ Franklin Pierce	1.20	.10		6.00	2.85	
820	15¢ James Buchanan	.75	.03		4.00	3.00	
821	16¢ Abraham Lincoln	1.50	.25		7.50	3.25	
822	17¢ Andrew Johnson	1.50	.12		7.50	3.40	
823	18¢ Ulysses S. Grant	2.25	.08		10.00	3.75	
824	19¢ Rutherford B. Hayes	1.50	.30		8.00	3.75	
825	20¢ James A. Garfield	1.10	.03		5.50	4.00	
826	21¢ Chester A. Arthur	1.60	.10		9.50	4.50	
827	22¢ Grover Cleveland	1.60	.50		11.00	4.75	
828	24¢ Benjamin Harrison	5.00	.25		22.00	4.75	
829	25¢ William McKinley	1.60	.03		8.00	6.00	
830	30¢ Theodore Roosevelt	8.50	.05		42.50	8.00	
831	50¢ William Howard Taft	12.00	.06		60.00	15.00	
	Perf. 11						
832	$1 Woodrow Wilson	18.00	.10		85.00	50.00	
832b	Wmkd. USIR	300.00	80.00				
833	$2 Warren G. Harding	60.00	6.00		245.00	95.00	
834	$5 Calvin Coolidge	225.00	5.50		925.00	160.00	

*This series was in use for approximately 16 years when the Liberty Series began replacing it. Various shades of these stamps are in existence due to the numerous reprintings.

835

836

837

838

852

853

854

855

856

857

858

		Un	U	#	PB	FDC	Q
	Issues of 1938, Perf. 11x10½						
835	3¢ Constitution Ratification, June 21	.25	.08		6.00	7.00	73,043,650
	Perf. 11						
836	3¢ Swedish-Finnish 300th Anniv.,						
	June 27	.25	.10	(6)	6.00	7.00	58,564,368
	In 1638, Swedish and Finnish settlers led by Peter Minuit etablished a settlement at Wilmington, Del.						
	Perf. 11x10½						
837	3¢ Northwest Territory, July 15	.25	.08		16.50	7.00	65,939,500
838	3¢ Iowa Territory 100th Anniv.,						
	Aug. 24	.25	.08		9.50	7.00	47,064,300
	Issues of 1939, Coil Stamps, Perf. 10 Vertically						
839	1¢ green Washington (804)	.25	.06			6.00	
840	1½¢ bistre brown						
	M. Washington (805)	.30	.06			6.00	
841	2¢ rose car. Adams (806)	.30	.05			7.00	
842	3¢ deep violet Jefferson (807)	.50	.04			8.00	
843	4¢ red violet Madison (808)	6.25	.20			9.00	
844	4½¢ dk. gray White House (809)	.50	.20			9.00	
845	5¢ bright blue Monroe (810)	5.00	.35			10.00	
846	6¢ red orange J.Q. Adams (811)	1.10	.20			10.50	
847	10¢ brown red Tyler (815)	12.50	.40			27.50	
	Perf. 10 Horizontally						
848	1¢ green Washington (804)	.70	.12			7.00	
849	1½¢ bistre brown						
	M. Washington (805)	1.20	.20			7.00	
850	2¢ rose car. Adams (806)	2.00	.20			8.00	
851	3¢ deep violet Jefferson (807)	2.00	.25			8.00	
	Perf. 10½x11						
852	3¢ Golden Gate Exposition, Feb. 18	.12	.06		1.65	6.00	114,439,600
853	3¢ New York World's Fair, Apr. 1	.15	.06		2.00	6.00	101,699,550
	Perf. 11						
854	3¢ Washington's Inauguration,						
	Apr. 30	.25	.10	(6)	4.75	6.00	72,764,550
	Perf. 11x10½						
855	3¢ Baseball Anniversary						
	100th, June 12	.22	.08		3.50	9.00	81,269,600
	Perf. 11						
856	3¢ Panama Canal, Aug. 15	.22	.08	(6)	6.00	6.00	67,813,350
	Perf. 10½x11						
857	3¢ 300th Anniv. of Printing, Sept. 25	.12	.08		1.65	6.00	71,394,750
	Perf. 11x10½						
858	3¢ 50th Anniv. of Statehood,						
	Nov. 2	.12	.08		1.65	5.50	66,835,000

		Un	U	#	PB	FDC	Q
	Famous Americans Issue, 1940, Perf. 10½x11						
	Authors						
859	1¢ Washington Irving	.08	.06		1.25	1.50	56,348,320
860	2¢ James Fenimore Cooper	.10	.08		1.50	1.60	53,177,110
861	3¢ Ralph Waldo Emerson	.12	.06		2.25	1.75	53,260,270
862	5¢ Louisa May Alcott	.35	.30		14.00	4.50	22,104,950
863	10¢ Samuel L. Clemens						
	(Mark Twain)	2.50	2.00		65.00	7.50	13,201,270
	Poets						
864	1¢ Henry W. Longfellow	.12	.08		1.85	1.50	51,603,580
865	2¢ John Greenleaf Whitier	.10	.08		2.25	1.50	52,100,510
866	3¢ James Russell Lowell	.18	.06		4.00	1.60	51,666,580
867	5¢ Walt Whitman	.35	.25		14.00	4.00	22,207,780
868	10¢ James Whitcomb Riley	3.50	2.50		65.00	7.50	11,835,530
	Educators						
869	1¢ Horace Mann	.09	.08		1.85	1.50	52,471,160
870	2¢ Mark Hopkins	.10	.06		1.65	1.50	52,366,440
871	3¢ Charles W. Eliot	.30	.06		3.75	1.60	51,636,270
872	5¢ Frances E. Willard	.50	.35		15.00	4.25	20,729,030
873	10¢ Booker T. Washington	2.50	1.75		40.00	7.50	14,125,580
	Scientists						
874	1¢ John James Audubon	.08	.06		1.50	1.50	59,409,000
875	2¢ Dr. Crawford W. Long	.10	.06		1.30	1.50	57,888,600
876	3¢ Luther Burbank	.10	.06		1.75	1.60	58,273,180
877	5¢ Dr. Walter Reed	.30	.25		12.00	4.00	23,779,000
878	10¢ Jane Addams	2.00	1.75		40.00	7.50	15,112,580

LOUISA MAY ALCOTT

It was Louisa May Alcott's father who wanted his girls to be "little women" and who encouraged Louisa to write what became her most popular book. But, ironically, Little Women *pays little attention to the father character, relegating him primarily to his study.*

The father's minor role reflects Alcott's ambivalence about her real father, a cold, moralistic man who was uncomfortable with his daughter's feisty temperament and with her inability (like that of her character, Jo) to fit the Victorian standard of passive womanhood.

Unlike her earlier works, Alcott found the writing of Little Women *a bore and was astonished by its huge success. Sadly, the book, which reflects her father's moralistic outlook, became her greatest burden, bringing unwanted acclaim and, to Alcott, evidence that her father's view of the world was, in fact, superior to her own. See Scott No. 862.*

859   860   861   862   863

864   865   866   867   868

869   870   871   872   873

874   875   876   877   878

MARK TWAIN

It was in San Francisco in the mid-1860s that Mark Twain—then nearly 30—came to realize that he would be a writer. The Bay City was a fitting place for such a decision, for it was then a flourishing literary center, home to Bret Harte, Ambrose Bierce and Henry George, as well as Twain.

Twain in turn gave life to the city in his books. Of a trip in the thick San Francisco fog he wrote: "We could not see the horse at all, and were obliged to steer by his ears, which stood up dimly out of the dense white mist."

Of the wind: "Behold, the same gust of wind that blows a lady's dress aside and exposes her ankle, fills your eyes so full of sand that you can't see it."

And of a quake in which he was caught one peaceful Sunday: "Such another destruction of mantle ornaments and toilet bottles as the earthquake created, San Francisco never saw before." Nor would the city ever see the likes of Twain again. See Scott No. 863.

LUTHER BURBANK

They called Luther Burbank "the wizard of horticulture," and there was, it seemed, something magical in his accomplishments. He grew hundreds of different kinds of apples on a single tree, transformed the black-berry to white, and turned the cactus from a useless desert plant into a spineless food for cattle.

The principles and techniques of plant breeding were known before Burbank's time. Yet no one before him had ever created new plants to order—"building them to fit a set of specifications," his biographers have said, "as if they were houses or ships or boardwalks."

For every success, of course, there were thousands of failures, which Burbank destroyed in bonfires. "It is better to run the risk of losing a perfected product," he said, "than to issue forth to the world a lot of second bests which have within them the power of self-perpetuation and multiplication, and which, if we do not destroy them now, will clutter the earth with inferiority and mediocrity." See Scott No. 876.

American agriculturist, Luther Burbank, circa 1920.

HORACE MANN

Horace Mann was a poor and sickly child with a tremendous thirst for knowledge. Although he spent much of his childhood performing hard manual labor, he also managed to immerse himself in books through the only source available in his home town of Franklin, Massachusetts: a small library founded by Benjamin Franklin. Despite the fact that the library stocked mostly histories and treatises on theology, Mann educated himself to the point where he could enter

1606

Brown University; he was graduated, in 1819, with highest honors.

After a career in law and politics, Mann returned, in 1837, to his first love: education. Appointed secretary of the newly created board of education of Massachusetts, he was determined to change the common belief that public education conflicted with the American ideals of self-improvement and individualism. Working with a remarkable intensity, he managed, in 11 years, to revolutionize the state's school system and, indirectly, public education in other states. His dedication, stemming from his boyhood days, rightly earned him the title, "the father of American public education." See Scott No. 869.

SAMUEL MORSE

924

In the fall of 1835, Robert G. Rankin, a lawyer, was walking past New York University when he heard his name called. He immediately recognized gray-haired Professor Samuel F.B. Morse, who took Rankin by the arm and said, "I wish you to go up into my sanctum and examine a piece of mechanism which, if you may not believe in, you, at least, will not laugh at."

Rankin and Morse climbed to the professor's third-floor room, full of the clutter of tools, wire and chemicals. The amused lawyer asked, "Well, professor, what are you at now? Magneticism, electricity, music?"

Morse launched into a long explanation of his "sending instrument," with electronic impulses that could be recorded at a distant point as dots, dashes and spaces. His friend listened politely, then remarked, "Well, professor, you have a pretty play! Theoretically true, but practically useful only as a mantel ornament."

The "mantel ornament" was the electromagnetic telegraph, the dots and dashes the "Morse code," which were to revolutionize world communication and immortalize the name of Samuel F.B. Morse. See Scott No. 890.

		Un	U	#	PB	FDC	Q
	1940 continued						
	Composers						
879	1¢ Stephen Collins Foster	.08	.06		1.50	1.50	57,322,790
880	2¢ John Philip Sousa	.10	.06		1.50	1.50	58,281,580
881	3¢ Victor Herbert	.15	.06		2.00	1.70	56,398,790
882	5¢ Edward MacDowell	.60	.30		15.00	4.00	21,147,000
883	10¢ Ethelbert Nevin	5.00	2.00		60.00	7.00	13,328,000
	Artists						
884	1¢ Gilbert Charles Stuart	.08	.06		1.10	1.50	54,389,510
885	2¢ James A. McNeill Whistler	.10	.06		1.10	1.50	53,636,580
886	3¢ Augustus Saint-Gaudens	.10	.06		1.25	1.60	55,313,230
887	5¢ Daniel Chester French	.40	.22		12.50	3.50	21,720,580
888	10¢ Frederic Remington	2.75	2.25		50.00	7.00	13,600,580
	Inventors						
889	1¢ Eli Whitney	.12	.08		3.00	1.50	47,599,580
890	2¢ Samuel F. B. Morse	.10	.06		1.75	1.50	53,766,510
891	3¢ Cyrus Hall McCormick	.20	.06		2.75	1.60	54,193,580
892	5¢ Elias Howe	1.50	.40		25.00	4.50	20,264,580
893	10¢ Alexander Graham Bell	12.00	3.25		145.00	12.00	13,726,580
	Issues of 1940, Perf. 11x10½						
894	3¢ Pony Express, Apr. 3	.60	.20		7.50	4.50	46,497,400
	Perf. 10½x11						
895	3¢ Pan American Union, Apr. 14	.45	.15		7.00	4.00	47,700,000
	Perf. 11x10½						
896	3¢ Idaho Statehood,						
	50th Anniversary, July 3	.20	.08		3.75	4.00	50,618,150
	Perf. 10½x11						
897	3¢ Wyoming Statehood,						
	50th Anniversary, July 10	.20	.08		3.25	4.00	50,034,400
	Perf. 11x10½						
898	3¢ Coronado Expedition, Sept. 7	.20	.08		3.25	4.00	60,943,700
	National Defense Issue, Oct. 16						
899	1¢ Statue of Liberty	.05	.04		.60	3.50	
900	2¢ Anti-aircraft Gun	.06	.03		.70	3.50	
901	3¢ Torch of Enlightenment	.12	.03		1.40	3.50	

879

880

881

882

883

884

885

886

887

888

889

890

891

892

893

894

895

896

897

898

899

900

901

902

903

904

905

906

907

908

909

910

911

912

913

914

915

916

917

918

919

920

921

		Un	U	#	PB	FDC	Q
	1940 continued						
	Perf. 10½x11						
902	3¢ Thirteenth Amendment,						
	Oct. 20	.30	.15		8.25	4.50	44,389,550
	Issue of 1941, Perf. 11x10½						
903	3¢ Vermont Statehood, Mar. 4	.22	.10		2.75	3.50	54,574,550
	Issues of 1942						
904	3¢ Kentucky Statehood, June 1	.15	.12		2.25	3.50	63,558,400
905	3¢ Win the War, July 4	.10	.03		.60	3.25	
906	5¢ Chinese Resistance, July 7	.50	.30		25.00	5.50	21,272,800

FRANKLIN ROOSEVELT

As a young boy in Hyde Park, New York, Franklin Roosevelt had a penchant for playing tricks. Once the future President went too far. He stretched a string across the top of the narrow stairs leading to the kitchen. His childhood nurse, Mamie, whom he loved dearly, stumbled over the string while carrying Franklin's supper tray. Fortunately she fell only a few steps and was merely shaken up. But young Franklin was severely punished.

Roosevelt developed many hobbies during his childhood. He collected stamps, books about the American Navy, models of ships and miniature children's books. His ability to while away many hours on his various interests was extremely helpful in later life while he recovered from his bout with polio.

The boy also loved animals, and there were always two or three horses in the family's stable. Eleanor Roosevelt recalled that "while we left the horses when we went to Campobello (their summmer home), I have taken many trips with birds, rabbits and dogs, as well as five children."

In 1950, five years after Roosevelt's death, most of his presidential papers were opened to the public during a ceremony at Hyde Park. Included among the nearly five million documents was a scrawled page written by the late President when he was 11. The essay, titled "Bird of the Hudson River Valley," displays more knowledge of birds than of spelling and punctuation. But it shows the abiding love Roosevelt had for all creatures. See Scott Nos. 930-933.

FDR, James Roosevelt, James P. Farley and Will Rogers share a hilarious moment.

	Un	U	#	PB	FDC	Q
Issues of 1943						
907	2¢ Allied Nations, Jan. 14	.08	.04		.50	3.00	1,671,564,200
908	1¢ Four Freedoms, Feb. 12	.06	.05		1.00	3.00	1,227,334,200
Overrun Countries Issue, 1943-44, Perf. 12						
909	5¢ Poland, June 22	.35	.20		15.00	6.00	19,999,646
910	5¢ Czechoslovakia, July 12	.30	.15		6.00	4.50	19,999,646
911	5¢ Norway, July 27	.25	.12		3.50	4.00	19,999,646
912	5¢ Luxembourg, Aug. 10	.25	.12		3.50	4.00	19,999,646
913	5¢ Netherlands, Aug. 24	.25	.12		3.50	4.00	19,999,646
914	5¢ Belgium, Sept. 14	.25	.12		3.50	3.75	19,999,646
915	5¢ France, Sept. 28	.25	.10		3.50	3.75	19,999,646
916	5¢ Greece, Oct. 12	.60	.25		25.00	3.75	14,999,646
917	5¢ Yugoslavia, Oct. 26	.35	.20		14.00	3.75	14,999,646
918	5¢ Albania, Nov. 9	.30	.20		8.50	3.75	14,999,646
919	5¢ Austria, Nov. 23	.30	.20		8.50	3.75	14,999,646
920	5¢ Denmark, Dec. 7	.30	.25		10.00	3.75	14,999,646
921	5¢ Korea, Nov. 2, 1944	.28	.25		12.50	5.50	14,999,646
Issues of 1944, Perf. 11x10½						
922	3¢ Transcontinental Railroad, May 10	.15	.10		2.00	4.00	61,303,000
923	3¢ Steamship, May 22	.12	.15		2.50	3.50	61,001,450
924	3¢ Telegraph, May 24	.12	.10		1.60	2.25	60,605,000
925	3¢ Philippines, Sept. 27	.12	.10		3.00	2.25	50,129,350
926	3¢ 50th Anniversary of Motion Picture, Oct. 31	.12	.10		2.00	2.25	53,479,400
Issues of 1945						
927	3¢ Florida Statehood, Mar. 3	.10	.08		1.00	2.25	61,617,350
928	5¢ United Nations Conference, Apr. 25	.12	.08		.70	2.00	75,500,000
Perf. 10½x11						
929	3¢ Iwo Jima (Marines), July 11	.10	.05		.60	2.00	137,321,000
Issues of 1945-46, Perf. 11x10½						
Franklin D. Roosevelt Issue						
930	1¢ F.D.R. and home at Hyde Park	.05	.05		.30	2.00	128,140,000
931	2¢ Roosevelt and "Little White House," Ga.	.08	.08		.50	2.00	67,255,000
932	3¢ Roosevelt and White House	.10	.06		.55	2.00	133,870,000
933	5¢ F.D.R., Globe and Four Freedoms, 1946	.12	.08		.75	2.00	76,455,400
934	3¢ U.S. Army in Paris, Sept. 28	.10	.05		.50	2.00	128,357,750
935	3¢ U.S. Navy, Oct. 27	.10	.05		.50	2.00	135,863,000
936	3¢ U.S. Coast Guard, Nov. 10	.10	.05		.50	2.00	111,616,700

922

923

924

925

926

927

928

929

930

931

932

933

934

935

936

937

938

939

940

941

942

943

944

945

946

947

949

950

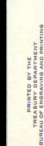

948

951

952

		Un	U	#	PB	FDC	Q
	1945-46 continued						
937	3¢ Alfred E. Smith, Nov. 26	.10	.04		.55	2.00	308,587,700
938	3¢ Texas Statehood, Dec. 29	.10	.05		.50	2.00	170,640,000
	Issues of 1946						
939	3¢ Merchant Marine, Feb. 26	.10	.05		.50	2.00	135,927,000
940	3¢ Veterans of World War II, May 9	.10	.04		.55	2.00	260,339,100
941	3¢ Tennessee Statehood, June 1	.10	.05		.50	2.00	132,274,500
942	3¢ Iowa Statehood, Aug. 3	.10	.05		.50	2.00	132,430,000
943	3¢ Smithsonian Institution, Aug. 10	.10	.05		.50	2.00	139,209,500
944	3¢ Kearny Expedition, Oct. 16	.10	.05		.50	2.00	114,684,450
	Issues of 1947, Perf. 10½x11						
945	3¢ Thomas A. Edison, Feb. 11	.10	.05		.50	2.00	156,540,510
	Perf. 11x10½						
946	3¢ Joseph Pulitzer, Apr. 10	.10	.05		.50	2.00	120,452,600
947	3¢ 100th Anniv. of the						
	Postage Stamp, May 17	.10	.05		.50	2.00	127,104,300
	Imperf.						
948	Souvenir sheet of two, May 19	2.25	.65			3.00	10,299,600
948a	5¢ blue, single stamp (1)	.35	.20				
948b	10¢ brn. org., single stamp (2)	.50	.25				

Issued in sheets of two with marginal inscription commemorating the 100th anniversary of U.S. postage stamps and the Centenary International Philatelic Exhibition, held in New York in 1947.

	Perf. 11x10½						
949	3¢ Doctors, June 9	.10	.05		.50	1.25	132,902,000
950	3¢ Utah, July 24	.10	.05		.50	1.25	131,968,000
951	3¢ U.S. Frigate Constitution, Oct. 21	.10	.05		.50	1.25	131,488,000
	Perf. 10½x11						
952	3¢ Everglades Nat'l Park, Dec. 5	.10	.05		.50	1.25	122,362,000

THE UNITED STATES MARINE CORPS

The word "marine" refers to the sea, and that's how the U.S. Marine Corps started —with men serving on naval ships as attack soldiers.

The U.S. Marine Corps was formed in 1775 on orders from the Continental Congress. Their first battle was fought several months later, in 1776, against the British in the Bahama Islands. Since then, the Marines have landed on foreign shores more than 300 times and have been among the first U.S. troops used in every naval battle fought.

During the 20th century, after World War I, the U.S. Marines trained to attack islands and seaports from ships at sea, working closely with air fighter support. In World War II, this training proved its worth as the Marines used the method to free many islands in the Pacific Ocean from the forces of Japan.

Called "leathernecks," after the stiff collars they wore years ago, the Marines still train to strike quickly and first. Helicopters have replaced naval landing craft, but the Marine motto, "Semper Fidelis—Always Faithful," remains the same. See Scott Nos. 929, 1315.

953

954

955

956

957

958

959

960

961

962

963

964

965

966

967

968

		Un	U	#	PB	FDC	Q
	Issues of 1948						
953	3¢ Dr. George Washington Carver,						
	Jan. 5	.10	.05		.50	1.25	121,548,000
	Perf. 11x10½						
954	3¢ Calif. Gold 100th Anniversary,						
	Jan. 24	.10	.05		.50	1.25	131,109,500
955	3¢ Mississippi Territory, Apr. 7	.10	.05		.50	1.25	122,650,500
956	3¢ Four Chaplains, May 28	.10	.05		.50	1.25	121,953,500
957	3¢ Wisconsin Statehood, May 29	.10	.05		.50	1.25	115,250,000
958	5¢ Swedish Pioneer, June 4	.15	.10		1.00	1.25	64,198,500
959	3¢ Progress of Women, July 19	.10	.05		.50	1.25	117,642,500
	Issued for the first Women's Rights Convention, held in 1848 at Seneca Falls, New York. The stamp shows three important leaders of the movement. Lucretia Mott, Carrie Chapman Catt and Elizabeth Stanton.						
	Perf. 10½x11						
960	3¢ William Allen White, July 31	.10	.06		.60	1.25	77,649,600
	Perf. 11x10½						
961	3¢ U.S.-Canada Friendship, Aug. 2	.10	.05		.50	1.25	113,474,500
962	3¢ Francis Scott Key, Aug. 9	.10	.05		.50	1.25	120,868,500
963	3¢ Salute to Youth, Aug. 11	.10	.06		.50	1.25	77,800,500
964	3¢ Oregon Territory, Aug. 14	.12	.10		1.20	1.25	52,214,000
	Perf. 10½x11						
965	3¢ Harlan Fiske Stone, Aug. 25	.15	.08		2.75	1.25	53,958,100
966	3¢ Palomar Mt. Obs., Aug. 30	.25	.10		4.00	1.75	61,120,010
	Perf. 11x10½						
967	3¢ Clara Barton, Sept. 7	.10	.08		.60	1.25	57,823,000
968	3¢ Poultry Industry, Sept. 9	.12	.08		.80	1.25	52,975,000

GEORGE WASHINGTON CARVER

During the Civil War, a slave boy and his mother were seized from a Missouri plantation owned by Moses Carver. A neighbor sent to retrieve the slaves caught up with them only after the mother had been sold. The boy was rescued by trading him for a $300 race horse. The sickly boy who some said was not worth the price, was George Washington Carver, the self-taught genius who revolutionized the agriculture of the South. Carver's boyhood was spent studying the woods around his home, nursing sick plants back to health, and helping farmers' wives from miles around with their gardens. Since the local school was open only to white children, the young "Plant Doctor" taught himself to read and write. He later opened a laundry, washing and scrubbing his way through a bachelor's and master's degree.

Lacking proper materials for his teaching and research, Carver turned ink bottles into bunsen burners and made beakers out of bottles from the dump. Carver created a thousand items of food, clothing and building materials. When he died in 1943, George Washington Carver was known throughout the world for his agricultural research and success. See Scott No. 953.

		Un	U	#	PB	FDC	Q
	1948 continued						
	Perf. 10½x11						
969	3¢ Gold Star Mothers, Sept. 21	.12	.08		.65	1.25	77,149,000
970	3¢ Fort Kearny, Sept. 22	.12	.08		.65	1.25	58,332,000
971	3¢ Volunteer Firemen, Oct. 4	.12	.08		.75	1.25	56,228,000
972	3¢ Five Indian Tribes, Oct. 15	.12	.08		.75	1.25	57,832,000
973	3¢ Rough Riders, Oct. 27	.12	.10		1.20	1.25	53,875,000
974	3¢ Juliette Low, Oct. 29	.12	.08		.65	1.25	63,834,000
	Perf. 10½x11						
975	3¢ Will Rogers, Nov. 4	.12	.08		1.00	1.25	67,162,200
976	3¢ Fort Bliss 100th Anniv., Nov. 5	.25	.08		5.25	1.25	64,561,000
	Perf. 11x10½						
977	3¢ Moina Michael, Nov. 9	.12	.08		.65	1.25	64,079,500
978	3¢ Gettysburg Address, Nov. 19	.12	.08		.70	1.25	63,388,000
	Perf. 10½x11						
979	3¢ American Turners, Nov. 20	.12	.08		.65	1.25	62,285,000
980	3¢ Joel Chandler Harris, Dec. 9	.12	.08		.75	1.25	57,492,610

CADILLAC LANDING AT DETROIT

On June 2, 1701, Antoine de la Mothe Cadillac left Montreal, Canada, with a party of fifty soldiers, fifty trappers and one hundred Indians in twenty-five canoes. It was the beginning of a bold adventure that would lead to the founding of the first French colony in the "west"—today the site of Detroit, Michigan.

Cadillac was also accompanied by his nine-year-old son Antoine, two priests, and Alphonse de Tonty, his second-in-command. Their party took the long, indirect route, going by way of the Ottawa River, Georgian Bay and Lake Huron. Lake Erie would have been faster, but the Iroquois controlled this great lake, and Cadillac did not want to annoy the powerful Indian tribe, which had not yet signed a peace treaty.

Late in the afternoon of July 23, 1701, the travelers reached the Detroit River. They paddled along slowly in their big canoes, looking for the perfect place to build their fort. The next day Cadillac's experienced eye found just the spot, where a fast-flowing creek ran parallel to the river, then turned and joined it. On this high ground protected by water on three sides, Cadillac built Fort Pontchartrain du Detroit. Detroit had become a permanent settlement. See Scott No. 1000.

970

971

969

972

973

974

975

976

977

978

979

981

982

980

983

984

985

986

987

988

989

990

991

992

993

994

995

996

997

998

999

1000

1001

1002

		Un	U	#	PB	FDC	Q
	Issues of 1949, Perf. 11x10½						
981	3¢ Minnesota Territory, Mar. 3	.10	.05		.50	1.25	99,190,000
982	3¢ Washington & Lee University,						
	Apr. 12	.10	.05		.50	1.25	104,790,000
983	3¢ Puerto Rico Election, Apr. 27	.10	.05		.50	1.25	108,805,000
984	3¢ Annapolis 300th Anniv., May 23	.10	.05		.50	1.25	107,340,000
985	3¢ Grand Army of the Republic,						
	Aug. 29	.10	.05		.50	1.25	117,020,000
	Perf. 10½x11						
986	3¢ Edgar Allan Poe, Oct. 7	.10	.05		.60	1.25	122,633,000
	Issues of 1950, Perf. 11x10½						
987	3¢ American Bankers Association,						
	Jan. 3	.10	.05		.50	1.25	130,960,00
	Perf. 10½x11						
988	3¢ Samuel Gompers, Jan. 27	.10	.05		.55	1.25	128,478,000
	The American labor leader (1850-1924) served as president of the American Federation of Labor.						
	National Capital 150th Anniv. Issue, Perf. 10½x11, 11x10½						
989	3¢ Statue of Freedom	.10	.05		.50	1.25	132,090,000
990	3¢ Executive Mansion	.10	.05		.50	1.25	130,050,000
991	3¢ Supreme Court Building	.10	.05		.50	1.25	131,350,000
992	3¢ U.S. Capitol Building	.10	.05		.50	1.25	129,980,000
	Perf. 11x10½						
993	3¢ Railroad Engineers, Apr. 29	.10	.05		.50	1.25	122,315,000
994	3¢ Kansas City, Mo., June 3	.10	.05		.50	1.25	122,170,000
995	3¢ Boy Scouts, June 30	.10	.06		.55	1.25	131,635,000
	Issued to honor the Boy Scouts of America whose Second National Jamboree was held in 1950 at Valley Forge, Pennsylvania.						
996	3¢ Indian Territory, July 4	.10	.05		.50	1.25	121,860,000
997	3¢ California Statehood, Sept. 9	.10	.05		.50	1.25	121,120,000
	Issues of 1951						
998	3¢ Confederate Veterans, May 30	.10	.05		.50	1.25	119,120,000
	The last reunion of the United Confederate Veterans took place in 1951 at Norfolk, Virginia.						
999	3¢ Nevada 100th Anniv., July 14	.10	.05		.50	1.25	112,125,000
1000	3¢ Landing of Cadillac, July 24	.10	.05		.50	1.25	114,140,000
	Detroit, the "Motor City," was founded by Antoine de la Mothe Cadillac in 1701.						
1001	3¢ Colorado Statehood, Aug. 1	.10	.05		.50	1.25	114,490,000
1002	3¢ American Chem. Society,						
	Sept. 4	.10	.05		.50	1.25	117,200,000

		Un	U	#	PB	FDC	Q
	1951 continued						
1003	3¢ Battle of Brooklyn, Dec. 10	.10	.05		.50	1.25	116,130,000
	Issues of 1952						
1004	3¢ Betsy Ross, Jan. 2	.10	.05		.50	1.25	116,175,000
1005	3¢ 4-H Club, Jan. 15	.10	.05		.50	1.25	115,945,000
1006	3¢ B&O Railroad, Feb. 28	.10	.05		.50	1.25	112,540,000
1007	3¢ American Auto. Assn., Mar. 4	.10	.05		.50	.85	117,415,000
1008	3¢ NATO, Apr. 4	.10	.03		.55	.85	2,899,580,000
1009	3¢ Grand Coulee Dam, May 15	.10	.05		.50	.85	114,540,000
1010	3¢ General Lafayette, June 13	.10	.05		.50	.85	113,135,000
	Perf. 10½x11						
1011	3¢ Mt. Rushmore Mem., Aug. 11	.10	.05		.50	.85	116,255,000
	Perf. 11x10½						
1012	3¢ Engineering, Sept. 6	.10	.05		.50	.85	113,860,000
1013	3¢ Service Women, Sept. 11	.10	.05		.50	.85	124,260,000
1014	3¢ Gutenberg Bible, Sept. 30	.10	.05		.50	.85	115,735,000
1015	3¢ Newspaper Boys, Oct. 4	.10	.05		.50	.85	115,430,000
1016	3¢ Red Cross, Nov. 21	.10	.05		.50	.85	136,220,000

MOUNT RUSHMORE

"Imagine, if you can, faces, the dimensions of a five-story building, carved on a mountain peak, where clouds fold about them like a great scarf and the moon hides behind a lock of hair. If I can discover the faces of Washington, Jefferson, Lincoln and Roosevelt within this mountain, they will, according to geologists, remain to tell the story of America for the next five million years."

That was the dream of Gutzon Borglum, the sculptor who envisioned the Mt. Rushmore National Memorial a half century ago. It was a dream that many people thought impractical, even impossible. One eastern newspaper wrote, "Borglum is about to destroy another mountain; thank God it is in South Dakota where no one will ever see it."

But the early criticism faded with the unveiling of the first 60-foot face—that of George Washington—on July 4, 1930. The enthusiastic response immediately established Mt. Rushmore as one of the nation's most popular shrines. Today more than two million people visit this unique "carving" each year, a tribute to Borglum's vision and to America's past and future. See Scott No. 1011.

The unfinished Lincoln and Gutzon Borglum.

1003

1004

1005

1006

1007

1008

1009

1010

1011

1012

1013

1014

1015

1016

		Un	U	#	PB	FDC	Q
Issues of 1953							
1017	3¢ National Guard, Feb. 23	.10	.05		.50	.85	114,894,600
1018	3¢ Ohio Statehood, Mar. 2	.10	.05		1.00	.85	118,706,000
1019	3¢ Washington Territory, Mar. 2	.10	.05		.55	.85	114,190,000
1020	3¢ Louisiana Purchase, Apr. 30	.10	.05		.50	.85	113,990,000
1021	5¢ Opening of Japan 100th Anniv.,						
	July 14	.15	.10		2.00	.85	89,289,600
1022	3¢ American Bar Assn., Aug. 24	.10	.05		.50	.85	114,865,000
	Issued for the American Bar Association's 75th anniversary, this stamp depicts four symbolic figures representing "Wisdom," "Justice," "Truth" and "Divine Inspiration."						
1023	3¢ Sagamore Hill, Sep. 14	.10	.05		.50	.85	115,780,000
	Sagamore Hill. Theodore Roosevelt's home in Oyster Bay, New York was opened as a national shrine in 1953.						
1024	3¢ Future Farmers, Oct. 13	.10	.05		.50	.85	115,244,600
1025	3¢ Trucking Industry, Oct. 27	.10	.05		.50	.85	123,709,000
1026	3¢ General Patton, Nov. 11	.10	.05		.50	.85	114,798,600
1027	3¢ New York City						
	300th Anniversary, Nov. 20	.10	.05		.50	.85	115,759,600
1028	3¢ Gadsden Purchase, Dec. 30	.10	.05		.50	.85	116,134,600
	The 1853 Gadsden Purchase adjusted the boundary between Mexico and the United States.						
Issues of 1954							
1029	3¢ Columbia University 200th Anniv.,						
	Jan. 4	.10	.05		.50	.85	118,540,000

THE GADSDEN PURCHASE

In 1853, James Gadsden, U.S. minister to Mexico, signed a treaty with Mexico agreeing to pay $10 million for a strip of land that is now largely the state of Arizona. "The Gadsden Purchase" created our southwestern boundary and represented the last addition of territory to the continental domain.

Ironically, when it came time to celebrate the centennial of this major acquisition, planners were puzzled to discover that reference books did not agree on the size of the area. Government publications put the purchase at 29,640 square miles.

But a surprisingly large number of historical texts, including the World Almanac, *the* Encylcopedia of American History, *and the* Dictionary of American History, *carried the figure of 45,535 square miles—a discrepancy of almost 16,000 square miles!*

The Library of Congress was asked to investigate. They found that part of the problem stemmed from the fact that the treaty cited a faulty map, which gave Mexico about 16,000 square miles which had already been settled by several thousand Americans. In June 1954, the Library announced the true figure was 29,640 square miles, ending a 100-year chain of error. See Scott No. 1028.

U.S. Minister, James Gadsden.

1017   1018   1019

1020   1021   1022

1023   1024   1025

1026   1027   1028

1029

1030

1031

1031A

1032

1033

1034

1035

1036

1037

1038

1039

1040

1041

1042

1042A

1043

1044

1044A

1045

1046

1047

1048

1049

		Un	U	#	PB	FDC	Q
	Liberty Issue, 1954-68, Perf. 11x10½, 10½x11						
1030	½¢ Benjamin Franklin, 1955	.05	.03		.30	.85	Unlimited
1031	1¢ George Washington, 1954	.05	.03		.25	.85	
1031A	1¼¢ Palace of the Governors,						
	Santa Fe, 1960	.05	.05		1.75	.85	
1032	1½¢ Mount Vernon, 1956	.05	.04		7.50	.60	
1033	2¢ Thomas Jefferson, 1954	.05	.03		.25	.60	
1034	2½¢ Bunker Hill Monument						
	and Massachusetts flag, 1959	.08	.05		2.00	.60	
1035	3¢ Statue of Liberty, 1954	.08	.03		.40	.60	
1035a	Booklet pane of 6	3.00	.50				
1036	4¢ Abraham Lincoln, 1954	.10	.03		.50	.60	
1036a	Booklet pane of 6	2.00	.50				
1037	4½¢ The Hermitage, 1959	.15	.08		1.75	.60	
1038	5¢ James Monroe, 1954	.17	.03		.75	.75	
1039	6¢ Theodore Roosevelt, 1955	.35	.03		1.75	.65	
1040	7¢ Woodrow Wilson, 1956	.25	.03		1.50	.70	
	Perf. 11						
1041	8¢ Statue of Liberty, 1954	.35	.06		5.75	.80	
1042	8¢ Statue of Liberty, redrawn, 1958	.30	.03		1.75	.60	
	Perf. 11x10½, 10½x11						
1042A	8¢ John J. Pershing, 1961	.25	.03		1.50	.60	
1043	9¢ The Alamo, 1956	.30	.04		1.50	.90	
1044	10¢ Independence Hall, 1956	.35	.03		1.65	.90	
	Perf. 11						
1044A	11¢ Statue of Liberty, 1961	.30	.06		1.50	.90	
	Perf. 11x10½, 10½x11						
1045	12¢ Benjamin Harrison, 1959	.45	.05		2.50	.90	
1046	15¢ John Jay, 1958	.60	.03		2.75	1.00	
1047	20¢ Monticello, 1956	.90	.03		4.50	1.20	
1048	25¢ Paul Revere, 1958	2.75	.03		14.00	1.30	
1049	30¢ Robert E. Lee, 1955	2.25	.08		10.00	1.50	

THE ALAMO

"Remember the Alamo" is a cry that echoes through history. For it is a cry not only of battle but of bravery—and tragedy.

In 1836, about 187 Texans, fighting for their independence from Mexico, resolved to halt Santa Anna's army of 5,000. They took their stand behind the thick walls of an abandoned mission called the Alamo.

The siege began on February 23 when the Mexican general demanded surrender. The Texans' reply was a cannon shot. Among the fighters was the great frontiersman, Davy Crockett, and some of his Tennessee boys.

The battle lasted 13 days. On March 6, the Mexican forces stormed the mission walls, killing every Alamo defender but losing almost 1,600 of their own men.

Forty-six days later the Texas army defeated the Mexican forces—and Texas was free. See Scott No. 1043.

		Un	U	#	PB	FDC	Q
	1954-68 Liberty Issue continued						
1050	40¢ John Marshall, 1955	3.75	.10		19.00	1.75	
1051	50¢ Susan B. Anthony, 1955	4.00	.04		20.00	5.00	
1052	$1 Patrick Henry, 1955	15.00	.06		75.00	9.50	
	Perf. 11						
1053	$5 Alexander Hamilton, 1956	150.00	5.50		725.00	67.50	
	Coil Stamps, Perf. 10 Vertically						
1054	1¢ dark green Washington						
	(1031), 1954	.25	.12			.75	
	Perf. 10 Horizontally						
1054A	1¼¢ turquoise, Palace of the						
	Governors, Santa Fe (1031A), 1960	.45	.10			.90	
	Perf. 10 Vertically						
1055	2¢ rose carmine Jefferson (1033), 1954	.10	.05			.75	
1056	2½¢ gray blue, Bunker Hill Monument						
	and Massachusetts flag (1034), 1959	.55	.20			1.20	
1057	3¢ deep violet Statue of Liberty						
	(1035), 1954	.15	.03			.75	
1058	4¢ red violet Lincoln (1036), 1958	.15	.04			.75	
	Perf. 10 Horizontally						
1059	4½¢ blue green Hermitage						
	(1037), 1959	2.75	.65			1.20	
	Perf. 10 Vertically						
1059A	25¢ green P. Revere (1048)	.70	.30			1.30	
	Issues of 1954, Perf. 11x10½						
1060	3¢ Nebraska Territory, May 7	.10	.05		.50	.75	115,810,000
1061	3¢ Kansas Territory, May 31	.10	.05		.50	.75	113,603,700
	Perf. 10½x11						
1062	3¢ George Eastman, July 12	.10	.05		.60	.75	128,002,000
	Perf. 11x10½						
1063	3¢ Lewis and Clark Expedition,						
	July 28	.10	.05		.50	.75	116,078,150
	Issues of 1955, Perf. 10½x11						
1064	3¢ Pennsylvania Academy of						
	Fine Arts, Jan. 15	.10	.05		.50	.75	116,139,800
	Perf. 11x10½						
1065	3¢ Land Grant Colleges, Feb. 12	.10	.05		.50	.75	120,484,800
1066	8¢ Rotary International, Feb. 23	.20	.12		1.75	.75	53,854,750
1067	3¢ Armed Forces Reserve, May 21	.10	.05		.50	.75	176,075,000
	Perf. 10½x11						
1068	3¢ New Hampshire, June 21	.10	.05		.50	.75	125,944,400
	Perf. 11x10½						
1069	3¢ Soo Locks, June 28	.10	.05		.50	.75	122,284,600
1070	3¢ Atoms for Peace, July 28	.15	.05		1.50	.75	133,638,850
1071	3¢ Fort Ticonderoga, Sept. 18	.10	.05		.50	.75	118,664,600

1050   1051   1052   1053

1060   1061   1062

1063   1065

1064

1066   1067

1068

1069   1070   1071

	Un	U	#	PB	FDC	Q
1955 continued						
Perf. 10½x11						
1072 3¢ Andrew W. Mellon, Dec. 20	.10	.05		.60	.75	112,434,000
Born in 1855, Andrew Mellon was a noted financier, industrialist and philanthropist.						
Issues of 1956						
1073 3¢ Benjamin Franklin, Jan. 17	.10	.05		.50	.75	129,384,550
Perf. 11x10½						
1074 3¢ Booker T. Washington, Apr. 5	.10	.05		.50	.75	121,184,600
Fifth International Philatelic Exhibition, Souvenir Sheet, Imperf.						
1075 Sheet of 2, Apr. 28	6.00	4.50			6.50	2,900,731
1075a 3¢ deep violet (1035)	1.35	.80				
1075b 8¢ dk. vio. bl. & car. (1041)	1.75	1.10				
Perf. 11x10½						
1076 3¢ New York Coliseum and						
Columbus Monument, Apr. 30	.10	.05		.50	.75	119,784,200
Wildlife Conservation Issue						
1077 3¢ Wild Turkey, May 5	.12	.05		.65	.75	123,159,400
1078 3¢ Pronghorn Antelope, June 22	.12	.05		.65	.75	123,138,800
1079 3¢ King Salmon, Nov. 9	.12	.05		.65	.75	109,275,000
Perf. 10½x11						
1080 3¢ Pure Food and Drug Laws,						
June 27	.10	.05		.50	.75	112,932,200
Chemist Harvey W. Wiley, shown on stamp, helped enact the first Pure Food and Drug Act in 1906.						
Perf. 11x10½						
1081 3¢ Wheatland, Aug. 5	.10	.05		.50	.75	125,475,000
Wheatland was the home of President James Buchanan (1791-1868). It is located in Lancaster, Pa.						
Perf. 10½x11						
1082 3¢ Labor Day, Sept. 3	.10	.05		.50	.75	117,855,000
Perf. 11x10½						
1083 3¢ Nassau Hall, Sept. 22	.10	.05		.50	.75	122,100,000
Constructed in 1756, Nassau Hall is Princeton University's most famous building.						
Perf. 10½x11						
1084 3¢ Devils Tower, Sept. 24	.10	.05		.50	.75	118,180,000
In 1906, Devils Tower in Wyoming became the first U.S. national monument.						
Perf. 11x10½						
1085 3¢ Children's Issue, Dec. 15	.10	.05		.50	.75	100,975,000
Issues of 1957						
1086 3¢ Alexander Hamilton, Jan. 11	.10	.05		.50	.75	115,299,450
Perf. 10½x11						
1087 3¢ Polio, Jan. 15	.10	.05		.50	.75	186,949,627
A tribute to the March of Dimes and the National Foundation for Infantile Paralysis.						
Perf. 11x10½						
1088 3¢ Coast and Geodetic Survey, Feb. 11	.10	.05		.50	.75	115,235,000
1089 3¢ Architects, Feb. 23	.10	.05		.50	.75	106,647,500

1072

1073

1074

1076

1077

1078

1079

1080

1081

1082

1083

1084

1085

1086

1087

1088

1089

1090

1091

1092

1093

1094

1095

1096

1097

1098

1099

KING SALMON

Each year thousands of King Salmon (or chinooks) make the long, arduous journey from the Pacific Ocean to the rivers in which they were born. The destination might be a narrow stream hidden in the mountains hundreds of miles from the ocean. But the salmon make their way unerringly to their home river, here to spawn and, most likely, to die.

The reason for the salmon's navigational prowess has baffled scientists for years. Early research indicated that their homing ability in fresh water is based mainly on the unique odor of each stream. But that doesn't explain the fishes' directional skills in the ocean. Biologists have proposed a number of theories, including such clues as magnetic fields and the position of the sun and stars. Some have suggested that the fishes have a built-in compass—a direction-finding ability imprinted on their chromosomes.

But all agree on one point: the salmon is an uncanny navigator, far superior to man with all his electronic aids. See Scott No. 1079.

		Un	U	#	PB	FDC	Q
	1957 continued						
	Perf. 10½x11						
1090	3¢ Steel Industry, May 22	.10	.05		.50	.75	112,010,000
	Perf. 11x10½						
1091	3¢ Int'l. Naval Review, June 10	.10	.05		.50	.75	118,470,000
1092	3¢ Oklahoma Statehood, June 14	.18	.05		.90	.75	102,230,000
1093	3¢ School Teachers, July 1	.10	.05		.50	.75	102,410,000
	Perf. 11						
1094	4¢ Flag Issue, July 4	.10	.05		.70	.75	84,054,400
	Perf. 10½x11						
1095	3¢ Shipbuilding, Aug. 15	.10	.05		.70	.75	126,266,000
	Perf. 11						
1096	8¢ Champion of Liberty, Aug. 31	.22	.15		1.90	.75	39,489,600
	Perf. 10½x11						
1097	3¢ Lafayette, Sept. 6	.10	.05		.50	.75	122,990,000
	Perf. 11						
1098	3¢ Wildlife Conservation, Nov. 22	.10	.05		.65	.75	174,372,800
	Perf. 10½x11						
1099	3¢ Religious Freedom, Dec. 27	.10	.05		.50	.75	114,365,000

MACKINAC BRIDGE

The prospect of linking the Straits of Mackinac, connecting the two sections of the State of Michigan, was long thought impossible. It was said that no man-made structure could possibly resist the ice pressure or the force of the storms of the upper peninsula.

Because of public skepticism, plans for the five-mile suspension bridge included extraordinary safety precautions. To ensure stability, three-quarters of the bridge's one million tons of concrete were built under water. The structure was designed to withstand 20 times the maximum ice pressure, and winds up to 966 miles per hour.

As a result, the bridge was possibly the safest ever built. During its construction (in the mid-1950s), Grover Denny, the construction superintendent, said to the designer, Dr. David B. Steinman, "Doctor, I believe that you have made an important mistake in a decimal point." Startled, Steinman asked, "What do you mean?" Denny replied, "Doctor, you have been telling people that this bridge is good for a century. But I want to go on record as saying that this bridge will be standing a thousand years from now!" See Scott No. 1109.

	Un	U	#	PB	FDC	Q
Issues of 1958						
1100 3¢ Gardening-Horticulture, Mar. 15	.10	.05		.50	.75	122,765,200
Perf. 11x10½						
1104 3¢ Brussels Fair, Apr. 17	.10	.05		.50	.75	113,660,200
Issued for the opening of the Brussels World's Fair, this stamp shows the United States Pavilion at the Fair.						
1105 3¢ James Monroe, Apr. 28	.10	.05		.60	.75	120,196,580
1106 3¢ Minnesota Statehood, May 11	.10	.05		.50	.75	120,805,200
Perf. 11						
1107 3¢ Geophysical Year, May 31	.15	.05		1.50	.75	125,815,200
Perf. 11x10½						
1108 3¢ Gunston Hall, June 12	.10	.05		.50	.75	108,415,200
Gunston Hall was the Virginia home of George Mason (1725-92) author of Virginia's constitution.						
Perf. 10½x11						
1109 3¢ Mackinac Bridge, June 25	.10	.05		.50	.75	107,195,200
1110 4¢ Champion of Liberty, July 24	.10	.05		.60	.75	115,745,280
Perf. 11						
1111 8¢ Champion of Liberty	.25	.15		6.00	.75	39,743,640
Simon Bolivar (1783-1830) liberated much of South America from Spanish domination.						
Perf. 11x10½						
1112 4¢ Atlantic Cable 100th Anniversary,						
Aug. 15	.10	.05		.50	.75	114,570,200
Lincoln 150th Anniv. Issue, 1958-59, Perf. 10½x11, 11x10½						
1113 1¢ Portrait by George Healy	.05	.05		.40	.75	120,400,200
1114 3¢ Sculptured Head						
by Gutzon Borglum	.10	.06		.60	.75	91,160,200
1115 4¢ Lincoln and Stephen Douglas						
Debating, 1958	.10	.05		.55	.75	114,860,200
1116 4¢ Statue in Lincoln Memorial						
by Daniel Chester French	.10	.05		.65	.75	126,500,000
Issues of 1958, Perf. 10½x11						
1117 4¢ Champion of Liberty, Sept. 19	.10	.05		.60	.75	120,561,280
Perf. 11						
1118 8¢ Champion of Liberty	.22	.12		4.25	.75	44,064,576
Lajos Kossuth (1802-1892), patriot of Hungary, was a leading figure in that nation's revolution.						
Perf. 10½x11						
1119 4¢ Freedom of Press, Sept. 22	.10	.05		.50	.75	118,390,200
Perf. 11x10½						
1120 4¢ Overland Mail, Oct. 10	.10	.05		.50	.75	125,770,200

1100

1104

1105

1106

1107

1108

1109

1110

1111

1112

1113

1114

1115

1116

1117

1118

1119

1120

1121

1122

1123

1124

1125

1126

1127

1128

1129

1130

1131

1132

1133

1134

1135

1136

1137

1138

		Un	U	#	PB	FDC	Q
	1958 continued						
	Perf. 10½x11						
1121	4¢ Noah Webster, Oct. 16	.10	.05		.50	.75	114,114,280
	Perf. 11						
1122	4¢ Forest Conservation, Oct. 27	.10	.05		.60	.75	156,600,200
	Perf. 11x10½						
1123	4¢ Fort Duquesne, Nov. 25	.10	.05		.50	.75	124,200,200
	Issues of 1959						
1124	4¢ Oregon Statehood, Feb. 14	.10	.05		.50	.75	120,740,200
	Perf. 10½x11						
1125	4¢ Champion of Liberty, Feb. 25	.10	.05		.55	.75	133,623,280
	Perf. 11						
1126	8¢ Champion of Liberty	.20	.12		2.25	.75	45,569,088
	Issued to honor José de San Martin (1778-1850), South American revolutionist.						
	Perf. 10½x11						
1127	4¢ NATO, Apr. 1	.10	.05		.50	.75	122,493,280
	Perf. 11x10½						
1128	4¢ Arctic Explorations, Apr. 6	.13	.05		.85	.75	131,260,200
	Admiral Peary conquered the North Pole by land in 1909. The submarine *Nautilus* conquered it by sea in 1958.						
1129	8¢ World Peace through World Trade,						
	Apr. 20	.20	.12		1.50	.75	47,125,200
1130	4¢ Nevada Silver, June 8	.10	.05		.50	.75	123,105,000
	In 1859, silver was discovered at Comstock Lode, Nevada. The rich mine yielded about $400 million worth of the precious metal.						
	Perf. 11						
1131	4¢ St. Lawrence Seaway, June 26	.10	.05		.50	.75	126,105,050
1132	4¢ 49-Star Flag, July 4	.10	.05		.50	.75	209,170,000
1133	4¢ Soil Conservation, Aug. 26	.10	.05		.65	.75	120,835,000
	Perf. 10½x11						
1134	4¢ Petroleum Industry, Aug. 27	.10	.05		.50	.75	115,715,000
	Oil was found at Titusville, Pa., in 1859 when Col. Edwin L. Drake hit "black gold" at 69½ feet.						
	Perf. 11x10½						
1135	4¢ Dental Health, Sept. 14	.10	.05		.50	.75	118,445,000
	Perf. 10½x11						
1136	4¢ Champion of Liberty, Sept. 29	.10	.05		.60	.75	111,685,000
	Perf. 11						
1137	8¢ Champion of Liberty	.20	.12		2.25	.75	43,099,200
	Ernst Reuter, honored here, was mayor of Berlin during the blockade of 1948-1949.						
	Perf. 10½x11						
1138	4¢ Dr. Ephraim McDowell, Dec. 3	.10	.05		.50	.75	115,444,000
	Dr. Ephraim McDowell (1771-1830) performed the first operation in ovarian surgery.						

1139

1140

1141

1142

1143

1144

1145

1146

1147

1148

1149

1150

1151

1152

	Un	U	#	PB	FDC	Q
Issues of 1960-61, Perf. 11, American Credo						
1139 4¢ Quotation from Washington's Farewell Address	.18	.05		1.00	.75	126,470,000
1140 4¢ B. Franklin Quotation	.18	.05		1.00	.75	124,560,000
1141 4¢ T. Jefferson Quotation	.18	.05		1.00	.75	115,455,000
1142 4¢ Francis Scott Key Quotation	.18	.05		1.00	.75	122,060,000
1143 4¢ Lincoln Quotation	.18	.05		1.00	.75	120,540,000
1144 4¢ Patrick Henry Quotation, 1961	.18	.05		1.00	.75	113,075,000
1145 4¢ Boy Scout Jubilee, Feb. 8	.10	.05		.50	.75	139,325,000
Perf. 10½x11						
1146 4¢ Olympic Winter Games, Feb. 18	.10	.05		.50	.75	124,445,000
1147 4¢ Champion of Liberty, Mar. 7	.10	.05		.60	.75	113,792,000
Perf. 11						
1148 8¢ Champion of Liberty	.20	.12		2.50	.75	44,215,200
Perf. 11x10½						
1149 4¢ World Refugee Year, Apr. 7	.10	.05		.50	.75	113,195,000
Perf. 11						
1150 4¢ Water Conservation, Apr. 18	.10	.05		.65	.75	121,805,000
Perf. 10½x11						
1151 4¢ SEATO, May 31	.10	.05		.50	.75	115,353,000
Perf. 11x10½						
1152 4¢ American Woman, June 2	.10	.05		.50	.75	111,080,000

PATRICK HENRY

Patrick Henry is generally regarded as one of the greatest orators of all time— but did this eloquent American statesman actually pen his most stirring words?

Two Ohio State University professors say, probably not. After scouring Virginia libraries a few years ago, the professors concluded that some of Henry's most famous speeches were probably written by his biographer, William Wirt. They say Henry was too busy making history to write down his speeches and that Wirt, who started the biography three years after Henry's death in 1799, fabricated many of Henry's words. They base their evidence on letters Wirt wrote expressing frustration at being unable to find witnesses to Henry's speeches.

But whether or not Wirt fantasized Henry's words, there is no doubt as to the authenticity of the great orator's most famous line. While Wirt may have written the rest of the speech, Henry penned the conclusion: "I know not what course others may take, but as for me, give me liberty or give me death!" See Scott No. 1144.

		Un	U	#	PB	FDC	Q
	1960-61 continued						
	Perf. 11						
1153	4¢ 50-Star Flag, July 4	.10	.05		.50	.75	153,025,000
	Perf. 11x10½						
1154	4¢ Pony Express 100th Anniv., July 19	.10	.05		.50	.75	119,665,000
	Perf. 10½x11						
1155	4¢ Employ the Handicapped, Aug. 28	.10	.05		.50	.75	117,855,000
1156	4¢ World Forestry Congress, Aug. 29	.10	.05		.50	.75	118,185,000
	Perf. 11						
1157	4¢ Mexican Independence, Sept. 16	.10	.05		.50	.75	112,260,000
1158	4¢ U.S.-Japan Treaty, Sept. 28	.10	.05		.50	.75	125,010,000
	Perf. 10½x11						
1159	4¢ Champion of Liberty, Oct. 8	.10	.05		.55	.75	119,798,000
	Perf. 11						
1160	8¢ Champion of Liberty	.20	.12		2.00	.75	42,696,000
	Issued to honor I.J. Paderewski (1860-1941). Polish pianist and statesman.						
	Perf. 10½x11						
1161	4¢ Sen. Taft Memorial, Oct. 10	.10	.05		.50	.75	106,610,000
	Perf. 11x10½						
1162	4¢ Wheels of Freedom, Oct. 15	.10	.05		.50	.75	109,695,000
	Issued in connection with the National Automobile Show, held in Detroit in 1960.						
	Perf. 11						
1163	4¢ Boy's Clubs of America, Oct. 18	.10	.05		.50	.75	123,690,000
1164	4¢ Automated P.O., Oct. 20	.10	.05		.50	.75	123,970,000
	Perf. 10½x11						
1165	4¢ Champion of Liberty, Oct. 26	.10	.05		.55	.75	124,796,000
	Perf. 11						
1166	8¢ Champion of Liberty	.20	.12		2.25	.75	42,076,800
	Baron Gustaf Mannerheim (1867-1951) was president of Finland from 1944 to 1946.						
1167	4¢ Camp Fire Girls, Nov. 4	.10	.05		.50	.75	116,210,000
	Perf. 10½x11						
1168	4¢ Champion of Liberty, Nov. 2	.10	.05		.55	.75	126,252,000
	Perf. 11						
1169	8¢ Champion of Liberty	.20	.12		2.25	.75	42,746,400
	Giuseppe Garibaldi (1807-1882) was a leader in the fight to unify all Italy.						
	Perf. 10½x11						
1170	4¢ Sen. George Memorial, Nov. 5	.10	.05		.50	.75	124,117,000
1171	4¢ Andrew Carnegie, Nov. 25	.10	.05		.50	.75	119,840,000
1172	4¢ John Foster Dulles Memorial,						
	Dec. 6	.10	.05		.55	.75	117,187,000
	Perf. 11x10½						
1173	4¢ Echo I—Communications for Peace,						
	Dec. 15	.55	.12		4.00	.75	124,390,000

1153

1154

1155

1156

1157

1158

1159

1160

1161

1162

1163

1164

1165

1166

1167

1168

1169

1170

1171

1172

1173

1174   1175   1176   1177

1178   1179   1180

1181   1182   1183

1184   1185   1186   1187

1191

1188   1189   1190

		Un	U	#	PB	FDC	Q
	Issues of 1961, Perf. 10½x11						
1174	4¢ Champion of Liberty, Jan. 26	.10	.05		.55	.75	112,966,000
	Perf. 11						
1175	8¢ Champion of Liberty	.20	.12		2.25	.75	41,644,200
	Pacifist Mahatma Gandhi (1869-1948) led India to freedom from the British in 1947.						
1176	4¢ Range Conservation, Feb. 2	.10	.05		.65	.75	110,850,000
	Perf. 10½x11						
1177	4¢ Horace Greeley, Feb. 3	.10	.05		.55	.75	98,616,000
	Civil War 100th Anniv. Issue, 1961-1965, Perf. 11x10½						
1178	4¢ Fort Sumter Centenary, 1961	.18	.05		1.25	.75	101,125,000
1179	4¢ Shiloh Centenary, 1962	.15	.05		1.00	.75	124,865,000
	Perf. 11						
1180	5¢ Gettysburg Centenary, 1963	.15	.05		1.00	.75	79,905,000
1181	5¢ Wilderness Centenary, 1964	.15	.05		1.00	.75	125,410,000
1182	5¢ Appomattox Centenary, 1965	.18	.05		1.10	.75	112,845,000
	Issue dates: #1178, Apr. 12, 1961; #1179, Apr. 7, 1962; #1180, July 1, 1963; #1181, May 5, 1964; #1182, Apr. 9, 1965.						
	Issues of 1961						
1183	4¢ Kansas Statehood, May 10	.10	.05		.60	.75	106,210,000
	Perf. 11x10½						
1184	4¢ Sen. George W. Norris, July 11	.10	.05		.55	.75	110,810,000
1185	4¢ Naval Aviation, Aug. 20	.10	.05		.55	.75	116,995,000
	Perf. 10½x11						
1186	4¢ Workmen's Comp., Sept. 4	.10	.05		.55	.75	121,015,000
	Perf. 11						
1187	4¢ Frederic Remington, Oct. 4	.15	.05		1.20	.75	111,600,000
	Perf. 10½x11						
1188	4¢ Republic of China, Oct. 10	.10	.05		.55	.75	110,620,000
	Issued for the 50th anniversary of the Republic of China. Stamp shows Sun Yat-sen (1866-1925), first president of China.						
1189	4¢ Naismith-Basketball, Nov. 6	.10	.05		.55	.75	109,110,000
	Perf. 11						
1190	4¢ Nursing, Dec. 28	.10	.05		.70	.75	145,350,000
	Issues of 1962						
1191	4¢ New Mexico Statehood, Jan. 6	.10	.05		.55	.75	112,870,000

		Un	U	#	PB	FDC	Q
	1962 continued						
1192	4¢ Arizona Statehood, Feb. 14	.16	.05		1.00	.75	121,820,000
1193	4¢ Project Mercury, Feb. 20	.20	.10		1.50	.85	289,240,000
	Issued for the first orbital flight of a U.S. astronaut. Flight made by Colonel John Glenn on Feb. 20, 1962.						
1194	4¢ Malaria Eradication, Mar. 30	.10	.05		.55	.75	120,155,000
	Perf. 10½x11						
1195	4¢ Charles Evans Hughes, Apr. 11	.10	.05		.55	.75	124,595,000
	Perf. 11						
1196	4¢ Seattle World's Fair, Apr. 25	.10	.05		.70	.75	147,310,000
1197	4¢ Louisiana Statehood, Apr. 30	.10	.05		.55	.75	118,690,000
	Perf. 11x10½						
1198	4¢ Homestead Act, May 20	.10	.05		.55	.75	122,730,000
1199	4¢ Girl Scout Jubilee, July 24	.10	.05		.55	.75	126,515,000
1200	4¢ Sen. Brien McMahon, July 28	.15	.05		1.00	.75	130,960,000
1201	4¢ Apprenticeship, Aug. 31	.10	.05		.55	.75	120,055,000
	Perf. 11						
1202	4¢ Sam Rayburn, Sept. 16	.10	.05		.55	.75	120,715,000
1203	4¢ Dag Hammarskjöld, Oct. 23	.12	.05		.70	.75	121,440,000
1204	4¢ Hammarskjöld Special Printing:						
	black, brown and yellow						
	(yellow inverted)	.18	.08		5.00	6.00	40,270,000
1205	4¢ Christmas Issue, Nov. 1	.10	.03		.50	.75	861,970,000
1206	4¢ Higher Education, Nov. 14	.10	.05		.55	.75	120,035,000
1207	4¢ Winslow Homer, Dec. 15	.15	.05		1.50	.75	117,870,000

DAG HAMMARSKJOLD

Those who would lead the world must themselves be exemplary members of the world. Such a man was Dag Hammarskjold, who served as Secretary-General of the U.N. from 1953 until his death in a plane crash over Africa in 1961.

Born in Sweden, Hammarskjold was a statesman of world class . . . and much more. He was a great reader, poet and translator, a hiker, a passionate mountain climber and a grand gourmet.

Though the world at large saw him as cool and distant, Hammarskjold's associates saw him refuse a private elevator, reject first-class travel and personally shake the hands of all 3,500 members of the U.N. staff. When he died, he bequeathed his summer home on the windswept moorlands of south Sweden to the world, and left unfinished a project to translate the work of philosopher Martin Buber. See Scott Nos. 1203-1204.

1192

1193

1194

1195

1196

1197

1198

1199

1200

1201

1202

1203

1204

1205

1206

1207

1208

1209

1213

1230

1231

1232

1233

1234

1235

1236

1237

1238

1239

1240

1241

1242

1243

1244

		Un	U	#	PB	FDC	Q
	Flag Issue of 1963						
1208	5¢ Flag over White House	.12	.03		.55	.75	
	Regular Issue of 1962-66, Perf. 11x10½						
1209	1¢ Andrew Jackson	.05	.03		.25	.75	
1213	5¢ George Washington	.12	.03		.65	.75	
1213a	Booklet pane of 5 + label	2.00	.75				
	Coil Stamps, Perf. 10 Vertically						
1225	1¢ green Jackson (1209)	.12	.03			.75	
1229	5¢ dark blue gray Washington (1213)	1.10	.03			.75	
	Issues of 1963, Perf. 11						
1230	5¢ Carolina Charter, Apr. 6	.12	.05		.60	.75	129,945,000
1231	5¢ Food for Peace—Freedom from Hunger,						
	June 4	.12	.05		.60	.75	135,620,000
1232	5¢ W. Virginia Statehood, June 20	.12	.05		.60	.75	137,540,000
1233	5¢ Emancipation Proclamation,						
	Aug. 16	.12	.05		.60	.75	132,435,000
1234	5¢ Alliance for Progress, Aug. 17	.12	.05		.60	.75	135,520,000
	Perf. 10½x11						
1235	5¢ Cordell Hull, Oct. 5	.12	.05		.60	.75	131,420,000
	Perf. 11x10½						
1236	5¢ Eleanor Roosevelt, Oct. 11	.12	.05		.60	.75	133,170,000
	Perf. 11						
1237	5¢ Science, Oct. 14	.20	.05		1.35	.75	130,195,000
1238	5¢ City Mail Delivery, Oct. 26	.12	.05		.60	.75	128,450,000
	Issued for the 100th anniversary of free city mail delivery.						
1239	5¢ Red Cross 100th Anniv., Oct. 29	.12	.05		.60	.75	118,665,000
1240	5¢ Christmas Issue, Nov. 1	.12	.03		.60	.75	1,291,250,000
1241	5¢ John James Audubon, Dec. 7	.15	.05		1.25	.75	175,175,000
	Issues of 1964, Perf. 10½x11						
1242	5¢ Sam Houston, Jan. 10	.12	.05		.60	.75	125,995,000
	Perf. 11						
1243	5¢ Charles M. Russell, Mar. 19	.15	.05		1.20	.75	128,925,000
	Perf. 11x10½						
1244	5¢ New York World's Fair, Apr. 22	.15	.05		1.65	.75	145,700,000

		Un	U	#	PB	FDC	Q
	1964 continued						
	Perf. 11						
1245	5¢ John Muir, Apr. 29	.12	.05		.60	.75	120,310,000
	Perf. 11 x 10½						
1246	5¢ Kennedy Memorial, May 29	.12	.05		.60	.75	511,750,000
	Perf. 10½ x 11						
1247	5¢ New Jersey 300th Anniv., June 15	.12	.05		.60	.75	123,845,000
	Perf. 11						
1248	5¢ Nevada Statehood, July 22	.12	.05		.60	.75	122,825,000
1249	5¢ Register and Vote, Aug. 1	.12	.05		.60	.75	453,090,000
	Perf. 10½ x 11						
1250	5¢ Shakespeare, Aug. 14	.12	.05		.60	.75	123,245,000
1251	5¢ Doctors Mayo, Sept. 11	.12	.05		.60	.75	123,355,000
1252	5¢ American Music, Oct. 15, Perf. 11	.12	.05		.60	.75	126,970,000
1253	5¢ Homemakers, Oct. 26, Perf. 11	.12	.05		.60	.75	121,250,000
	Christmas Issue, Nov. 9						
1254	5¢ Holly, Perf. 11	1.50	.05		7.50	.75	351,940,000
1255	5¢ Mistletoe, Perf. 11	1.50	.05		7.50	.75	351,940,000
1256	5¢ Poinsettia, Perf. 11	1.50	.05		7.50	.75	351,940,000
1257	5¢ Sprig of Conifer, Perf. 11	1.50	.05		7.50	.75	351,940,000
1257b	Block of four, #1254-1257	6.50	.60				
	Perf. 10½ x 11						
1258	5¢ Verrazano-Narrows Bridge, Nov. 21	.12	.05		.60	.75	120,005,000
	Perf. 11						
1259	5¢ Fine Arts, Dec. 2	.12	.05		.75	.75	125,800,000
	Perf. 10½ x 11						
1260	5¢ Amateur Radio, Dec. 15	.12	.05		.75	.75	122,230,000

POINSETTIA

1256

The poinsettia isn't really a house plant, and the flower isn't really a flower. In its natural state, the poinsettia is a shrub, and can grow to a height of twelve feet. The flower of the poinsettia is actually tiny and yellow, and is barely noticeable amidst the large, brightly-colored modified-leaf bracts that surround each one.

The poinsettia was named in honor of Joel Roberts Poinsett, who introduced the plant to the United States. A student of law, gunnery, medicine, mathematics and science, Poinsett distinguished himself as a master diplomat, both at home and abroad. As Secretary of War, Minister to Mexico, member of the South Carolina Legislature and private citizen, Poinsett was known for his charisma, his insatiable appetite for literature and scientific discovery, his strong opinions and his mastery in public speaking. Born in Charleston, South Carolina, he died in his home state in 1851. The poinsettia lives on in homes across America during the Christmas season each year. See Scott No. 1256.

1245

1246

1247

1248

1249

1250

1251

1252

1253

1257b

1258

1259

1260

1261

1262

1263

1264

1265

1266

1267

1268

1269

1270

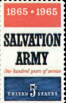

1271

1272

1273

1274

1275

1276

		Un	U	#	PB	FDC	Q
	Issues of 1965, Perf. 11						
1261	5¢ Battle of New Orleans, Jan. 8	.12	.05		.75	.75	115,695,000
1262	5¢ Physical Fitness-Sokol, Feb. 15	.12	.05		.75	.75	115,095,000
1263	5¢ Crusade Against Cancer, Apr. 1	.12	.05		.75	.75	119,560,000
	Perf. 10½x11						
1264	5¢ Churchill Memorial, May 13	.12	.05		.75	.75	125,180,000
	Perf. 11						
1265	5¢ Magna Carta, June 15	.12	.05		.75	.75	120,135,000
1266	5¢ Intl. Cooperation Year, June 26	.12	.05		.75	.75	115,405,000
	Issued for International Cooperation Year and the 20th anniversary of the United Nations.						
1267	5¢ Salvation Army, July 2	.12	.05		.75	.75	115,855,000
	Perf. 10½x11						
1268	5¢ Dante Alighieri, July 17	.12	.05		.75	.75	115,340,000
1269	5¢ Herbert Hoover, Aug. 10	.12	.05		.75	.75	114,840,000
	Perf. 11						
1270	5¢ Robert Fulton, Aug. 19	.12	.05		.75	.75	116,140,000
1271	5¢ Settlement of Florida, Aug. 28	.12	.05		1.00	.75	116,900,000
	Established in 1565, St. Augustine, Florida, was the first permanent European Settlement in the U.S.						
1272	5¢ Traffic Safety, Sept. 3	.12	.05		1.00	.75	114,085,000
1273	5¢ John Singleton Copley, Sept. 17	.18	.05		1.25	.75	114,880,000
1274	11¢ International Telecommunication Union,						
	Oct. 6	.50	.25		15.00	.75	26,995,000
1275	5¢ Adlai E. Stevenson, Oct. 23	.12	.05		.75	.75	128,495,000
1276	5¢ Christmas Issue, Nov. 2	.12	.03		.60	.75	1,139,930,000

ADLAI STEVENSON AND THE U.N.

Always known for his wit, Adlai Stevenson managed to maintain his sense of humor throughout his final years as U.S. Ambassador to the United Nations. Often the target of his wit was himself.

When Stevenson arrived at the U.N. in 1961, he was taken on a tour of the Security Council chambers. After spotting the United States nameplate, he was informed that he was next in line for the Council's rotating presidency. Shaking his head, the twice-defeated U.S. Presidential candidate lamented, "That's the way it is. When I want the presidency, I can't have it; when I don't, I can."

Later in his U.N. career, Stevenson noted that he was known by almost everyone who had served at the U.N., and that 98 percent of them had been pro-Democratic Party during his unsuccessful presidential campaigns. "I've often said," Stevenson remarked, "it was a shame I ran for President of the wrong country." See Scott No. 1275.

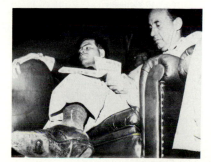

Photo Credit: Wideworld Photos

		Un	U	#	PB	FDC	Q
Issues of 1965-78, Prominent Americans, Perf. 11x10½, 10½x11							
1278	1¢ Thomas Jefferson, 1968	.03	.03		.20	.35	
1278a	Booklet pane of 8, 1968	1.00	.25				
1278b	Booklet pane of 4, 1971	.75	.20				
1279	1¼¢ Albert Gallatin, 1967	.20	.05		22.50	.35	
1280	2¢ Frank Lloyd Wright, 1966	.04	.03		.30	.35	
1280a	Booklet pane of 5 + label, 1968	1.20	.40				
1280c	Booklet pane of 6, 1971	1.00	.35				
1281	3¢ Francis Parkman, 1967	.06	.03		.70	.35	
1282	4¢ Abraham Lincoln, 1965	.08	.03		.40	.35	
1283	5¢ George Washington, 1966	.10	.03		.50	.45	
1283B	5¢ Washington redrawn, 1967	.12	.03		1.00	.45	
1284	6¢ Franklin D. Roosevelt, 1966	.12	.03		.65	.45	
1284b	Booklet pane of 8, 1967	1.50	.50				
1284c	Booklet pane of 5 + label, 1968	1.25	.50				
1285	8¢ Albert Einstein, 1966	.16	.05		1.25	.50	
1286	10¢ Andrew Jackson, 1967	.25	.03		1.30	.60	
1286A	12¢ Henry Ford, 1968	.30	.03		1.75	.50	
1287	13¢ John F. Kennedy, 1967	.30	.05		1.65	.65	
1288	15¢ Oliver Wendell Holmes, 1968	.30	.06		1.50	.60	
1288B	15¢ dk. rose claret Holmes (1288),						
	Perf. 10, 1978	.30	.05			.75	
1288c	Booklet pane of 8, 1978	2.40					
1289	20¢ George C. Marshall, 1967	.40	.06		2.00	.80	
1290	25¢ Frederick Douglass, 1967	.50	.03		2.50	1.00	
1291	30¢ John Dewey, 1968	.60	.08		3.00	1.20	
1292	40¢ Thomas Paine, 1968	.80	.10		4.00	1.60	
1293	50¢ Lucy Stone, 1968	1.00	.04		5.00	2.50	
1294	$1 Eugene O'Neill, 1967	2.00	.08		10.00	5.00	
1295	$5 John Bassett Moore, 1966	10.00	2.00		50.00	45.00	
	No. 1288B issued only in booklets.						
Coil Stamps, Issues of 1966-78, Perf. 10 Horizontally							
1297	3¢ violet Parman (1281), 1975	.12	.03			.75	
1298	6¢ gray brown F.D.R. (1284), 1967	.50	.05			.75	
	Perf. 10 Vertically						
1299	1¢ green Jefferson (1278), 1968	.06	.03			.75	
1303	4¢ black Lincoln (1282), 1966	.15	.03			.75	
1304	5¢ blue Washington (1283), 1966	.15	.03			.75	
1305	6¢ Franklin D. Roosevelt, 1968	.20	.03			.75	
1305E	15¢ rose claret Holmes (1288), 1978	.30	.03			.75	
1305C	$1 dull purple Eugene O'Neill						
	(1294), 1973	2.25	.20			3.00	

1278   1279   1280   1281   1282

1283   1283B   1284   1285   1286

1286A   1287   1288   1289

1290   1291   1292   1293   1294

1295   1305

306

1307

1308

1309

1310

1312

1313

1314

1311

1315

1316

1317

1318

1319

		Un	U	#	PB	FDC	Q
	Issues of 1966, Perf. 11						
1306	5¢ Migratory Bird Treaty, Mar. 16	.15	.05		1.00	.75	116,835,000
1307	5¢ Humane Treatment of Animals,						
	Apr. 9	.15	.05		.90	.75	117,470,000
1308	5¢ Indiana Statehood, Apr. 16	.12	.05		.75	.75	123,770,000
1309	5¢ American Circus, May 2	.12	.05		.90	.75	131,270,000
	Sixth International Philatelic Exhibition Issues						
1310	5¢ Stamped Cover, May 21	.12	.05		.90	.75	122,285,000
	Imperf.						
1311	5¢ Souvenir Sheet, May 23	.40	.15			.75	14,680,000
	Perf. 11						
1312	5¢ Bill of Rights, July 1	.12	.05		.75	.75	114,160,000
	Perf. 10½ x 11						
1313	5¢ Polish Millennium, July 30	.15	.05		.90	.75	128,475,000
	Perf. 11						
1314	5¢ National Park Service, Aug. 25	.12	.05		.75	.75	119,535,000
1315	5¢ Marine Corps Reserve, Aug. 29	.12	.05		1.00	.75	125,110,000
1316	5¢ General Federation of Women's						
	Clubs, Sept. 12	.12	.05		1.00	.75	114,853,200
1317	5¢ Johnny Appleseed, Sept. 24	.12	.05		1.00	.75	124,290,000
1318	5¢ Beautification of America, Oct. 5	.15	.05		1.75	.75	128,460,000
1319	5¢ Great River Road, Oct. 21	.12	.05		1.00	.75	127,585,000

JOHNNY APPLESEED

"Johnny Appleseed": crackpot or prophet? Businessman or hippie?

The legend of "Johnny Appleseed" has survived nearly 200 years. But the myth remains stronger than the man, and few have been able to untangle truth from tradition.

Historians agree that "Johnny Appleseed" was born John Chapman in 1774 in Leominster, Mass., and that he spent much of the next 70 years wandering westward, planting his beloved appleseeds. But some see "Appleseed" as a deranged fanatic, others as a colorful character who wore a saucepan for a hat. One historian refers to him as "America's first beatnik, an early hippie who had a little Robin Hood in him." Another contends that he was not a crackpot, but a businessman who owned a number of orchards and farms and held title to land in half a dozen places.

But myth and fact do converge on one thing: "Johnny Appleseed" undoubtedly did more than any other man to bring fruitful orchards to this country's wild frontier. See Scott No. 1317.

		Un	U	#	PB	FDC	Q
1966 continued							
1320	5¢ Savings Bond—Servicemen,						
	Oct. 26	.12	.05		1.00	.75	115,875,000
1321	5¢ Christmas Issue, Nov. 1	.12	.03		.75	.75	1,173,547,420
1322	5¢ Mary Cassatt, Nov. 17	.20	.05		2.75	.75	114,015,000
Issues of 1967							
1323	5¢ National Grange, Apr. 17	.12	.05		.90	.75	121,105,000
	The National Grange, a farm organization, was created in 1867.						
1324	5¢ Canada 100th Anniv., May 25	.12	.05		.90	.75	132,045,000
1325	5¢ Erie Canal, July 4	.12	.05		.90	.75	118,780,000
1326	5¢ "Peace"—Lions, July 5	.12	.05		.90	.75	121,985,000
1327	5¢ Henry David Thoreau, July 12	.12	.05		.90	.75	111,850,000
1328	5¢ Nebraska Statehood, July 29	.12	.05		.90	.75	117,225,000
1329	5¢ Voice of America, Aug. 1	.12	.05		1.20	.75	111,515,000
1330	5¢ Davy Crockett, Aug. 17	.12	.05		1.00	.75	114,270,000
Space Accomplishments Issue, Sep. 29							
1331	5¢ Space-Walking Astronaut	1.75	.25				60,432,500
1331a	Pair, #1331-1332	5.50	2.50		17.50	8.00	
1332	5¢ Gemini 4 Capsule and Earth	1.75	.25		17.50		60,432,500
1333	5¢ Urban Planning, Oct. 2	.15	.05		3.00	.75	110,675,000
1334	5¢ Finnish Independence, Oct. 6	.15	.05		3.50	.75	110,670,000
Perf. 12							
1335	5¢ Thomas Eakins, Nov. 2	.18	.05		3.00	.75	113,825,000
Perf. 11							
1336	5¢ Christmas Issue, Nov. 6	.12	.04		.60	.75	1,208,700,000
1337	5¢ Mississippi Statehood, Dec. 11	.15	.05		2.50	.75	113,330,000
Issues of 1968-71							
1338	6¢ Flag and White House	.12	.03		.60	.75	

DAVY CROCKETT

Legend has it that Davy Crockett, famous bear hunter, frontiersman and one-time congressman, died a heroic death defending the Alamo.

But now an historian questions that myth. In 1978, Dan Kilgore, a former president of Texas State Historical Society, published a book titled How Did Davy Die? *The author contends that Crockett surrendered or was captured at the Alamo, then executed by conquering Mexican troops. Kilgore bases his contention on the recently translated diary of a lieutenant colonel in the Mexican army. He says that statements from seven Mexican soldiers back up his account.*

Kilgore also casts doubt on Crockett's motives in going to defend the Alamo. The popular story is that Crockett went to Texas because of his love of liberty. Kilgore suggests that the frontiersman joined the combatants because of the humiliation he suffered when he lost his bid for reelection to Congress in 1835.

No matter what the true version, chances are that Davy Crockett and the ideas of freedom he represented will always be remembered—and for very good reasons. See Scott No. 1330.

1320

1321

1322

1323

1324

1325

1326

1327

1328

1329

1330

1331a

1333

1334

1335

1336

1337

1338

		Un	U	#	PB	FDC	Q
	1968-71 continued						
	Perf. 11x10½						
1338D	6¢ dark blue, red & green (1338), 1970	.12	.03	(20)	3.25	.75	
1338F	8¢ multicolored (1338), 1971	.16	.03	(20)	3.50	.75	
	Coil Stamps of 1969-71, Perf. 10 Vertically						
1338A	6¢ dark blue, red & green (1338), 1969	.12	.03			.75	
1338G	8¢ multicolored (1338), 1971	.16	.03			.75	
	Issues of 1968, Perf. 11						
1339	6¢ Illinois Statehood, Feb. 12	.18	.05		1.00	.75	141,350,000
1340	6¢ HemisFair '68, Mar. 30	.18	.05		1.00	.75	144,345,000
1341	$1 Airlift, Apr. 4	6.00	2.50		32.50	6.50	
	Issued to pay for airlift of parcels to and from servicemen overseas.						
1342	6¢ "Youth"—Elks, May 1	.18	.05		1.00	.75	147,120,000
1343	6¢ Law and Order, May 17	.18	.05		1.00	.75	⊦30,125,000
1344	6¢ Register and Vote, June 27	.18	.05		1.00	.75	158,700,000
	Historic Flag Series, July 4						
1345	6¢ Ft. Moultrie Flag (1776)	.80	.35		5.50	3.00	23,153,000
1346	6¢ Ft. McHenry Flag (1795-1818)	.80	.35				23,153,000
1347	6¢ Washington's Cruisers Flag (1775)	.80	.35				23,153,000
1348	6¢ Bennington Flag (1777)	.80	.35				23,153,000
1349	6¢ Rhode Island Flag (1775)	.80	.35				23,153,000
1350	6¢ First Stars and Stripes Flag (1777)	.80	.35				23,153,000
1351	6¢ Bunker Hill Flag (1775)	.80	.35				23,153,000
1352	6¢ Grand Union Flag (1776)	.80	.35				23,153,000
1353	6¢ Phila. Light Horse Flag (1775)	.80	.35				23,153,000
1354	6¢ First Navy Jack (1775)	.80	.35				23,153,000

FIRST STARS AND STRIPES

"Resolved, that the flag of the United States be made of thirteen stripes, alternate red and white; that the Union be thirteen stars, white in a blue field, representing a new constellation."

That resolution, recorded by Congress on June 14, 1777, is the one certainly in a maze of contradictions and legend surrounding the origin of the American flag.

We've all heard, for example, how George Washington called on Betsy Ross and commissioned her to make the first flag. But at the time the general is said to have come calling, he was in fact off fighting the British in New Jersey.

A congressional representative from New Jersey—one Francis Hopkinson—claimed credit for the design of the flag, among other designs he submitted to Congress in 1780. He asked at first only for a quarter cask of wine in return, but later upped the ante to several thousand dollars. Congress denied his request, saying that others were involved in the design and that Hopkinson could not claim "the sole merit."

For many years, in fact, the design remained loosely defined, the arrangement and shape of the stars and stripes left to individual fancy. Not until 1912, when the design was standardized under President Taft, did all Americans rally 'round the same flag. See Scott No. 1350.

1339

1340

1341

1342

1343

1344

1345

1346

1347

1348

1349

1350

1351

1352

1353

1354

1355

1356

1357

1358

1359

1360

1361

1362

1363

1364

1368a

1369

1370

		Un	U	#	PB	FDC	Ω
1354a	Strip of ten, #1345-1354	10.00	6.50	(20)	22.50	15.00	
	Perf. 12						
1355	5¢ Walt Disney, Sept. 11	.20	.05		1.75	.75	153,015,000
	Perf. 11						
1356	6¢ Father Marquette, Sept. 20	.20	.05		1.10	.75	132,560,000
1357	6¢ Daniel Boone, Sept. 26	.20	.05		1.10	.75	130,385,000
1358	6¢ Arkansas River, Oct. 1	.20	.05		1.10	.75	132,265,000
1359	6¢ Leif Erikson, Oct. 9	.20	.05		1.20	.75	128,710,000
	Perf. 11x10½						
1360	6¢ Cherokee Strip, Oct. 15	.20	.05		1.65	.75	124,775,000
	Perf. 11						
1361	6¢ John Trumbull, Oct. 18	.25	.05		2.75	.75	128,295,000
1362	6¢ Waterfowl Conservation, Oct. 24	.30	.05		3.50	.75	142,245,000
1363	6¢ Christmas Issue, Nov. 1	.20	.04	(10)	2.75	.75	1,410,580,000
1364	6¢ American Indian, Nov. 4	.40	.05		3.50	.75	125,100,000
	Issues of 1969, Beautification of America, Jan. 16						
1365	6¢ Capitol, Azaleas and Tulips	2.00	.15		13.50	2.00	48,142,500
1366	6¢ Washington Monument,						
	Potomac River and Daffodils	2.00	.15		13.50	2.00	48,142,500
1367	6¢ Poppies and Lupines						
	along Highway	2.00	.15		13.50	2.00	48,142,500
1368	6¢ Blooming Crabapples						
	along Street	2.00	.15		13.50	2.00	48,142,500
1368a	Block of four, #1365-1368	8.50	3.50		13.50	5.00	
1369	6¢ American Legion, Mar. 15	.20	.05		1.10	.75	148,770,000
1370	6¢ Grandma Moses, May 1	.25	.05		1.35	.75	139,475,000

LEIF ERIKSON

In 1963, a Norwegian explorer uncovered the remains of a small settlement near L'Anse aux Meadows, Newfoundland. Some of the houses contained "ember pits" similar to those found in Norse houses in Greenland, and at least one house had a great hall in the Viking style. Radiocarbon dating of charcoal from the ruins indicates that they were occupied about 1000 A.D.—just when Leif the Lucky, son of Erik the Red, and his fellow Vikings are said to have set sail from Greenland to North America. Are these the remains of Leif's settlement?

No one really knows the site of what Leif called "Vinland the Good," which has been placed everywhere from the northern tip of Labrador down to the Carolinas. But neither does anyone any longer doubt its existence. Viking artifacts have been found scattered along the East Coast and as far inland as North Dakota. Meanwhile, the search continues. The saga of the Viking sea rover, begun centuries before Columbus, is not yet over. See Scott No. 1359.

		Un	U	#	PB	FDC	Q
	1969 continued						
1371	6¢ Apollo 8, May 5	.30	.06		3.50	1.00	187,165,000
1372	6¢ W. C. Handy, May 17	.20	.05		1.00	.75	125,555,000
1373	6¢ California Settlement, July 16	.20	.05		1.00	.75	144,425,000
1374	6¢ John Wesley Powell, Aug. 1	.20	.05		1.00	.75	135,875,000
1375	6¢ Alabama Statehood, Aug. 2	.20	.05		1.00	.75	151,110,000
	Botanical Congress Issue						
1376	6¢ Douglas Fir (Northwest)	2.75	.15		15.00	2.00	39,798,750
1377	6¢ Lady's Slipper (Northeast)	2.75	.15		15.00	2.00	39,798,750
1378	6¢ Ocotillo (Southwest)	2.75	.15		15.00	2.00	39,798,750
1379	6¢ Franklinia (Southeast)	2.75	.15		15.00	2.00	39,798,750
1379a	Block of four, #1376-1379	12.00	3.50		15.00	5.00	
	Perf. 10½x11						
1380	6¢ Dartmouth College Case, Sept. 22	.20	.05		1.35	.60	129,540,000
	Perf. 11						
1381	6¢ Professional Baseball, Sept. 24	.25	.05		1.75	.75	130,925,000
1382	6¢ Intercollegiate Football, Sept. 26	.25	.05		1.85	.75	139,055,000
1383	6¢ Dwight D. Eisenhower, Oct. 14	.20	.05		1.00	.75	150,611,200
	Perf. 11x10½						
1384	6¢ Christmas Issue, Nov. 3	.18	.03	(10)	2.25	.75	1,709,795,000
1384a	Precanceled	.30	.06				

"A Winter Sunday in Norway, Maine," shown on stamp, was painted around 1870 by an unknown artist.

| 1385 | 6¢ Hope for Crippled, Nov. 20 | .18 | .05 | | 1.00 | .75 | 127,545,000 |
| 1386 | 6¢ William M. Harnett, Dec. 3 | .18 | .05 | | 1.20 | .75 | 145,788,800 |

D.D. EISENHOWER

Operation Overload, *the Allied invasion of German-occupied France, was to be the most ambitious military undertaking in man's history. If the operation was a success, the man who commanded it could take much of the credit for the defeat of Nazi Germany.*

Almost everyone thought the appointment would go to George C. Marshall (Chief of Staff under President Franklin Roosevelt)—including General Dwight D. Eisenhower, Allied commander in the Mediterranean. What made Eisenhower unhappy, however, were reports that he would replace Marshall in Washington. Eisenhower had no patience with politicians. He could not bear to continue an argument "after logic had made the opposition's position untenable, yet politicians persist against all logic." He was anxious to avoid such a fate.

But problems arose over Marshall's impending appointment. After months of indecision and conflicting reports, Eisenhower was summoned to meet Roosevelt in Tunis. The President turned to the general and said, "Well, Ike, you are going to command OVERLOAD." Ike's response was to take charge of perhaps the largest invasion plan of any war. See Scott No. 1383.

1371

1372

1373

1374

1375

1379a

1380

1381

1382

U.S. 6c POSTAGE

DWIGHT D. EISENHOWER

1383

HOPE
FOR THE CRIPPLED

1385

1384

1384a

1386

AMERICAN BALD EAGLE | AFRICAN ELEPHANT HERD

1391

HAIDA CEREMONIAL CANOE | THE AGE OF REPTILES

1390a

1392

1393   1393D   1394   1396   1397

1398   1399   1400

1405

1406

1407   1408   1409

		Un	U	#	PB	FDC	Q
	Issues of 1970, Natural History, May 6						
1387	6¢ American Bald Eagle	.30	.12		3.75	2.00	50,448,550
1388	6¢ African Elephant Herd	.30	.12		3.75	2.00	50,448,550
1389	6¢ Tlingit Chief in Haida Ceremonial						
	Canoe	.30	.12		3.75	2.00	50,448,550
1390	6¢ Brontosaurus, Stegosaurus and						
	Allosaurus from Jurassic Period	.30	.12		3.75	2.00	50,448,550
1390a	Block of four, #1387-1390	1.35	.75		3.75	3.00	
1391	6¢ Maine Statehood, July 9	.18	.05		1.10	.75	171,850,000
	Perf. 10½x11						
1392	6¢ Wildlife Conservation, July 20	.18	.05		1.10	.75	142,205,000
	Issues of 1970-74, Perf. 11x10½, 10½x11, 11						
1393	6¢ Dwight D. Eisenhower, 1970	.12	.03		.60	.75	
1393a	Booklet pane of 8	1.00	.50				
1393b	Booklet pane of 5 + label	.85	.35				
1393D	7¢ Benjamin Franklin, 1972	.14	.03		1.35	.75	
1394	8¢ Eisenhower, 1971	.16	.03		1.00	.75	
1395	8¢ Eisenhower, 1971	.16	.03			.75	
1395a	Booklet pane of 8, 1971	1.50	1.25				
1395b	Booklet pane of 6, 1971	1.00	.75				
1395c	Booklet pane of 4 + 2 labels, -72	1.00	.50				
1395d	Booklet pane of 7 + label, 1972	1.25	1.00				
1396	8¢ U.S. Postal Service, 1971	.25	.03	(12)	7.50	.75	
1397	14¢ Fiorello H. LaGuardia, 1972	.28	.03		2.35	.85	
1398	16¢ Ernie Pyle, 1971	.32	.03		2.35	.75	
1399	18¢ Dr. Elizabeth Blackwell, 1974	.36	.06		1.80	1.00	
1400	21¢ Amadeo P. Giannini, 1973	.42	.06		2.10	1.00	
	Coil Stamps, Perf. 10 Vertically						
1401	6¢ dark blue gray Eisenhower						
	(1393), 1970	.20	.03			.75	
1402	8¢ deep claret Eisenhower (1395), -71	.22	.03			.75	
	Issues of 1970, Perf. 11						
1405	6¢ Edgar Lee Masters, Aug. 22	.18	.05		1.00	.75	137,660,000
1406	6¢ Woman Suffrage, Aug. 26	.18	.05		1.00	.75	135,125,000
1407	6¢ South Carolina, Sept. 12	.18	.05		1.00	.75	135,895,000
1408	6¢ Stone Mountain Mem., Sept. 19	.18	.05		1.00	.75	132,675,000
1409	6¢ Fort Snelling, Oct. 17	.18	.05		1.00	.75	134,795,000

		Un	U #		PB	FDC	Q
	Perf. 11x10½, Anti-Pollution Issue, Oct. 28						
1410	6¢ Save Our Soil	.85	.13	(10)	9.50	1.50	40,400,000
1411	6¢ Save Our Cities	.85	.13				40,400,000
1412	6¢ Save Our Water	.85	.13				40,400,000
1413	6¢ Save Our Air	.85	.13				40,400,000
1413a	Block of four, #1410-1413	3.75	2.25	(10)	9.50	3.00	
	Christmas Issue, Nov. 5, Perf. 10½x11						
1414	6¢ Nativity, by Lorenzo Lotto	.20	.03	(8)	3.00	1.20	638,730,000
1414a	Precanceled	.35	.08				358,245,000
	Perf. 11x10½						
1415	6¢ Tin and Cast-Iron Locomotive	1.10	.10	(8)	12.00	1.40	122,313,750
1415a	Precanceled	1.75	.15				109,912,500
1416	6¢ Toy Horse on Wheels	1.10	.10				122,313,750
1416a	Precanceled	1.75	.15				109,912,500
1417	6¢ Mechanical Tricycle	1.10	.10				122,313,750
1417a	Precanceled	1.75	.15				109,912,500
1418	6¢ Doll Carriage	1.10	.10				122,313,750
1418a	Precanceled	1.75	.15				109,912,500
1418b	Block of four, #1415-1418	4.75	.90	(8)	12.00	3.00	
1418c	Block of four, precanceled	8.00	1.75		37.50	3.00	
	Perf. 11						
1419	6¢ United Nations, Nov. 20	.18	.05		1.25	.75	127,610,000
1420	6¢ Landing of the Pilgrims, Nov. 21	.18	.05		1.25	.75	129,785,000
	Disabled Veterans and Servicemen Issue, Nov. 24						
1421	6¢ Disabled American Veterans						
	Emblem	.30	.10			.75	67,190,000
1421a	Pair, #1421-1422	.70	.30		7.00	.60	
1422	6¢ U.S. Servicemen	.30	.10		7.00	.75	67,190,000
	Issues of 1971						
1423	6¢ American Wool Industry, Jan. 19	.18	.05		1.00	.75	135,305,000
1424	6¢ Gen. Douglas MacArthur, Jan. 26	.18	.05		1.00	.75	134,840,000
1425	6¢ Blood Donor, Mar. 12	.18	.05		1.00	.75	130,975,000
	Perf. 11x10½						
1426	8¢ Missouri 150th Anniv., May 8	.20	.05	(12)	3.50	.75	161,235,000

1414

1413a

1419

1418b

1420   1421a   1423   1424

1425   1426

1430a

1431

1432

1433

1434

1435

1436

1437

1438

1439

	Un	U	#	PB	FDC	Q
Perf. 11, Wildlife Conservation Issue, June 12						
1427 8¢ Trout	.30	.10		2.25	1.50	43,920,000
1428 8¢ Alligator	.30	.10		2.25	1.50	43,920,000
1429 8¢ Polar Bear and Cubs	.30	.10		2.25	1.50	43,920,000
1430 8¢ California Condor	.30	.10		2.25	1.50	43,920,000
1430a Block of four, #1427-1430	1.30	.85		2.25	3.00	
1431 8¢ Antarctic Treaty, June 23	.25	.05		1.65	.75	138,700,000
1432 8¢ American Revolution						
200th Anniversary, July 4	.85	.05		7.50	.75	138,165,000
1433 8¢ John Sloan, Aug. 2	.22	.05		1.65	.75	152,125,000
Decade of Space Achievements Issue, Aug. 2						
1434 8¢ Earth, Sun, Landing Craft						
on Moon Pair	.25	.10				88,147,500
1434a Pair, #1434-1435	.60	.35		2.25	1.20	
1435 8¢ Lunar Rover and Astronauts	.25	.10		2.25	1.20	88,147,500
1436 8¢ Emily Dickinson, Aug. 28	.18	.05		1.25	.75	142,845,000
1437 8¢ San Juan, Sept. 12	.18	.05		1.25	.75	148,755,000
Perf. 10½x11						
1438 8¢ Prevent Drug Abuse, Oct. 5	.18	.05	(6)	1.85	.75	139,080,000
1439 8¢ CARE, Oct. 27	.18	.05	(8)	2.10	.75	130,755,000

WHALING SHIPS

Despite worldwide efforts to protect the endangered whale, outlaw ships continue to comb the seas in pursuit of valuable whale meat. But in one case, the whalers' greed proved their undoing.

In June of 1978, the trawler Tonna *set out to hunt finback whales in the North Atlantic. By late July, the vessel rode low in the water, weighed down by 450 tons of whale meat. The* Tonna *was headed for home when the lookout spotted a big finback ahead. The trawler gave chase, and the crew fired a grenade-tipped harpoon into the fleeing whale. The grenade exploded deep within the animal, and the sea turned red as the whale thrashed to its death.*

As winches were hauling the 66-foot-long creature on board, the carcass suddenly rolled over against the rail. The fishing vessel couldn't handle the huge weight and careened onto its side. The sea poured into the open portholes, and the crew watched in horror as the electric winch froze, killing any hope of releasing the dead whale. In desperation the captain ordered his men to cut up the carcass. But a tropical storm came up suddenly, and huge waves engulfed the already crippled ship. As the Tonna *sank into the sea, the crew scrambled into life rafts. But the captain, who had spent most of his life pursuing the dwindling number of whales, refused to abandon ship. He—and the dead whale that had defeated him—went down with the* Tonna.

See Scott No. 1441.

		Un	U	#	PB	FDC	Q
	Perf. 11, Historic Preservation Issue, Oct. 29						
1440	8¢ Decatur House, Washington, D.C.	.30	.12		2.25	1.20	42,552,000
1441	8¢ Whaling Ship *Charles W. Morgan*	.30	.12				42,552,000
1442	8¢ Cable Car, San Francisco, Calif.	.30	.12				42,552,000
1443	8¢ San Xavier del Bac Mission, Ariz.	.30	.12				42,552,000
1443a	Block of four, #1440-1443	1.30	.75		2.25	3.00	
	Perf. 10½x11, Christmas Issue, Nov. 10						
1444	8¢ Adoration of the Shepherds,						
	by Giorgione	.18	.03	(12)	2.50	.75	1,074,350,000
1445	8¢ Partridge in a Pear Tree,						
	by Jamie Wyeth	.18	.03	(12)	2.50	.75	979,540,000
	Issues of 1972, Perf. 11						
1446	8¢ Sidney Lanier, Feb. 3	.18	.05		1.00	.75	137,355,000
	Perf. 10½x11						
1447	8¢ Peace Corps, Feb. 11	.18	.05	(6)	1.50	.75	150,400,000
	National Parks 100th Anniversary Issue, Perf. 11						
1448	2¢ Hulk of Ship, Apr. 5	.06	.06		2.50	1.25	172,730,000
1449	2¢ Cape Hatteras Lighthouse, Apr. 5	.06	.06				172,730,000
1450	2¢ Laughing Gulls on Driftwood,						
	Apr. 5	.06	.06				172,730,000
1451	2¢ Laughing Gulls and Dune, Apr. 5	.06	.06				172,730,000
1451a	Block of four, Cape Hatteras,						
	#1448-1451	.25	.30		2.50	1.25	
1452	6¢ Wolf Trap Farm, June 26	.16	.04		1.25	.75	104,090,000
1453	8¢ Yellowstone, Mar. 1	.18	.05		1.00	.75	164,096,000
1454	15¢ Mt. McKinley, July 28	.35	.22		2.50	.75	53,920,000
C84	11¢ City of Refuge, May 3	.30	.15		2.75	.50	

Note: Beginning with this issue, the U.S.P.S. began to offer stamp collectors first day cancellations affixed to 8x10½ inch souvenir pages. The pages are similar to the stamp announcements that have appeared on post office bulletin boards since Scott No. 1132.

		Un	U	#	PB	FDC	Q
1455	8¢ Family Planning, Mar. 18	.16	.05		1.00	.75	153,025,000
.	**Perf. 11x10½, American Revolution Bicentennial Issue, Jul. 4,**						
	Craftsmen in Colonial America						
1456	8¢ Glassmaker	.30	.08		3.00	1.00	50,472,500
1457	8¢ Silversmith	.30	.08				50,472,500
1458	8¢ Wigmaker	.30	.08				50,472,500
1459	8¢ Hatter	.30	.08				50,472,500
1459a	Block of four, #1456-1459	1.35	.60		3.00	2.50	
	Olympic Games Issue, Aug. 17						
1460	6¢ Bicycling and Olympic Rings	.12	.04	(10)	2.00	.75	67,335,000
1461	8¢ Bobsledding	.16	.05	(10)	2.25	.85	179,675,000
1462	15¢ Running	.30	.18	(10)	4.00	1.00	46,340,000

1444

HISTORIC PRESERVATION

1443a

1445

1446

1447

1451a

1452

National Parks Centennial
1453

National Parks Centennial
1454

C84

1455

1460

1461

1462

C85

1459a

1463

1467a

1468

1469

1470

1471

1473

1474

	Un	U	#	PB	FDC	Q
1972 continued						
C85 11¢ Skiing and Olympic Rings,						
Aug. 17	.25	.15	(10)	3.50	.50	
1463 8¢ P.T.A. 75th Anniv., Sept. 15	.16	.05		1.00	.75	180,155,000
Perf. 11, Wildlife Conservation Issue, Sep. 20						
1464 8¢ Fur Seals	.25	.08		1.40	1.50	49,591,200
1465 8¢ Cardinal	.25	.08				49,591,200
1466 8¢ Brown Pelican	.25	.08				49,591,200
1467 8¢ Bighorn Sheep	.25	.08				49,591,200
1467a Block of four, #1464-1467	1.10	.60		1.40	3.00	

Note: With this issue the U.S.P.S. introduced the "American Commemorative Series" Stamp Panels. Each panel contains a block of four mint stamps, mounted with text, and background illustrations.

	Un	U	#	PB	FDC	Q
Perf. 11x10½						
1468 8¢ Mail Order 100th Anniv., Sept. 27	.16	.05	(12)	2.75	.75	185,490,000
Perf. 10½x11						
1469 8¢ Osteopathic Medicine, Oct. 9	.16	.05	(6)	1.35	.75	162,335,000
Perf. 11						
1470 8¢ American Folklore Issue, Oct. 13	.16	.05		1.00	.75	162,789,950
Perf. 10½x11, Christmas Issue, Nov. 9						
1471 8¢ Angel from "Mary,						
Queen of Heaven"	.16	.03	(12)	2.75	.75	1,003,475,000
1472 8¢ Santa Claus	.16	.03	(12)	2.75	.75	1,017,025,000
Perf. 11						
1473 8¢ Pharmacy, Nov. 11	.16	.05		1.00	.75	165,895,000
1474 8¢ Stamp Collecting, Nov. 17	.16	.05		1.00	.75	166,508,000

CABLE CARS

Cable cars, with their squealing brakes, clanging bells, and groaning cables, first climbed the steep hills of what famous American city?

The answer: Pittsburgh. Pittsburgh? So claim the Pittsburgh city fathers who recently celebrated the designation of their cable car system as a National Historic Landmark. Not surprisingly, the allegation ruffled the feathers of some San Franciscans, who insist that their famed cars are most historic.

The Steel City cites these facts to back its claim: Pittsburgh began operating a "coal-carrying incline" in 1854, just a few years after the California Gold Rush. In 1870, the city inaugurated the first "passenger incline," operating on a cable car system similar to San Francisco's. This was three years earlier than the first trip of the San Francisco cable car on August 2, 1873.

But no matter who was really first, it seems highly unlikely that San Francisco will ever relinquish its popular image as home of America's cable car. See Scott No. 1442.

		Un	U	#	PB	FDC	Q
	Issues of 1973, Perf. 11x10½						
1475	8¢ Love, Jan. 26	.16	.05	(6)	1.35	.75	330,055,000
	Perf. 11						
	American Revolution Bicentennial Issues, Communications in Colonial America						
1476	8¢ Printer and Patriots Examining						
	Pamphlet, Feb. 16	.20	.05		1.35	.75	166,005,000
1477	8¢ Posting a Broadside, Apr. 13	.20	.05		1.35	.75	163,050,000
1478	8¢ Postrider, June 22	.20	.05		1.35	.75	159,005,000
1479	8¢ Drummer, Sept. 28	.20	.05		1.35	.75	147,295,000
	Boston Tea Party, July 4						
1480	8¢ British Merchantman	.22	.10		1.35	1.75	49,068,750
1481	8¢ British Three-master	.22	.10				49,068,750
1482	8¢ Boats and Ship's Hull	.22	.10				49,068,750
1483	8¢ Boat and Dock	.22	.10				49,068,750
1483a	Block of four, Boston Tea Party,						
	#1480-1483	.95	.70		1.35	3.75	
	American Arts Issue						
1484	8¢ George Gershwin, Feb. 28	.16	.05	(12)	2.75	.75	139,152,000
1485	8¢ Robinson Jeffers, Aug. 13	.16	.05	(12)	2.75	.75	128,048,000
1486	8¢ Henry Ossawa Tanner, Sept. 10	.16	.05	(12)	2.75	.75	146,008,000
1487	8¢ Willa Cather, Sept. 20	.16	.05	(12)	2.75	.75	139,608,000
1488	8¢ Nicolaus Copernicus, Apr. 23	.16	.05		.80	.75	159,475,000

COPERNICUS

"The earth revolve around the sun? Why, it's downright revolutionary! The man's a fool!" Such (loosely translated) was the reaction of Martin Luther and more than a few others to the theories of Nicolaus Copernicus in the early 16th century.

To be sure, Copernicus wasn't the first to suggest it: a Greek named Aristarchus had done so 17 centuries earlier. But his theories had long since been forgotten, and those of Ptolemy had held sway over most of the intervening time: An Earth-

centered universe surrounded by revolving spherical shells did, after all, fit well with the idea of a creator whose chief work was mankind.

No one knows exactly when—or even why—Copernicus first realized that the apparent movement of the heavenly bodies around the Earth could as well be due to the Earth's spinning on its axis. His theories did explain what the eye could see (the telescope was not invented till 60 years after his death) . . . but so, however clumsily, did those of Ptolemy.

Copernicus's theory, in fact, had remarkably little impact in its time. It was left to men like Kepler and Newton to confirm his work and win that battle in the next century. See Scott No. 1488.

1475

1476

1477

1478

1479

1483a

1484

1485

1486

1487

1488

		Un	U	#	PB	FDC	Q
Perf. 10½x11, Postal Service Employees Issue, Apr. 30							
1489	8¢ Stamp Counter	.20	.12			1.10	48,602,000
1490	8¢ Mail Collection	.20	.12				48,602,000
1491	8¢ Letter Facing Conveyor	.20	.12				48,602,000
1492	8¢ Parcel Post Sorting	.20	.12				48,602,000
1493	8¢ Mail Cancelling	.20	.12				48,602,000
1494	8¢ Manual Letter Routing	.20	.12				48,602,000
1495	8¢ Electronic Letter Routing	.20	.12				48,602,000
1496	8¢ Loading Mail on Truck	.20	.12				48,602,000
1497	8¢ Mailman	.20	.12				48,602,000
1498	8¢ Rural Mail Delivery	.20	.12				48,602,000
1498a	Strip of ten, #1489-1498	2.25	1.75 (10)		2.25	6.00	

MARCONI

It was on a vacation in the Italian Alps that 19-year-old Guglielmo Marconi first conceived the idea of wireless telegraphy. Heinrich Hertz, the discoverer of radio waves, had just died, and Marconi was inspired by an article on his work.

"It seemed to me," Marconi later said, "that if the radiation could be increased, developed, and controlled, it would be possible to signal across space for considerable distances."

He returned home and began to experiment in the attic of his parents' villa near Bologna. His skeptical father, Giuseppe, feared he was harboring a "dabbler," and challenged the boy to a test. He would support his son if Guglielmo could transmit the three dots of the letter S in Morse code from the house to a receiver on the lawn.

To the father's surprise, the clicks came through. It was a distance of only a few yards, but it marked the beginning of a new era in communications. Just six years later, the first wireless signal would cross the vast Atlantic Ocean. See Scott No. 1500.

U.S. POSTAL SERVICE 8¢   U.S. POSTAL SERVICE 8¢   U.S. POSTAL SERVICE 8¢   U.S. POSTAL SERVICE 8¢   U.S. POSTAL SERVICE 8¢

Nearly 27 billion U.S. stamps are sold yearly to carry your letters to every corner of the world.

People Serving You

Mail is picked up from nearly a third of a million local collection boxes, as well as your mailbox.

People Serving You

More than 87 billion letters and packages are handled yearly—almost 300 million every delivery day.

People Serving You

The People in your Postal Service handle and deliver more than 500 million packages yearly.

People Serving You

Thousands of machines, buildings, and vehicles must be operated and maintained to keep your mail moving.

People Serving You

1489   1490   1491   1492   1493

U.S. POSTAL SERVICE 8¢   U.S. POSTAL SERVICE 8¢   U.S. POSTAL SERVICE 8¢   U.S. POSTAL SERVICE 8¢   U.S. POSTAL SERVICE 8¢

The skill of sorting mail manually is still vital to delivery of your mail.

People Serving You

Employees use modern, high-speed equipment to sort and process huge volumes of mail in central locations.

People Serving You

Thirteen billion pounds of mail are handled yearly by postal employees as they speed your letters and packages.

People Serving You

Our customers include 54 million urban and 12 million rural families, plus 9 million businesses.

People Serving You

Employees cover 4 million miles each delivery day to bring mail to your home or business.

People Serving You

1494   1495   1496   1497   1498

1499

1500

1501

1502

C86

1503

1504

1505

1506

1507

1508

1509

1510

1511

	Un	U	#	PB	FDC	Q
Perf. 11						
1499 8¢ Harry S. Truman, May 8	.16	.05		1.00	.75	157,052,800
Electronics Progress Issue, July 10						
1500 6¢ Marconi's Spark Coil and Gap	.12	.10		1.25	.75	53,005,000
1501 8¢ Transistor and						
Printed Circuit Board	.16	.05		1.00	.75	159,775,000
1502 15¢ Microphone, Speaker,						
Vacuum Tube, TV Camera	.30	.20		2.25	.80	39,005,000
C86 11¢ De Forest Auditions, July 10	.30	.15		1.75	.50	
1503 8¢ Lyndon B. Johnson, Aug. 27	.16	.05	(12)	2.50	.75	152,624,000
Issues of 1973-74, Rural America Issue						
1504 8¢ Angus and Longhorn Cattle,						
by F.C. Murphy, Oct. 5, 1973	.16	.05		1.00	.75	145,840,000
1505 10¢ Chautauqua centenary,						
Aug. 6, 1974	.20	.05		1.00	.75	151,335,000
1506 10¢ Kansas hard winter wheat						
centenary, Aug. 16, 1974	.20	.05		1.00	.75	141,085,000
Perf. 10½x11, Christmas Issue, Nov. 7, 1973						
1507 8¢ Madonna and Child by Raphael	.16	.03	(12)	2.10	.75	885,160,000
1508 8¢ Christmas Tree in Needlepoint	.16	.03	(12)	2.10	.75	939,835,000
Issue of 1973-74, Perf. 11x10½						
1509 10¢ 50-Star and 13-Star Flags, 1973	.20	.03	(20)	4.50	.75	
1510 10¢ Jefferson Memorial						
and Signature, 1973	.20	.03		1.00	.75	
1510b Booklet pane of 5 + label, 1973	1.00	.30				
1510c Booklet pane of 8, 1973	1.60	.30				
1510d Booklet pane of 6, 1974	1.20	.30				
1511 10¢ Mail Transport; "ZIP", 1974	.20	.03	(8)	1.80	.75	

ROBINSON JEFFERS

Poet Robinson Jeffers could aptly be termed "an eccentric pessimist."

The poet and his wife lived in relative solitude in a granite house he built himself in Carmel, California. Working in an isolated stone tower overlooking the ocean, Jeffers wrote by kerosene lamp until 1949, when he finally allowed his house to be connected to electric lines—the last in Carmel to switch to electricity. He relented only because his wife could no longer find wicks for their lamps and stoves.

A profound pessimist, Jeffers was absorbed with tragedy and attracted to the doom-filled Greek epics. "Civilization is a transient sickness," he wrote, and "humanity is needless." Perhaps his best-known work was an adaptation of Euripides' Medea, *starring Judith Anderson, the biggest theatrical success of 1947.*

But despite his idiosyncrasies and his negative outlook, Jeffers was one of the most honored of American writers and poets. A critic wrote that although the philosophy "is negative, repetitive, dismal," the poetry "is positive as any creative expression must be." And of his 1950 drama, The Tower Beyond Tragedy, *the* New York Times *wrote, "Call it a masterpiece and you cannot be wrong. For the Jeffers poem is written in lines of fire." See Scott No. 1485.*

	Un	U	#	PB	FDC	Q
1973-74 continued						
Coil Stamps, Perf. 10 Vertically						
1518 6.3¢ Bells, Oct. 1, 1974	.13	.07			.75	
1519 10¢ red & blue Flags (1509), 1973	.20	.03			.75	
1520 10¢ blue Jefferson Memorial (1510),-73	.20	.03			.75	
Issues of 1974, Perf. 11						
1525 10¢ V.F.W. Emblem, Mar. 11	.20	.05		1.25	.75	143,930,000
Perf. 10½x11						
1526 10¢ Robert Frost, Mar. 26	.20	.05		1.00	.75	145,235,000
Perf. 11						
1527 10¢ Cosmic Jumper and Smiling Sage,						
by Peter Max, Apr. 18	.20	.05	(12)	2.60	.75	135,052,000
Perf. 11x10½						
1528 10¢ Horses Rounding Turn, May 4	.20	.05	(12)	2.60	.75	156,750,000
Perf. 11						
1529 10¢ Skylab II, May 14	.20	.05		1.00	.75	164,670,000
Centenary of UPU Issue, June 6						
1530 10¢ Michelangelo, by Raphael	.20	.10			1.10	23,769,600
1531 10¢ "Five Feminine Virtues,"						
by Hokusai	.20	.10				23,769,600
1532 10¢ Old Scraps,						
by John Frederick Peto	.20	.10				23,769,600
1533 10¢ The Lovely Reader,						
by Jean Liotard	.20	.10				23,769,600
1534 10¢ Lady Writing Letter, by Terborch	.20	.10				23,769,600
1535 10¢ Inkwell and Quill,						
by Jean Chardin	.20	.10				23,769,600
1536 10¢ Mrs. John Douglas,						
by Thomas Gainsborough	.20	.10				23,769,600
1537 10¢ Don Antonio Noriega, by Goya	.20	.10				23,769,600
1537a Block or strip of 8, #1530-37	1.60	1.75	(16)	3.40	4.25	

SKYLAB

For six years, America's first manned space station—Skylab—circled the globe. The space mission was unprecedented—and so was its return.
Despite tracking stations, radar and electronic computers, America's space scientists could not predict even roughly where the nine-story, 77.5-ton Skylab would fall. (The situation inevitably led to the Chicken Little cry, "The Skylab is falling! The Skylab is falling!" Skylab parties sprang up all over the country, with feathers and beaks the dress of the day. Newspapers offered awards for Skylab remnants— which readers began bringing in even before the space station fell.)

Luckily, of 16 possible orbits, Skylab chose the safest, and on July 12, 1979, the huge laboratory landed mostly over water, with some pieces falling over Australia's nearly unpopulated interior. It was a fiery finish, but no one was hurt— and the groundwork was laid for even more sophisticated space voyages in the future. See Scott No. 1529.

1518

1519

1520

1525

1526

1527

1528

1529

1537a

		Un	U	#	PB	FDC	Q
	1974 continued						
	Mineral Heritage Issue, June 13						
1538	10¢ Petrified Wood	.20	.10		1.25	1.50	41,803,200
1539	10¢ Tourmaline	.20	.10				41,803,200
1540	10¢ Amethyst	.20	.10				41,803,200
1541	10¢ Rhodochrosite	.20	.10				41,803,200
1541a	Block of 4, #1538-1541	.80	.60		1.25	3.00	
	Nos. 1538-1541 printed in blocks of four in panes of 48.						
1542	10¢ Fort Harrod, June 15	.20	.05		1.00	.75	156,265,000
	American Revolution Bicentennial, First Continental Congress, July 4						
1543	10¢ Carpenter's Hall	.20	.10		1.20	1.10	48,896,250
1544	10¢ "We ask but for Peace,						
	Liberty and Safety"	.20	.10				48,896,250
1545	10¢ "Deriving their Just Powers"	.20	.10				48,896,250
1546	10¢ Independence Hall	.20	.10				48,896,250
1546a	Block of four, #1543-1546	.80	.60		1.20	3.00	
	Nos. 1543-1546 printed in blocks of four in panes of 50.						
1547	10¢ Molecules and Drops of Gasoline						
	and Oil, Sept. 22	.20	.05		1.00	.75	148,850,000
1548	10¢ The Headless Horseman, Oct. 10	.20	.05		1.00	.75	157,270,000
1549	10¢ Little Girl, Oct. 12	.20	.05		1.00	.75	150,245,000
	Christmas Issues, 1974						
1550	10¢ Angel, Oct. 23	.20	.03	(10)	2.20	.75	835,180,000
1551	10¢ Sleigh Ride, by Currier and Ives,						
	Oct. 23	.20	.03	(12)	2.60	.75	882,520,000
1552	10¢ Weather Vane; precanceled,						
	Nov. 15	.25	.08	(20)	5.50	.75	213,155,000
	Imperf. Self-adhesive						

PETRIFIED FOREST

Indian legend tells of a hungry goddess, cold and exhausted, who came upon hundreds of logs lying on the ground. She killed a rabbit with a club, then set upon making a fire, intent on preparing dinner. But the logs were too wet to burn. Incensed, she cursed the spot, turning the logs into stone so they could never burn.

The legend refers to the region now known as the Petrified Forest, an incredible display of petrified wood that is part of the Painted Desert in northern Arizona. Although the region was millions of years in the making, it was almost unknown to man until the early 1880s.

Unfortunately, discovery of the area also brought a threat to its existence. Souvenir hunters, gem collectors and commercial jewelers invaded the forest. They blasted open entire logs looking for the amethyst crystals that were often inside.

Alarmed, the citizens of Arizona petitioned Congress to make the area a national reserve. In 1906, President Theodore Roosevelt created the Petrified Forest National Monument. Not until 1962, however, did it officially become part of the National Park System. See Scott No. 1538.

1541a

1542

1546a

1547

1548

Retarded Children
Can Be Helped

Christmas

i551

1552

Benjamin West
American artist
10 cents U.S. postage

1553

Paul Laurence
Dunbar
American poet
10 cents U.S. postage

1554

MOVIEMAKER   US 10 c
D.W. GRIFFITH

1555

PIONEER ★ JUPITER
US 10c

1556

MARINER 10 ★ VENUS/MERCURY
US 10c

1557

collective bargaining
out of conflict...accord
UNITED STATES
10c

1558

Contributors To The Cause   U.S. 8c
Sybil Ludington ★ *Youthful Heroine*

1559

YOUTHFUL HEROINE
On the dark night of April 26, 1777,
16-year-old Sybil Ludington rode
her horse "Star" alone through the
Connecticut countryside rallying
her father's militia to repel a
raid by the British on Danbury.

Contributors To The Cause...   US 10c
Salem Poor ★ *Gallant Soldier*

GALLANT SOLDIER
The conspicuously courageous
actions of black foot soldier
Salem Poor at the Battle of
Bunker Hill on June 17, 1775,
earned him citations for his
bravery and leadership ability.

1560

Contributors To The Cause...   US 10c
Haym Salomon ★ *Financial Hero*

FINANCIAL HERO
Businessman and broker Haym
Salomon was responsible for
raising most of the money
needed to finance the American
Revolution and later to save
the new nation from collapse.

1561

Contributors To The Cause...   US 18c
Peter Francisco ★ *Fighter Extraordinary*

FIGHTER EXTRAORDINARY
Peter Francisco's strength
and bravery made him a
legend around campfires.
He fought with distinction
at Brandywine, Yorktown
and Guilford Court House.

1562

Lexington & Concord 1775 by Sandham
US Bicentennial 10cents

1563

Bunker Hill 1775 by Trumbull
US Bicentennial 10c

1564

	Un	U	#	PB	FDC	Q
Issues of 1975						
American Art Issue, Perf. 10½x11, 11						
1553 10¢ Benjamin West, Self-portrait,						
Feb. 10	.20	.05	(10)	2.20	.75	156,995,000
1554 10¢ Paul Laurence Dunbar, May 1	.20	.05	(10)	2.20	.75	146,365,000
1555 10¢ D. W. Griffith, May 27	.20	.05		1.00	.75	148,805,000
Space Issue, Perf. 11						
1556 10¢ Pioneer 10, Feb. 28	.20	.05		1.00	.80	173,685,000
1557 10¢ Mariner 10, Apr. 4	.20	.05		1.00	.80	158,600,000
1558 10¢ "Labor and Management", Mar. 13	.20	.05	(8)	1.80·	.75	153,355,000
American Bicentennial Issues, Contributors to the Cause, Mar. 25, Perf. 11x10½						
1559 8¢ Sybil Ludington	.16	.13	(10)	1.75	.75	63,205,000
1560 10¢ Salem Poor	.20	.05	(10)	2.20	.75	157,865,000
1561 10¢ Haym Salomon	.20	.05	(10)	2.20	.75	166,810,000
1562 18¢ Peter Francisco	.36	.20	(10)	4.00	.75	44,825,000
Perf. 11						
1563 10¢ "Birth of Liberty",						
by Henry Sandham, April 19	.20	.05	(12)	2.60	.75	144,028,000
Perf. 11x10½						
1564 10¢ Battle of Bunker Hill,						
by John Trumbull, June 17	.20	.05	(12)	2.60	.75	139,928,000

HAYM SALOMON

In the midst of the Revolutionary War, a dusty horseback rider, in Continental Army uniform, appeared at a synagogue in Philadelphia, interrupting Yom Kippur services. "I am a courier from General Washington," he said. "Is Haym Salomon here?"

A slight figure stepped forward, read the message and responded, "Tell General Washington that his appeal shall not be in vain." Then Salomon turned to his fellow worshippers: "The General is in urgent need of $200,000." Salomon pledged his entire fortune; the other worshippers pledged more. When the entire amount was raised, the congregation returned to its services.

This story illustrates the generosity and influence of a little known war hero, a Polish merchant and banker who helped finance America's revolution. Haym Salomon not only kept the nation in finances through the sale of subsidies to France and Holland, he also turned his commission over to the U.S. and underwrote many of the expenses of Lafayette's army.

Salomon died in 1785, penniless; his obituary must read: "Gentleman, Scholar, Patriot—A Banker whose only interest was the interest of his Country."
See Scott No. 1561.

		Un	U	#	PB	FDC	Q
	Military Uniforms, July 4, Perf. 11						
1565	10¢ Soldier with Flintlock Musket,						
	Uniform Button	.20	.08	(12)	2.60	.90	44,963,750
1566	10¢ Sailor with Grappling Hook,						
	First Navy Jack, 1775	.20	.08				44,963,750
1567	10¢ Marine with Musket,						
	Full-rigged Ship	.20	.08				44,963,750
1568	10¢ Militiaman with Musket,						
	Powder Horn	.20	.08				44,963,750
1568a	Block of 4, #1565-1568	.80	.50	(12)	2.60	2.40	
	Apollo-Soyuz Space Issue, July 15, Perf. 11x10½						
1569	10¢ Apollo and Soyuz after Docking,						
	and Earth	.20	.10			.85	80,931,600
1569a	Pair, #1569-1570	.40	.25	(12)	2.60	2.00	
1570	10¢ Spacecraft before Docking,						
	Earth and Project Emblem	.20	.10				80,931,600
1571	10¢ Worldwide Equality for Women,						
	Aug. 26	.20	.05	(6)	1.40	.75	145,640,000
	Postal Service Bicentennial Issue, Sep. 3						
1572	10¢ Stagecoach and Trailer Truck	.20	.08	(12)	2.60	.75	42,163,750
1573	10¢ Old and New Locomotives	.20	.08				42,163,750
1574	10¢ Early Mail Plane and Jet	.20	.08				42,163,750
1575	10¢ Satellite for Transmission						
	of Mailgrams	.20	.08				42,163,750
1575a	Block of 4, #1572-1575	.80	.50	(12)	2.60	2.40	
	Perf. 11						
1576	10¢ World Peace, Sept. 29	.20	.05		1.00	.75	146,615,000
	Banking and Commerce Issue, Oct. 6						
1577	10¢ Engine Turning, Indian Head Penny						
	and Morgan Silver Dollar	.20	.08			.75	73,098,000
1577a	Pair, #1577-1578	.40	.20		1.00	1.00	
1578	10¢ Seated Liberty, Quarter, $20 Gold						
	(Double Eagle), Engine Turning	.20	.08		1.00	.75	73,098,000

CONTINENTAL ARMED FORCES

When George Washington took command of the Continental forces in 1775, it was a mixed band of federal and colonial soldiers, of patriots, adventurers and mercenaries. While in battle they could (sometimes) act as one, their differences frequently found expression in hand-to-hand encounters between the army's ardent patriots and those of lesser zeal. A New Englander, according to one account, "felt no hesitation, when meeting a half-hearted Nova Scotia volunteer . . . in knocking him down on the spot without pretext or preliminary explanation."

Yet all their differences became insignificant in the face of the hardship of camp life and the excitement of battle. Men bred to city life or to the rugged individualism of pioneers soon learned the skills of group survival, the spirit of an army. See Scott No. 1568a.

1568a

1569a

1571

1575a

1576

1577a

1579

1580

1581

1582

1583

1584

1591

1592

1593

1595d

1596

1598

1599

1603

1604

1605

1606

		Un	U	#	PB	FDC	Q
Christmas Issue, Oct. 14, Perf. 11							
1579	(10¢) Madonna by Domenico						
	Ghirlandaio	.20	.03	(12)	2.60	.75	739,430,000
1580	(10¢) Christmas Card,						
	by Louis Prang, 1878	.20	.03	(12)	2.60	.75	878,690,000
1580b	Perf. 10½x11	.50	.05				
Issues of 1975-79, Americana, Perf. 11x10½							
1581	1¢ Inkwell & Quill, 1977	.03	.03		.15	.40	
1582	2¢ Speaker's Stand, 1977	.04	.03		.20	.40	
1584	3¢ Early Ballot Box, 1977	.06	.03		.30	.40	
1585	4¢ Books, Bookmark, Eyeglasses,	.08	.04		.40	.40	
	Size: 17½x20½mm., 1977						
1590	9¢ Capitol Dome (1591), 1977	.25	.20			1.00	
1590a	Perf. 10	12.50	5.00				
	Size: 18½x22½mm.						
1591	9¢ Capitol Dome, 1975	.18	.03		.90	.60	
1592	10¢ Comtemplation of Justice, 1977	.20	.03		1.00	.60	
1593	11¢ Printing Press, 1975	.22	.03		1.10	.60	
1594	12¢ Torch	.24	.03				
1595	13¢ Liberty Bell, 1975	.26	.03			.60	
1595a	Booklet pane of 6	1.60	.50				
1595b	Booklet pane of 7 + label	1.80	.50				
1595c	Booklet pane of 8	2.10	.50				
1595d	Booklet pane of 5 + label, 1976	1.30	.50				
1596	13¢ Eagle and Shield, 1975	.26	.03	(12)	3.38	.60	
Perf. 11							
1597	15¢ Fort McHenry Flag, 1978	.30	.03	(6)	2.10	.65	
Perf. 11x10½							
1598	15¢ Fort McHenry Flag (1597), 1978	.30	.03			.65	
1598a	Booklet pane of 8	2.40					
1599	16¢ Head of Liberty, 1978	.32	.03		1.60	.65	
1603	24¢ Old North Church, 1975	.48	.09		2.40	.75	
1604	28¢ Fort Nisqually, 1978	.56	.08		2.80	1.10	
1605	29¢ Sandy Hook Lighthouse, 1978	.58	.08		2.90	1.10	
1606	30¢ One-room Schoolhouse	.60	.08		3.00	1.10	

No. 1590 is on white paper. No. 1591 on gray paper. Nos. 1590 and 1590a, 1595, 1598 issued only in booklets. Additional American Series, see No. 1813.

		Un	U	#	PB	FDC	Q
1608	50¢ Whale Oil Lamp	1.00	.25		5.00	1.25	
1610	$1 Candle and Rushlight Holder	2.00	.25		10.00	3.00	
1611	$2 Kerosene Table Lamp	4.00	1.00		20.00	4.75	
1612	$5 Railroad Lantern	10.00	2.00		50.00	10.00	
	Coil Stamps, Perf. 10 Vertically						
1613	3.1¢ Guitar	.08	.03			.40	
1614	7.7¢ Saxhorns, 1976	.16	.08			.60	
1615	7.9¢ Drum, 1976	.16	.08			.60	
1615C	8.4¢ Piano, 1978	.18	.08			.60	
1616	9¢ Capitol Dome (1591), 1976	.18	.03			.60	
1617	10¢ Contemplation of Justice						
	(1592), 1977	.20	.03			.60	
1618	13¢ Liberty Bell (1595), 1975	.26	.03			.65	
1618C	15¢ Fort McHenry Flag (1597), 1978	.30	.08			.65	
1619	16¢ Head of Liberty (1599), 1978	.32	.03			.60	
	Perf. 11x10½						
1622	13¢ Flag over Independence Hall,-75	.26	.03	(20)	5.50	.65	
1623	13¢ Flag over Capitol, 1977	.26	.03			1.00	
1623a	Booklet pane of 8	2.00					
1623b	Perf. 10	1.00	.50				
1623c	Booklet pane of 8, Perf. 10	40.00					
	Nos. 1623, 1623b issued only in booklets						
	Coil Stamp, Perf. 10 Vertically						
1625	13¢ Flag over Independence Hall						
	(1622), 1975	.26	.03			.65	
	Issues of 1976						
1629	13¢ Drummer Boy	.26	.08				73,151,666
1630	13¢ Old Drummer	.26	.08				73,151,666
1631	13¢ Fifer	.26	.08				73,151,666
1631a	Spirit of 76, #1629-1631	.78	.40	(12)	3.40	1.75	
1632	Interphil	.26	.06		1.30	.65	157,825,000

LIBERTY BELL

The famous Liberty Bell began its life as an engineer's nightmare. Commissioned by the Province of Pennsylvania in 1751, the bell was cast the next year by the respected Whitechapel Foundry in London. On the state assembly's order a biblical phrase was inscribed inside: "Proclaim liberty throughout all the land unto all the inhabitants thereof." The next year Philadelphians gathered in the State House yard to hear the new bell ring out. On the first strike, however, it cracked, the only Whitechapel's bell to have done so in 400 years.

Two Philadelphians recast the bell. But instead of ringing melodically, the bell gave out a "bonk." The third recasting was successful—and on July 4, 1776, the bell rang its most famous peal, summoning patriots for the first public reading of the Declaration of Independence.

The bell rang for the last time in 1846, when it cracked beyond repair. But despite its flaws—or more probably because of them—the Liberty Bell had already won a permanent place in American history. See Scott No. 1618.

1614

1615

1608

1610

1611

1612

1615c

1622

1631a

1623a

Interphil

1632

		Un	U	#	PB	FDC	Q
American Bicentennial, State Flags Issue, Feb. 23, 1976							
1633	13¢ Delaware	.45	.30			1.75 ea.	8,720,100
1634	13¢ Pennsylvania	.45	.30				8,720,100
1635	13¢ New Jersey	.45	.30				8,720,100
1636	13¢ Georgia	.45	.30				8,720,100
1637	13¢ Connecticut	.45	.30				8,720,100
1638	13¢ Massachusetts	.45	.30				8,720,100
1639	13¢ Maryland	.45	.30				8,720,100
1640	13¢ South Carolina	.45	.30				8,720,100
1641	13¢ New Hampshire	.45	.30				8,720,100
1642	13¢ Virginia	.45	.30				8,720,100
1643	13¢ New York	.45	.30				8,720,100
1644	13¢ North Carolina	.45	.30				8,720,100
1645	13¢ Rhode Island	.45	.30				8,720,100
1646	13¢ Vermont	.45	.30				8,720,100
1647	13¢ Kentucky	.45	.30				8,720,100
1648	13¢ Tennessee	.45	.30				8,720,100
1649	13¢ Ohio	.45	.30				8,720,100
1650	13¢ Louisiana	.45	.30				8,720,100
1651	13¢ Indiana	.45	.30				8,720,100
1652	13¢ Mississippi	.45	.30				8,720,100
1653	13¢ Illinois	.45	.30				8,720,100

GEORGIA

One of Georgia's most important contributions to the nation was the invention of the cotton gin. But this far-reaching event occurred almost by accident.

Eli Whitney had traveled to Savannah in 1792 to tutor a wealthy family. When he arrived, the position was filled. Soon after he met Mrs. Nathanael Greene, a wealthy widow who invited Whitney to visit her estate. During the visit, one of Mrs. Greene's friends remarked, "The man who can invent a machine to separate the lint of cotton from the seed will make a fortune." Mrs. Greene turned to Whitney and said, "Anyone who can fix a watch as you fixed mine has the ability to create any type of machine; you are that man."

Whitney set up a small workshop and spent the winter working. He managed to make a machine that separated the seeds, but couldn't find a way of keeping the lint from clinging to the roller. According to legend, Mrs. Greene went to her dressing table, picked up a brush, and held it against the roller. The result—the first successful cotton gin, a device that revolutionized the country's economy. See Scott No. 1632.

1633
1634
1635
1636
1637
1638
1639
1640
1641
1642
1643
1644
1645
1646
1647
1648
1649
1650
1651
1652
1653

1654	1655	1656
1657	1658	1659
1660	1661	1662
1663	1664	1665
1666	1667	1668
1669	1670	1671
1672	1673	1674

1675

1676

1677

1678

1679

1680

1681

1682

OKLAHOMA

The word "Oklahoma" is rooted in the Choctaw Indian Language and means "red people." The territory was originally set aside as a haven for the American Indian tribes displaced by white settlement.

In 1870, a strong movement began to open the Indian lands for white settlement. Boom companies were hastily organized to promote settlement, and rumors generated numerous false starts. Finally, President Harrison issued a proclamation opening the Indian lands as of April 22, 1889. The appointed hour was noon, and no settler who set foot on Indian land before noon could ever own any acreage. Settlers lined up by the thousands, witnesses at hand, to stake their claims to free 160-acre plots. Oklahoma City had a population of less than 100 that morning; by nightfall, it was a city of 10,000. Many were disappointed, but many beat out the competition by ruse, by speed, and by luck. The Indian lands were "boomed," and Oklahoma was settled at last by one of the wildest stampedes the buffalo lands had ever seen. See Scott No. 1678.

	Un	U	#	PB	FDC	Q
1976 continued						
1654 13¢ Alabama	.45	.30			1.75 ea.	8,720,100
1655 13¢ Maine	.45	.30				8,720,100
1656 13¢ Missouri	.45	.30				8,720,100
1657 13¢ Arkansas	.45	.30				8,720,100
1658 13¢ Michigan	.45	.30				8,720,100
1659 13¢ Florida	.45	.30				8,720,100
1660 13¢ Texas	.45	.30				8,720,100
1661 13¢ Iowa	.45	.30				8,720,100
1662 13¢ Wisconsin	.45	.30				8,720,100
1663 13¢ California	.45	.30				8,720,100
1664 13¢ Minnesota	.45	.30				8,720,100
1665 13¢ Oregon	.45	.30				8,720,100
1666 13¢ Kansas	.45	.30				8,720,100
1667 13¢ West Virginia	.45	.30				8,720,100
1668 13¢ Nevada	.45	.30				8,720,100
1669 13¢ Nebraska	.45	.30				8,720,100
1670 13¢ Colorado	.45	.30				8,720,100
1671 13¢ North Dakota	.45	.30				8,720,100
1672 13¢ South Dakota	.45	.30				8,720,100
1673 13¢ Montana	.45	.30				8,720,100
1674 13¢ Washington	.45	.30				8,720,100
1675 13¢ Idaho	.45	.30				8,720,100
1676 13¢ Wyoming	.45	.30				8,720,100
1677 13¢ Utah	.45	.30				8,720,100
1678 13¢ Oklahoma	.45	.30				8,720,100
1679 13¢ New Mexico	.45	.30				8,720,100
1680 13¢ Arizona	.45	.30				8,720,100
1681 13¢ Alaska	.45	.30				8,720,100
1682 13¢ Hawaii	.45	.30				8,720,100
1682a Sheet of 50, #1633-1682	25.00		(50)	32.50	32.50	

CALIFORNIA

Until 1848, the people of what is now the State of California led a quiet, peaceful life. Cattle, horses and sheep ranged freely. The climate was mild, the soil fruitful. Crime was rare and the pace leisurely.

Then gold was discovered, and the peaceful pace turned into a stampede. Hordes of fortune hunters descended on the state from as far away as Europe and China. The gold rush was one of the largest mass movements of people in the 19th century. Within two years, the population of California grew from 13,000 to 100,000.

The result was chaos. The old society collapsed with the deluge of adventurers, and the public put out a cry for law and order. The result: a constitution was adopted, a legislature and governor elected, and, on September 9, 1859, California was admitted as the 31st state of the union. See Scott No. 1663.

DECLARATION OF INDEPENDENCE

Even after Americans had fought and died in the Battles of Bunker Hill, Lexington and Concord, the colonists still tried to secure their rights as Englishmen. As the war progressed, however, the breach between Great Britain and its American colonies widened. The

1694a

colonists began to realize that a complete break with England was necessary to gain the liberties they desired. The cry for independence mounted throughout the land.

In January 1776, Thomas Paine wrote in Common Sense *that "Tis time to part." The idea of separation from the Crown grew and the Continental Congress appointed a committee to prepare a charter of independence. Thomas Jefferson was selected to write a draft of the declaration.*

On July 4, 1776, in one of history's most eloquent documents, it was officially declared "these United Colonies are, and of Right ought to be Free and Independent States." To justify these actions, the king of England was charged with a "history of repeated injuries and usurpation." The Declaration of Independence boosted morale and rallied Americans to the cause of liberty by proclaiming "that all men are created equal, that they are endowed by their Creator with certain inalienable Rights, that among these are Life, Liberty and the Pursuit of Happiness." Throughout the years the Declaration of Independence has continued to serve as a source of pride to Americans and as a source of inspiration to millions of oppressed people everywhere in their quest for freedom. See Scott Nos. 627, 1687, 1691-1694.

Thomas Jefferson's rough draft of the Declaration of Independence.

	Un	U	#	PB	FDC	Q
1976 continued						
1683 13¢ Bell's Telephone Patent						
Application, Mar. 10	.26	.06		1.30	.65	159,915,000
1684 13¢ Ford-Pullman Monoplane						
and Laird Swallow Biplane, Mar. 19	.26	.06	(10)	2.90	.65	156,960,000
1685 13¢ Various Flasks, Separatory Funnel,						
Computer Tape, Apr. 6	.26	.06	(12)	3.40	.65	158,470,000
American Bicentennial Issues, Souvenir Sheets, May 29						
Sheets of 5 Stamps Each						
1686 13¢ Surrender of Cornwallis at Yorktown,						
by John Trumbull	4.50				6.00	1,990,000
1687 18¢ Declaration of Independence,						
by John Trumbull	6.00				7.50	1,983,000

COMMERCIAL AVIATION

On January 1, 1914, a cheering throng of 3000 followed a carnival band to a yacht basin in St. Petersburg, Florida. Amid the revelry, the St. Petersburg-Tampa Airboat Line conducted an auction to determine who would be the world's first airline passenger. The winner: ex-mayor A.C. Pheil, who paid $400 for that privilege.

Pheil donned goggles and football helmet and climbed into the open cockpit of the aircraft—a 36-foot biplane of plywood, spruce and linen. Pilot Tony Jannus, who specialized in steady flying rather than the more popular stunt-flying, made his way through a maze of wires and sat down beside him. Jannus revved the six-cylinder, 75-horsepower engine, and the pusher-type propeller began to spin. As the crowd roared, the 1400-pound airboat skimmed along Tampa Bay and rose into the air. Twenty-three minutes later it beached at the Tampa waterfront—an 18-mile journey that normally took 12 hours by rail. Just ten years after the Wright brothers flew their fragile aircraft, commercial aviation was born. See Scott No. 1684.

Official First Day Cover

50 YEARS OF SCHEDULED AIRLINE SERVICE

Air Transport Association of America

CHICAGO, IL
MAR
19
1976
60656

Commercial Aviation
1926-1976

FIRST DAY OF ISSUE

1683

1684

1685

The Surrender of Lord Cornwallis at Yorktown
From a Painting by John Trumbull

1686

The Declaration of Independence, 4 July 1776 at Philadelphia
From a Painting by John Trumbull

1687

Washington Crossing the Delaware
From a Painting by Emanuel Leutze / Eastman Johnson

1688

Washington Reviewing His Ragged Army at Valley Forge
From a Painting by William T. Trego

1689

	Un	U	#	PB	FDC	Q
1976 continued						
1688 24¢ Washington Crossing the Delaware,						
by Emanuel Leutze/						
Eastman Johnson	7.50				8.50	1,953,000
1689 31¢ Washington Reviewing Army						
at Valley Forge, by William T. Trego	9.00				9.50	1,903,000

WASHINGTON CROSSING THE DELAWARE

Emanuel Leutze's well-known painting, "Washington Crossing the Delaware," has given that historic event the aura of a legend. But even without the painting's inspiration, the crossing would be long remembered . . . for it proved to be a turning point in the war for independence.

Things looked bleak for the American forces as 1776 drew to a close. Defeats had been many and troops were few, cold and hungry. Washington's small army shivered in their camp on the Pennsylvania side of the Delaware, while across the river in Trenton, ample troops of Hessian mercenaries prepared to celebrate Christmas, resting up for an attack on Philadelphia. Washington knew he must strike now, while he could take the enemy by surprise—and while he still had the men do it.

The Delaware would not be easy to cross. Huge ice boulders and jagged, swiftly moving ice floes blocked the way; to crash through the ice at Trenton would be dangerous and would destroy any chance of surprise. But several miles up the river, at McKonkey's Ferry, the current was gentler and the ice less threatening. Here, on Christmas day, Washington concentrated his troops.

Among those men was a regiment of seasoned sailors, Colonel John Clover's Marblehead fishermen. On 60-foot, double-ended boats discovered hidden in creeks or beached along the shore, the fishermen ferried 2,400 men and 18 cannon across 300 yards of water.

The Hessians were taken completely by surprise—1,000 of them were captured, wounded, or killed, while the Americans suffered barely a scratch. More important still was the restored American morale. This proof that trained Hessians could be defeated, that land invasion could be beaten back, changed the minds of many who had been ready to desert. And George Washington went down in history as one of the world's great military strategists. See Scott No. 1688.

		Un	U	#	PB	FDC	Q
	1976 continued						
1690	13¢ Franklin and Map						
	of North America, 1776, June 1	.26	.06		1.30	.65	164,890,000
	American Bicentennial Issue, Declaration of Independence, by Trumbull, July 4						
1691	13¢	.26	.08				51,008,750
1692	13¢	.26	.08				51,008,750
1693	13¢	.26	.08				51,008,750
1694	13¢	.26	.08			.65	51,008,750
1694a	Strip of 4, #1691-1694	1.10	.50	(20)	5.50	2.00	
	Each stamp shows part of painting. Stamps are numbered from left to right.						
	Olympic Games Issue, July 16						
1695	13¢ Diving	.26	.06			.70	46,428,750
1696	13¢ Skiing	.26	.06			.70	46,428,750
1697	13¢ Running	.26	.06			.70	46,428,750
1698	13¢ Skating	.26	.06			.70	46,428,750
1698a	Block of 4, #1695-1698	1.10		(12)	3.40	2.00	
1699	13¢ Clara Maass, Aug. 18	.26	.06	(12)	3.40	.65	130,592,000
1700	13¢ Adolph S. Ochs, Sept. 18	.26	.06		1.30	.65	158,332,800
	Christmas Issue, Oct. 27						
1701	13¢ Nativity,						
	by John Singleton Copley	.26	.03	(12)	3.40	.65	809,955,000

SPIRIT OF ST. LOUIS

Nearly everyone knows Charles Lindbergh as the aviator who, in the single-engine Spirit of St. Louis, *made the first solo, non-stop transatlantic flight. Few, however, recall that Lindy, the "Lone Eagle," did some of his best flying without wings, as a reluctant parachutist.*

One jump was a bit more suspenseful than most. Unable to land in Chicago because of a dense fog, Lindbergh ran out of fuel before he could locate a beacon light. He bailed out at 5,000 feet, but in his rush, forgot to cut off the plane's ignition.

Without the pilot's weight the plane nosed down, allowing the small bit of remaining fuel to enter the carburetor and restart the engine. As he drifted down through the fog, Lindbergh heard the noise of the engine grow louder and softer, louder and softer. The plane, it seemed, was in hot pursuit of its pilot, circling him and ready to pounce!

Lindbergh, needless to say, escaped its clutches and landed without a scratch. See Scott No. 1710.

1690

1694a

1699

1700

1701

1698a

1706
1707
1708
1709

1702

1703

1704

1705

1710

1711

1715a

1716

1720a

1721

		Un	U	#	PB	FDC	Q
Christmas Issue, Oct. 27, 1976 continued							
1702	13¢ "Winter Pastime",						
	by Nathaniel Currier	.26	.03	(10)	2.86	.65	481,685,000
1703	13¢ as 1702	.26	.03	(20)	5.70	.65	481,685,000

No. 1702 has overall tagging. Lettering at base is black and usually ½mm. below design. As a rule, no "snowflaking" in sky or pond. Pane of 50 has margins on 4 sides with slogans. No. 1703 has block tagging the size of the printed area. Lettering at base is gray black and usually ¾mm. below design. "Snowflaking" generally in sky and pond. Pane of 50 has margin only at right or left, and no slogans.

		Un	U	#	PB	FDC	Q
Issues of 1977 American Bicentennial, Perf. 11							
1704	13¢ Washington,						
	by Charles Wilson Peale, Jan. 3	.26	.06	(10)	2.90	.65	150,328,000
1705	13¢ Tin Foil Phonograph, Mar. 23	.26	.06		1.30	.65	176,830,000
Pueblo Indian Art Issue, Apr. 13							
1706	13¢ Zia Pot	.26	.06	(10)	3.00	.65	48,994,000
1707	13¢ San Ildefonso Pot	.26	.06				48,994,000
1708	13¢ Hopi Pot	.26	.06				48,994,000
1709	13¢ Acoma Pot	.26	.06				48,994,000
1709a	Block of 4, #1706-1709	1.05	.25	(10)	3.00	2.00	
1710	13¢ Spirit of St. Louis, May 20	.26	.06	(12)	3.65	.65	208,820,000
1711	13¢ Columbine and Rocky Mountains,						
	May 21	.26	.06	(12)	3.65	.65	192,250,000
Butterfly Issue, June 6							
1712	13¢ Swallowtail	.26	.06	(12)	3.65	.65	54,957,500
1713	13¢ Checkerspot	.26	.06				54,957,500
1714	13¢ Dogface	.26	.06				54,957,500
1715	13¢ Orange Tip	.26	.06				54,957,500
1715a	Block of 4, #1712-1715	1.05	.25	(12)	3.65	2.00	
American Bicentennial Issues							
1716	13¢ Marquis de Lafayette, June 13	.26	.06		1.30	.65	159,852,000
Skilled Hands for Independence, July 4							
1717	13¢ Seamstress	.26	.06	(12)	3.65	.65	47,077,500
1718	13¢ Blacksmith	.26	.06				47,077,500
1719	13¢ Wheelwright	.26	.06				47,077,500
1720	13¢ Leatherworker	.26	.06				47,077,500
1720a	Block of 4, #1717-1720	1.05	.25	(12)	3.65	2.00	
Perf. 11x10½							
1721	13¢ Peace Bridge and Dove, Aug. 4	.26	.06		1.30	.65	163,625,000

US Bicentennial 13 cents

1722

1723a

1725

1726

1727

US Bicentennial 13 cents

1728

1729

1730

1731

1732

1733

1734

1735

1738

1744

		Un	U	#	PB	FDC	Q
	1977 continued						
	American Bicentennial Issue, Perf. 11						
1722	13¢ Herkimer at Oriskany,						
	by Yohn Frederick, Aug. 6	.26	.06	(10)	3.10	.65	156,296,000
	Energy Issue, Oct. 20						
1723	13¢ Energy Conservation	.26	.06			.65	79,338,000
1723a	Pair, #1723-1724	.52	.12	(12)	3.65	1.20	
1724	13¢ Energy Development	.26	.06			.65	79,338,000
	American Bicentennial Issues						
1725	13¢ Farm House, Sept. 9	.26	.06		1.30	.65	154,495,000
	First civil settlement in Alta, California, 200th anniversary.						
1726	13¢ Articles of Confederation, Sept. 30	.26	.06		1.30	.65	168,050,000
	200th anniversary of the Drafting of the Articles of Confederation, York Town, Pa.						
1727	13¢ Movie Projector and						
	Phonograph, Oct. 6	.26	.06		1.30	.65	156,810,000
	American Bicentennial Issue						
1728	13¢ Surrender of Saratoga,						
	by John Trumbull, Oct. 7	.26	.06	(10)	3.10	.65	153,736,000
	Christmas Issue, Oct. 21						
1729	13¢ Washington at Valley Forge	.26	.03	(20)	5.70	.65	882,260,000
1730	13¢ Rural Mailbox	.26	.03	(10)	3.10	.65	921,530,000
	Issues of 1978, Perf. 11						
1731	13¢ Carl Sandburg, Jan. 6	.26	.06		1.30	.65	156,580,000
	Capt. Cook Issue, Jan. 20						
1732	13¢ Capt. Cook	.26	.06		1.30	.70	101,095,000
1732a	Pair, #1732-1733	.55	.20			1.50	
1733	13¢ "Resolution" and "Discovery"	.26	.03		1.30	.65	101,095,000
1734	13¢ Indian Head Penny, 1877, Jan. 11	.26	.03		1.30	.70	
1735	(15¢) Eagle (A), May 22	.30	.03		1.50	.65	
	Perf. 11x10½						
1736	(15¢) orange Eagle (1735), May 22	.30	.03			.65	
1736a	Booklet pane of 8	2.40					
1737	15¢ Roses, July 11	.30	.03				
1737a	Booklet pane of 8	2.40					
	Nos. 1736 and 1737 issued only in booklets.						
	Coil Stamp, Perf. 10 Vertically						
1743	(15¢) orange Eagle (1735), May 22	.30	.03			.65	
	Perf. 11						
1744	13¢ Harriet Tubman, Feb. 1	.26	.06	(12)	3.65	.65	156,555,000

		Un	U	#	PB	FDC	Q
American Folk Art Issue, American Quilts, Mar. 8, 1978							
1745	13¢ Basket design, red & orange	.26	.06	(12)	3.65	.65	41,295,600
1746	13¢ Basket design, red	.26	.06				41,295,600
1747	13¢ Basket design, orange	.26	.06				41,295,600
1748	13¢ Basket design, black	.26	.06				41,295,600
1748a	Block of 4, #1745-1748	1.05	.30	(12)	3.65	2.00	
American Dance Issue, Apr. 26							
1749	13¢ Ballet	.26	.06	(12)	3.65	.65	39,399,600
1750	13¢ Theater	.26	.06				39,399,600
1751	13¢ Folk Dance	.26	.06				39,399,600
1752	13¢ Modern Dance	.26	.06				39,399,600
1752a	Block of 4, #1749-1752	1.05	.30	(12)	3.65	2.00	
1753	13¢ French Alliance, May 4	.26	.06		1.30	.65	102,920,000
Perf. 10½x11							
1754	13¢ Dr. Papanicolaou with Microscope,						
	May 13	.26	.06		1.30	.65	152,355,000
Performing Arts Issue, Perf. 11							
1755	13¢ Jimmie Rodgers, May 24	.26	.06	(12)	3.65	.65	94,625,000
1756	15¢ George M. Cohan, July 3	.30	.06	(12)	4.20	.65	151,570,000
1757	13¢ Souvenir sheet of 8, June 10	2.25				3.50	15,170,400
1758	15¢ Photographic Equipment, June 26	.30	.06	(12)	4.20	.65	163,200,000
1759	15¢ Viking I Landing on Mars, July 20	.30	.06		1.50	.65	158,880,000

EARLY PHOTOGRAPHIC EQUIPMENT

In 1881, George Eastman was getting ready for a Carribean vacation when he learned of a new photographic process available in England. Eastman never went to the Carribean; instead he traveled to England to learn more about this new "dry plate" process. On his return to America he conducted experiments on his mother's kitchen table, inventing a far more convenient and light sensitive form of photography.

Eastman's invention set the stage for the hand-held camera. No longer did the camera announce itself with its familiar tripod legs and bellows. And no longer did photographers have to carry cumbersome tents for on-site processing of their still-wet sensitized plates. The new camera was an innocuous box, sometimes masque-rading as a workman's toolbox, doctor's satchel, or even a hat or walking stick. The most popular hidden camera was the 1886 vest camera, a round metal can that was hung under a vest and took pictures through a buttonhole.

The hidden cameras were a fad that soon faded. But the Eastman process gave birth to the kind of "candid" photography we know today. See Scott No. 1758.

1748a

1752a

1753

1754

1755

1756

Canadian International Philatelic Exhibition
Toronto

This tribute features wildlife that share the Canadian-United States border.

Cette émission souvenir est consacrée à la faune vivant près
de la frontière entre les Etats-Unis et le Canada.

Postmaster General of the United States

1757

Photography USA 15c

1758

Viking missions to Mars

Expanding human knowledge USA 15c

1759

763a 1767a

768 1769

1770

1771 1773

1772 1774

1772

	Un	U	#	PB	FDC	Q
1978 continued						
American Owls, Aug. 26						
1760 15¢ Great Gray Owl	.30	.06		1.50	.65	46,637,500
1761 15¢ Saw-whet Owl	.30	.06				46,637,500
1762 15¢ Barred Owl	.30	.06				46,637,500
1763 15¢ Great Horned Owl	.30	.06				46,637,500
1763a Block of 4, #1760-1763	1.25	.30		1.50	2.00	
American Trees, Oct. 9						
1764 15¢ Giant Sequoia	.30	.06	(12)	4.20	.65	42,034,000
1765 15¢ White pine	.30	.06				42,034,000
1766 15¢ White Oak	.30	.06				42,034,000
1767 15¢ Gray Birch	.30	.06				42,034,000
1767a Block of 4, #1764-1767	1.25	.30	(12)	4.20	2.00	
Christmas Issue, Oct. 18						
1768 15¢ Madonna and Child	.30	.03	(12)	4.20	.65	963,370,000
1769 15¢ Hobby Horse	.30	.03	(12)	4.20	.65	916,800,000
Issues of 1979, Perf. 11						
1770 15¢ Robert F. Kennedy, Jan. 12	.30	.06		1.50	.65	159,297,600
1771 15¢ Martin Luther King, Jr., Jan. 13	.30	.06	(12)	4.20	.65	166,435,000
1772 15¢ Internt'l Year of the Child, Feb. 15	.30	.06		1.50	.65	162,535,000
Perf. 10½x11						
1773 15¢ John Steinbeck, Feb. 27	.30	.06		1.50	.65	155,000,000
1774 15¢ Albert Einstein, Mar. 4	.30	.06		1.50	.65	157,310,000
American Folk Art Issue, Apr. 19, Pennsylvania Toleware						
1775 15¢ Coffeepot	.30	.06	(10)	3.50	.65	43,524,000
1776 15¢ Tea Caddy	.30	.06				43,524,000
1777 15¢ Sugar Bowl	.30	.06				43,524,000
1778 15¢ Coffeepot	.30	.06				43,524,000
1778a Block of 4, #1775-1778	1.20		(10)	3.50	2.00	174,096,000

ALBERT EINSTEIN

"You will never amount to anything," an exasperated Munich high school teacher told the student. At the time, it seemed a reasonable assumption. The boy hadn't even begun to talk until the age of three, and at sixteen he was asked to leave school because of his poor performance. Yet Albert Einstein would go on to change forever our ideas of space and time with his theories of relativity.

Just as Einstein's revolutionary scientific ideas collided violently with accepted belief, so did his pacifist political views. After the outbreak of World War I, he appealed to scientists of all nations to oppose nationalism and work for peace. He traveled widely, lecturing not only on relativity, but also in favor of a Jewish homeland in Palestine. When Hitler came to power in Germany he was out of the country . . . and never returned. Though he urged President Roosevelt to develop an atomic bomb to fight the Nazis, his final project was a plea to scientists to halt nuclear armament.

"I would teach peace rather than war," Einstein wrote. "I would inculcate love rather than hate." See Scott Nos. 1285, 1774.

		Un	U	#	PB	FDC	Q
	1979 continued						
	American Architecture Issue, June 4						
1779	15¢ Virginia Rotunda	.30	.06		1.50	.65	41,198,400
1780	15¢ Baltimore Cathedral	.30	.06		1.50	.65	41,198,400
1781	15¢ Boston State House	.30	.06		1.50	.65	41,198,400
1782	15¢ Philadelphia Exchange	.30	.06		1.50	.65	41,198,400
1782a	Block of 4, #1779-1782	1.20				2.00	164,793,600
	Endangered Flora Issue, June 7						
1783	15¢ Persistent Trillium	.30	.06	(12)	4.20	.65	40,763,750
1784	15¢ Hawaiian Wild Broadbean	.30	.06			.65	40,763,750
1785	15¢ Contra Costa Wallflower	.30	.06			.65	40,763,750
1786	15¢ Antioch Evening Primrose	.30	.06			.65	40,763,750
1786a	Block of 4, #1783-1786	1.25				2.00	163,055,000
1787	15¢ Seeing Eye Dogs, June 15	.30	.06	(20)	6.50	.65	161,860,000
1788	15¢ Special Olympics, Aug. 9	.30	.06	(10)	3.50	.65	165,775,000
1789	15¢ John Paul Jones,						
	by Charles Willson Peale, Sept. 23	.30	.06	(10)	3.50	.65	160,000,000
	Olympic Games Issue, Oct.						
1790	10¢ Javelin	.20	.05	(12)	2.75	.60	67,195,000
1791	15¢ Running	.30	.06	(12)	4.25	.65	46,726,250
1792	15¢ Swimming	.30	.06	(12)	4.25	.65	46,726,250
1793	15¢ Canoeing	.30	.06			.65	46,726,250
1794	15¢ Equestrian	.30	.06			.65	46,726,250
1794a	Block of 4, #1791-1974	1.25	.30			2.00	187,650,000
C97	31¢ High Jump	.62	.30			1.15	
	Christmas Issue, Oct. 18						
1799	15¢ Virgin and Child, by Gerard David	.30	.05	(12)	4.25	.65	873,710,000
1800	15¢ Santa Claus	.30	.05	(12)	4.25	.65	931,880,000
1801	15¢ Will Rogers, Nov. 4	.30	.06	(12)	4.25	.65	161,290,000
1802	15¢ Vietnam Veterans, Nov. 11	.30	.06	(10)	3.50	.65	172,740,000

GUIDE DOGS

Many people assume that the most important thing a guide dog learns is to obey his blind master's commands: to sit, to turn right or left, to go forward.

But even more important than the dog's ability to obey is his ability to disobey. Guide dogs are trained not to follow a command if it will lead their masters into danger. A trained dog will not, for example, obey a "forward" command if it will take his master into an obstacle or a busy street.

Guide dogs begin their training at the age of about 14 months, going through an intensive three- to five-month course. The most important part of the training comes when dog and master learn to work together.

Only a small proportion of blind people (about 10 percent) are temperamentally suited to work with guide dogs. But those who can use a dog find they are blessed not only with a pair of eyes but with something even more valuable: good judgment. See Scott No. 1787.

Architecture USA 15c — Jefferson 1743-1826 Virginia Rotunda
Architecture USA 15c — Latrobe 1764-1820 Baltimore Cathedral
Architecture USA 15c — Bulfinch 1763-1844 Boston State House
Architecture USA 15c — Strickland 1788-1854 Philadelphia Exchange

1782a

Endangered Flora 15c — PERSISTENT TRILLIUM
Endangered Flora 15c — HAWAIIAN WILD BROADBEAN
Endangered Flora 15c — CONTRA COSTA WALLFLOWER
Endangered Flora 15c — ANTIOCH DUNES EVENING PRIMROSE

1786a

USA 15c
Seeing For Me

1787

Special Olympics
Skill·Sharing·Joy
USA 15c

1788

I have not yet begun to fight
John Paul Jones
US Bicentennial 15c

1789

Olympics 1980 Decathlon
USA 10c

1790

Airmail Olympics 1980
USA 31c

C97

Gerard David National Gallery
Christmas USA 15c

1799

USA 15c Olympics 1980
USA 15c Olympics 1980
USA 15c Olympics 1980
USA 15c Olympics 1980

1794a

Christmas 15c USA

1800

WILL ROGERS
Performing Arts USA 15c

1801

USA·15c
HONORING VIETNAM VETERANS
NOV·11·1979

1802

1742a

1798a

1803

1804

1811

1813

1805
1806

1807
1808

1809
1810

		Un	U	#	PB	FDC	Q
	1980 Issues **Windmills, Feb. 7, Perf. 11**						
1738	15¢ Virginia, 1720	.30	.03			.65	
1739	15¢ Rhode Island, 1790	.30	.03			.65	
1740	15¢ Massachusetts, 1793	.30	.03			.65	
1741	15¢ Illinois, 1860	.30	.03			.65	
1742	15¢ Texas, 1890	.30	.03			.65	
1742a	Booklet pane of 10	3.00	.60			6.50	
	Winter Olympic Games Issue, Feb. 1						
1795	15¢ Speed Skating	.30	.06	(12)	4.25	.65	
1796	15¢ Downhill Skiing	.30	.06	(12)	4.25	.65	
1797	15¢ Ski Jump	.30	.06			.65	
1798	15¢ Hockey Goaltender	.30	.06			.65	
1798a	Block of 4, #1795-1798	1.25	.30			2.00	208,295,000
	Perf. 11½ x 11½						
1803	15¢ W.C. Fields, Jan. 29	.30	.06	(12)	4.25	.65	168,995,000
	Perf. 11						
1804	15¢ Benjamin Banneker, Feb. 15	.30	.06	(12)	4.25	.65	160,000,000
	Letter Writing Issue, Feb. 25						
1805	15¢ Letter Preserve Memories	.30	.06	(36)	11.00	.65	
1806	15¢ P.S. Write Soon	.30	.06	(36)	11.00	.65	
1807	15¢ Letters Lift Spirits	.30	.06	(36)	11.00	.65	
1808	15¢ P.S. Write Soon	.30	.06	(36)	11.00	.65	
1809	15¢ Letters Shape Opinions	.30	.06	(36)	11.00	.65	
1810	15¢ P.S. Write Soon	.30	.06	(36)	11.00	.65	
1810a	15¢ Strip of 6, #1805-1810	1.80	.36			3.00	232,134,000
	Perf. 10						
1811	1¢ Americana Type Coil, March 6	.03	.03			.65	
1813	3.5¢ Coil, June 23	.08	.03			.65	

ANNE SULLIVAN

Helen Keller called her, simply, "Teacher." But Anne Sullivan was much more. She was Helen's constant companion, closest friend and window to the outside world.

Helen called the day of Annie's arrival "my soul's birthday," and perhaps it was that for Teacher, too. For Anne Sullivan had led a bleak life. Born in desperate poverty, she lost her parents and much of her sight by the age of five, and spent the rest of her childhood in the squalor of the state poorhouse, where her brother Jimmie died of tuberculosis.

With Helen, a new world opened up to Anne, just as she opened the world to Helen. Hand-in-hand they attended Radcliffe, traveled the world, wrote books and speeches, and befriended the famous and powerful. It was a life neither could have led alone, but together they were unstoppable. See Scott No. 1824.

		Un	U	#	PB	FDC	Q
	1980 continued						
	Perf. 10½x11						
1821	15¢ Frances Perkins, April 10	.30	.06		1.50	.65	163,510,000
	Perf. 11						
1822	15¢ Dolley Madison, May 20	.30	.06		1.50	.65	256,620,000
1823	15¢ Emily Bissell, May 31	.30	.06		1.50	.65	95,695,000
1824	15¢ Helen Keller/Anne Sullivan,						
	June 27	.30	.06		1.50	.65	153,975,000
1825	15¢ Veterans Administration, July 21	.30	.06		1.50	.65	160,000,000
1826	15¢ General Bernardo de Galvez,						
	July 23	.30	.06		1.50	.65	103,850,000
	Coral Reefs Issue, Aug. 26						
1827	15¢ Brain Coral	.30	.06	(12)	4.50		
1828	15¢ Elkhorn Coral	.30	.06				
1829	15¢ Chalice Coral	.30	.06	(12)	4.50		
1830	15¢ Finger Coral	.30	.06			.65	
1830a	Block of 4, #1827-1830	1.20	.24			2.00	204,715,000
1831	15¢ Organized Labor, Sept. 1	.30	.06	(12)	4.50	.65	166,545,000
1832	15¢ Edith Wharton, Sept. 5	.30	.06		1.50	.65	163,310,000

CORAL REEFS

Yellow, orange, purple, green, tan . . . the coral reefs are gardens in the sea, home to animals from starfish to sea anemones, drawing tourists to the world's warm waters. An odd role, when you think of it, for a mass of skeletons.

Coral is the limestone remains of millions of tiny sea animals called polyps. Living together in colonies, the coral polyps draw calcium from the water and, with the help of algae, secrete an outer skelton of calcium carbonate (limestone). When the polyps die, their skeletons are left behind in the form of domes or branching trees, tiny pipe organs or irregular crusts.

Sometimes coral builds up in the form of barriers and ridges called coral reefs. The most famous of these is the Great Barrier Reef of Australia, more than 1,250 miles long, which forms a barrier between the shoreline and the open sea.

Atolls, too, are coral reefs—ring-shaped islands of coral surrounding a body of water called a lagoon. Atolls must have a ridge on which to grow—a submerged mudbank or the rim of a sunken volcano. While they are rare in the Atlantic, they flourish in the Pacific and Indian Oceans.

See Scott Nos. 1827-1830.

Frances Perkins
USA 15c

1821

1822

Emily Bissell
Crusader Against Tuberculosis
USA 15c

1823

HELEN KELLER
ANNE SULLIVAN

1824

1825

Gen. Bernardo de Gálvez
Battle of Mobile 1780

1826

1830a

Organized Labor
Proud and Free
USA 15c

1831

Edith Wharton
USA 15c

1832

Glow by Josef Albers USA 15c
Learning
never ends
1833

Tlingit
Indian Art USA 15c

Bella Coola
Indian Art USA 15c

Heiltsuk, Bella Bella
Indian Art USA 15c

Chilkat Tlingit
Indian Art USA 15c

1837a

Richardson 1838-1886 Trinity Church Boston
Architecture USA 15c

Renwick 1818-1895 Smithsonian Washington
Architecture USA 15c

AJ Davis 1803-1892 Lyndhurst Tarrytown NY
Architecture USA 15c

Furness 1839-1912 Penn Academy Philadelphia
Architecture USA 15c

1841a

Christmas USA 15c
1842

USA 15c
Season's Greetings
1843

		Un	U	#	PB	FDC	Q
	1980 continued						
1833	15¢ American Education, Sept. 12	.30	.06			.65	160,000,000
	Indian Art—Masks Issue, Sept. 25						
1834	15¢ Bella Bella	.30	.06	(10)	3.50	.65	
1835	15¢ Chilkat	.30	.06			.65	
1836	15¢ Tlingit	.30	.06			.65	
1837	15¢ Bella Coola	.30	.06			.65	
1837a	Block of 4, #1834-1837	1.20	.25			2.00	152,404,000
	American Architecture Issue, Oct. 9						
1838	15¢ Smithsonian	.30	.06				
1839	15¢ Trinity Church	.30	.06				
1840	15¢ Pennsylvania Academy of Fine Arts	.30	.06				
1841	15¢ Lyndhurst	.30					
1841a	Block of 4, #1838-1841	1.20	.24				152,720,000
1842	15¢ Christmas Stained Glass Windows, Oct. 16	.30	.03			.65	692,500,000
1843	15¢ Christmas Antique Toys, Oct. 16	.30	.03			.65	718,715,000

SMITHSONIAN

Archie Bunker's chair. The Wright brothers' Kitty Hawk Flyer. *Bamboo-eating pandas. Moonrocks. A Panamanian jungle preserve. Paintings by Winslow Homer.*

What do these items have in common? They are all part of the Smithsonian Institution (sometimes known as "the nation's attic"), which has accumulated more than 70 million cataloged items in its 123-year history. The outgrowth of a half-million-dollar legacy from James Smithson, a wealthy English mineralogist, the Smithsonian today is a unique complex of museums and art galleries (and a zoo) in Washington, D.C., plus a number of bureaus, observatories and research laboratories around the world.

One of the most famous items in the collection arrived at the Smithsonian in a curious fashion. In 1958, a museum curator received a registered package via U.S. Mail. When he opened the package, the curator was astonished to find the Hope Diamond, the largest blue diamond (44.5 carats) in the world. The famous gem had arrived unannounced (but insured for $1 million), the gift of a New York jeweler to the Smithsonian's National Gem Collection. See Scott No. 1838.

1851

1874

1875

1816

Dahlia USA 18c

Lily USA 18c

Rose USA 18c

Camellia USA 18c

1879 a

1890

1891

1893 a

The Gift of Self

USA 18c

American Red Cross
1881-1981

1910

George Mason

USA 18c

1850

SAVINGS AND LOANS

SAVE

USA 18c

1911

SEQUOYAH

The son of a Cherokee mother and British father, Sequoyah was convinced that literacy was the source of the white man's power. Though he could neither read nor write and knew no language but Cherokee, Sequoyah set out in 1803, at the age of 30, to invent a system of writing for his people.

At first he tried to create a symbol for each word. But the method was too elaborate, and not even he could remember what each one meant. Finally he hit upon the idea of creating a symbol for each syllable in the language—86 in all. His symbols included letters of the English alphabet, some turned upside down, and some symbols on his own.

Mockery and doubt greeted Sequoyah's first attempts to introduce his new language. But eventually he won over the doubters. In 1824, portions of the Bible appeared in the Cherokee langage, and four years later a bilingual newspaper, the Cherokee Phoenix, was published.

Even though illiterate, Sequoyah had become the only man in history to create a written language single-handedly. See Scott No. 1851.

		Un	U
Great Americans Issue, Dec. 27, 1980			
1851	19¢ Sequoyah	.38	.05
Issues of 1981			
1874	15¢ Everett Dirksen, Jan. 4	.30	.06
1875	15¢ Whitney Moore Young, Jr. Jan. 30	.30	.06
	18¢ Eagle (B) *		
	18¢ Eagle (B) Coil *		
	18¢ Eagle (B) Booklet *		
	Booklet Pane of 8 *		
Americana Issue, April 8, 1981			
1816	12¢ Freedom of Conscience	.24	.05
	12¢ Freedom of Conscience Coil	.24	.05
Flower Issue, April 23			
1876	18¢ Red Rose	.36	.06
1877	18¢ Camelia	.36	.06
1878	18¢ Dahlia	.36	.06
1879	18¢ Lily	.36	.06
1879a	Block of 4	1.44	.24
Flag Issue, April 24			
1890	18¢ For Amber Waves of Grain	.36	.03
1891	18¢ From Sea to Shining Sea (Coil)	.36	.03
1892	6¢ U.S.A.	.12	.03
1893	18¢ For Purple Mountains Majesty	.36	.03
1893a	Booklet Pane of 8	2.64	
1910	18¢ American Red Cross	.36	.06
Great Americans Issue, May 7			
1850	18¢ George Mason	.36	.03
1911	18¢ Savings & Loan Associations, May 8	.36	.06

*Information not available at presstime

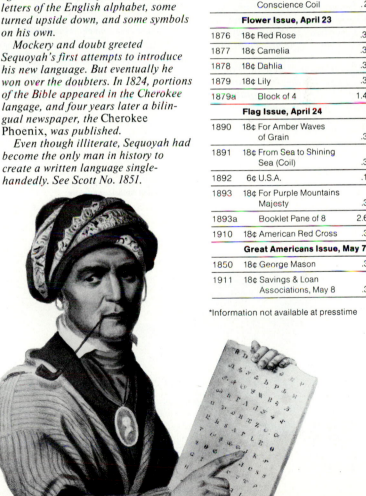

ELECTRIC CARS

At the height of their popularity, about 1900, electric automobiles were widely used for both public and private transportation, especially in large cities. New York City boasted a fleet of electric cabs, and cab stands all over town sported battery chargers for drivers to use between fares.

In those years the electric cars were more than a means of transportation; they were considered a social asset, and the ads appealed to snob instincts. One company promoted its vehicle as "the only car for a lady"; ads featured fashionable women seated in the shiny, spotless electric, with the headline, "no crank, no grease, no fumes." Another company advertised the "Stately, Stylish Electric Stanhope . . . the aristocrat of motors."

But while the electrics were fashionably clean and quiet, they had serious limitations: they were heavy, capable of only limited speed, and expensive— and they could go for only 40 to 60 miles before they needed recharging. Moreover, most Americans lived and worked on farms, and few rural communities had the electric power to recharge batteries.

The popularity of the electric car began to wane after 1912 when gasoline cars became easier to operate and offered higher speeds. By 1930, the internal combustion engine reigned supreme, and the once popular electric car was dead. See Scott No. 1905.

		Un	U
Wildlife Issue, May 14			
1880	18¢ Bighorned Sheep	.36	.03
1881	18¢ Puma	.36	.03
1882	18¢ Harbor Seal	.36	.03
1883	18¢ Bison	.36	.03
1884	18¢ Brown Bear	.36	.03
1885	18¢ Polar Bear	.36	.03
1886	18¢ Elk	.36	.03
1887	18¢ Moose	.36	.03
1888	18¢ White-tailed Deer	.36	.03
1889	18¢ Pronghorned Antelope	.36	.03
1889a	Booklet Pane of 10	3.60	
Transportation Issue, May 18			
1906	18¢ Surrey with Fringe on Top (Coil)	.36	.03
Space Achievement Issue, May 21			
1912	18¢ Exploring the Moon	.36	.06
1913	18¢ Benefiting Mankind	.36	.06
1914	18¢ Benefiting Mankind	.36	.06
1915	18¢ Understanding the Sun	.36	.06
1916	18¢ Probing the Planets	.36	.06
1917	18¢ Benefiting Mankind	.36	.06
1918	18¢ Benefiting Mankind	.36	.06
1919	18¢ Comprehending the Universe	.36	.06
1919a	Block of 8	3.00	1.00
Great Americans Issue			
1849	17¢ Rachel Carson, May 28	.34	.03
1859	35¢ Dr. Charles Drew, June 3	.70	.08
1920	18¢ Professional Management, June 18	.36	.06
Transportation Issue, June 25			
1905	17¢ Electric Car (Coil)	.34	.03

1889a

1906   1849   1859

1919a

1920   1905

Save Wetland Habitats
Save Grassland Habitats
Save Mountain Habitats
Save Woodland Habitats

1924a

Disabled doesn't mean Unable

1925

Edna St. Vincent Millay

American Poet

1926

Alcoholism You can beat it! USA 18c

1927

Architecture USA 18c
Architecture USA 18c
Architecture USA 18c
Architecture USA 18c

USA 18c
James Hoban White House Architect

Bobby Jones

USA 18c

Babe Zaharias

USA

		Un	U
Wildlife Habitat Issue, June 26			
1921	18¢ Wetland Habitats	.36	.06
1922	18¢ Grassland Habitats	.36	.06
1923	18¢ Mountain Habitats	.36	.06
1924	18¢ Woodland Habitats	.36	.06
1924a	Block of 4	1.50	.30
1925	18¢ International Year of the Disabled,* June 29		
1926	Edna St. Vincent Millay,* July 10		
1927	Alcoholism,* Aug. 19		

	Un	U
American Architecture Issue, Aug. 28		
Biltmore*		
Palace of Fine Arts*		
NYU Library*		
Bank*		
Block of 4*		
James Hoban*		
Bobby Jones, Sept. 22*		
Babe Zaharias, Sept. 22*		
Pair*		

*Information not available at presstime

BABE DIDRIKSON ZAHARIAS

When all is said and done, when all the scores are totaled, the official times are in, it is unlikely that any athlete, male or female, will have surpassed the achievements of Babe Didrikson Zaharias.

Everything she touched—every sport she set her mind to—turned to gold. She conquered basketball and tennis, bowling and golf, and just about every event in track and field. In 1922, she set new Olympic and world records in the javelin throw and hurdles. She took up golf in the late 1930s, and went on to win more than 50 major golf tournaments—the last of them, the National Women's Open and the Tam O'Shanter All-America in 1954, after a major cancer operation. Her victory was one of the greatest comebacks in the history of sports. In 1950, the Associated Press named Babe the outstanding woman athlete of the first half of the century.

The big question, of course, is why. Are phenomenal athletes like this born or made? And the answer is, naturally, both. Undoubtedly, Babe Didrikson was born with a great talent, but her championships came only with a great deal of work. As she said of her first major golf tournament, she kept drilling until there was "tape all over my hands, and blood all over the tape."

EDNA ST. VINCENT MILLAY

Poet Edna St. Vincent Millay was ruthlessly critical of her own work, often agonizing for days over a single, imperfect line.

Her self-criticism led to a meticulous concern about the way her works appeared in print. In 1946, she wrote her publishers, "It occurs to me with something of dismay, that, if I were dead—instead of being, as I am, alive and kicking, and I said kicking—the firm of Harper and Brothers might conceivably . . . alter one word in one of my poems. This you must never do."

Millay refused to allow any but her best works to be published. In 1947, she wrote her publishers, "The fact is, I have too much pride and too much faith in myself as a dramatist, to permit the publication in one volume of seven dramatic works of mine, of which only three . . . are good plays." She added that "it will do no good to me or to Harper's, when I bring out a book of new lyrics, good lyrics, to have this book preceded by a book of bad poems."

But despite her perfectionist attitude and her poor health, Millay turned out a respectable number of works. When she died in 1950 at the age of 58, she had managed to write six plays, an opera libretto and eleven volumes containing about 500 poems. See Scott No. 1926

DESERT PLANTS

American cactus growth, late 19th Century drawing.

*Information not available at presstime

Those who have never seen the desert may picture it as a vast and barren wasteland. Far from it. In fact, most deserts are alive with an astonishing variety of plant and animal life.

True, the desert is a harsh, inhospitable environment, with extremes of temperature and very little rainfall. But many species have learned, over the eons, to withstand such conditions— and no family has learned these lessons better than the Cactaceae, the true cacti. Their fleshy stems and branches have evolved specifically to store water, while their thick, nearly poreless skin helps keep it from evaporating.

Most cacti are known for their spines, which may be long or short, curved or straight, rigid as thorns or soft as hair. Most also have brilliant flowers, called "silk flowers" because of their resemblance to bright fabric. While they may last only a few days, the flowers are frequently large (up to a foot in diameter) and come in nearly every color of the rainbow.

Though we think of the cactus as a desert plant, they can be found in almost every part of the western hemisphere, from Canada to the tip of South America, from coastal areas to jungles to the Andes Mountains. In habitat, in shape, and in variety, the cactus is unrivaled.

The Giant Saguaro, the largest native cactus in North America, often attains a height of 60 feet and weighs as much as three tons.

John Hanson
President Continental Congress
USA 18c

SPACE ACHIEVEMENT

Issuance of the long-awaited Space Achievement stamps on May 21, 1981, marked an unusual format for U.S. stamps. In the center of the design is a block of four large stamps depicting the Space Shuttle taking off, being boosted into orbit, circling the earth and landing. On either side of the block of four is a vertically oriented pair of smaller stamps highlighting other U.S. space achievements. The stamps on the left side of the design feature the Apollo missions and Pioneer II. The upper left stamp depicts an astronaut on the Moon, while the lower left stamp shows the Pioneer II space vehicle. The upper right stamp is the Skylab space workshop, and at the lower right is the Space Telescope, which is scheduled to be carried into space by the Space Shuttle in mid-1985.

Besides the American Commemorative Panel (pictured below—for more information, see page 265), the U.S. Postal Service has also issued a special Space Achievement Folder (see page 272 for more information) to display these unique stamps.

AMERICAN COMMEMORATIVES

In May of 1961, after years of speculation and scientific testing, the United States sent astronaut Alan B. Shepard, Jr. to take a closer look at the wonders of unexplored space.

His mission, though it lasted just fifteen minutes and journeyed only 116 miles into the sky, was significant for two reasons: One—it proved that man could indeed survive outside the earth's atmosphere, and two—that he could venture farther still.

In the twenty years since that historic first flight, this country has sent more than thirty manned spacecrafts into orbit, plus countless fact-finding satellites. We have put men on the moon, seen them walk in space, sent cameras to photograph the surfaces of other planets, launched scientific laboratories into orbit and most recently—designed and flown a reusable 80-ton space vehicle that may ultimately shuttle people and payload to and from Earth's orbit.

The success of the Space Shuttle Columbia's voyage is particularly noteworthy for what it may eventually mean to man's future endeavors in space: scientific satellites can be retrieved or refurbished; entire laboratories and personnel transported; manned, military "command" posts established. The possibilities are infinite.

Though still in its infant stages, the United States Space Program can be credited with providing us with volumes of information about the complex physical processes which govern the Earth. Hopefully we will learn more about our planet in order to better manage and provide for it.

The steel line engraving of the male figure and a globe surrounded by electronic equipment, appeared on certificates issued by the American Bank Note Company, Twin Industries Corporation, Eitel McCullough, Inc., Sanders Associates, Inc., and The Lamson & Sessions Company. The "Woman with Globe" scene was used on stock certificates issued by Superscope, Inc., in 1973 and 1980.

Space Achievement

Stamps printed by the Bureau of Engraving and Printing, Washington, D.C.

Copyright 1981 United States Postal Service

No 143 in a series

May 29, 1981 / Printed in U.S.A.

RACHEL CARSON

If one person can be said to have given birth to the contemporary ecology movement, surely it must be Rachel Carson. Part biologist, part poet, she gained world fame with the publication three decades ago of The Sea Around Us. In that book she warned eloquently of the threat posed by our own activities to the life that arose in, and is sustained by, the sea.

Always, Carson's chief concern was the relation of life to its environment. In the late 1950s, she began collecting data on the effects of deadly poisons—especially synthetic insecticides—on the "living community." The result was Silent Spring, an exposé of the destruction already wrought—and still to come—by the forces of modern man.

1849

"It is not my contention that chemical insecticides must never be used," she wrote. "I do contend that we have put poisonous . . . chemicals indiscriminately into the hands of persons largely or wholly ignorant of their potentials for harm. We have allowed these chemicals to be used with little or no advance investigation of their effect on soil, water, wildlife, and man himself. Future generations are unlikely to condone our lack of prudent concern for the integrity of the natural world that supports all life." See Scott No. 1849.

CHARLES DREW

Blood played a major—and a symbolic—role in the short, brilliant career of Dr. Charles R. Drew.

Drew achieved fame as a pioneer in blood preservation, and equal renown as a crusading teacher known to his students at Howard University as "Big Red." The nickname grew from his sudden wrath, so intense when roused that it turned his pale complexion blood red within seconds.

Born in 1904 in Washington, D.C., Drew became fascinated with blood groups while a medical student at McGill University in Montreal. His thesis on banked-blood (on graduation from Columbia-Presbyterian Medical Center, New York City, 1940) was well-timed. It established him as a recognized authority and led to his work on the "Blood for Britain" project which shipped lifesaving plasma overseas during World War II.

But Drew's most enduring medical contribution began in 1941 when he was named director of surgery at Howard University's medical school in his hometown. In nine years he infused new life into the department, training a vanguard of surgeons who altered the image and visibility of black surgeons in America. His work was shouldered by the generation of doctors he had helped prepare when his career was ended in April, 1950, by a fatal auto accident—two months short of his 46th birthday. See Scott No. 1859.

1859

AIR MAIL STAMPS
SPECIAL DELIVERY STAMPS

		Un	U	#	PB	FDC	Q
	Air Post Stamps						
	For prepayment of postage on all mailable matter sent by airmail. All unwatermarked.						
	Issue of 1918, Perf. 11						
C1	6¢ Curtiss Jenny	225.00	40.00	(6)	2,250.00	*15,000.00*	3,395,854
C2	16¢ Curtiss Jenny	275.00	52.50	(6)	4,850.00	*15,000.00*	3,793,887
C3	24¢ Curtiss Jenny	275.00	60.00	(6)	1,250.00	*17,500.00*	2,134,888
C3a	Center Inverted		*145,000.00*				
	Issue of 1923						
C4	8¢ Wooden Propeller and						
	Engine Nose	75.00	22.50	(6)	1,200.00	650.00	6,414,576
C5	16¢ Air Service Emblem	275.00	55.00	(6)	6,250.00	1,150.00	5,309,275
C6	24¢ De Havilland Biplane	350.00	35.00	(6)	7,000.00	1,250.00	5,285,775
	Issue of 1926-27						
C7	10¢ Map of U.S.						
	and Two Mail Planes	8.50	.50	(6)	125.00	90.00	42,092,800
C8	15¢ olive brown (C7)	9.50	2.75	(6)	150.00	100.00	15,597,307
C9	20¢ yellow green (C7)	30.00	2.25	(6)	325.00	120.00	17,616,350
	Issue of 1927						
C10	10¢ Lindbergh's "Spirit of						
	St. Louis," June 18	21.00	3.50	(6)	325.00	35.00	20,379,179
C10a	Booklet pane of 3	140.00	*60.00*				
	Nos. C1-C10 inclusive were also available for ordinary postage.						
	Issue of 1928						
C11	5¢ Beacon on Rocky Mountains,						
	July 25	10.00	.65	(6)	100.00	50.00	106,887,675
C12	5¢ Winged Globe, Feb. 10	23.50	.55	(6)	400.00	16.00	97,641,200
	Graf Zeppelin Issue, Apr. 19						
C13	65¢ Zeppelin over Atlantic Ocean	800.00	600.00	(6)	7,250.00	2,850.00	93,536
C14	$1.30 Zeppelin between						
	Continents	1,850.00	1,000.00	(6)	16,500.00	2,500.00	72,428
C15	$2.60 Zeppelin Passing Globe	2,850.00	1,500.00	(6)	24,500.00	3,750.00	61,296
	Issued for use on mail carried on the first Europe-Pan-American round-trip flight of Graf Zeppelin, May 1930.						
	Issues of 1931-32, Perf. 10½x11						
C16	5¢ violet (C12)	11.50	.50		250.00	300.00	57,340,050
C17	8¢ olive bistre (C12)	5.00	.30		90.00	20.00	76,648,803

C1 C2 C3 C3a

C4 C5 C6

C7 C10

C11

C12 C13

C14 C15

		Un	U	#	PB	FDC	Q
	Issue of 1933, Perf. 11						
C18	50¢ Century of Progress, Oct. 2	250.00	150.00	(6)	2,250.00	300.00	324,070
	Issue of 1934, Perf. 10½x11						
C19	6¢ dull orange (C12), July 1	4.25	.10		45.00	*175.00*	302,205,100
	Issue of 1935, Perf. 11						
C20	25¢ Transpacific, Nov. 22	4.50	1.75	(6)	75.00	37.50	10,205,400
	Issue of 1937						
C21	20¢ The "China Clipper," over the						
	Pacific, Feb. 15	30.00	3.00	(6)	350.00	35.00	12,794,600
C22	50¢ carmine (C21)	27.50	6.50	(6)	325.00	35.00	9,285,300
	Issue of 1938						
C23	6¢ Eagle Holding Shield,						
	Olive Branch, and Arrows, May 14	.65	.06		12.50	15.00	349,946,500
	Issue of 1939						
C24	30¢ Transatlantic, May 16	20.00	1.75	(6)	375.00	27.50	19,768,150
	Issues of 1941-44, Perf. 11x10½						
C25	6¢ Twin-motor Transport Plane, 1941	.18	.03		1.00	1.50	4,476,527,700
C25a	Booklet pane of 3	6.50	*1.00*				
C26	8¢ olive green (C25), 1944	.25	.05		1.50	3.00	1,744,876,650
C27	10¢ violet (C25), 1941	1.75	.20		20.00	4.00	67,117,400
C28	15¢ brown carmine (C25), 1941	4.50	.35		24.00	6.00	78,434,800
C29	20¢ bright green (C25), 1941	3.75	.30		22.50	6.50	42,359,850
C30	30¢ blue (C25), 1941	4.00	.30		25.00	11.00	59,880,850
C31	50¢ orange (C25), 1941	24.00	4.00		200.00	27.50	11,160,600
	Singles from No. C25a are imperf. at sides or imperf. at sides and bottom.						
	Issue of 1946						
C32	5¢ DC-4 Skymaster, Sept. 25	.15	.04		.75	1.25	864,753,100
	Issues of 1947, Perf. 10½x11						
C33	5¢ DC-4 Skymaster, Mar. 26	.15	.04		.75	1.00	971,903,700
	Perf. 11x10½						
C34	10¢ Pan American Union Building,						
	Washington, D.C., Aug. 30	.40	.06		2.50	·1.50	207,976,550
C35	15¢ Statue of Liberty						
	and New York Skyline, Aug. 20	.55	.05		2.85	2.25	756,186,350
C36	25¢ Plane over San Francisco-						
	Oakland Bay Bridge, July 30	1.25	.12		7.50	2.75	132,956,100
	Issues of 1948						
	Coil Stamp, Perf. 10 Horizontally						
C37	5¢ carmine (C33), Jan. 15	2.00	1.10			1.25	Unlimited
	Perf. 11x10½						
C38	5¢ New York City, July 31	.22	.20		25.00	1.35	38,449,100
	Issued for the 50th anniversary of the consolidation of the five boroughs of New York City.						

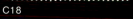

C18

C20

C21

C23

C24

C25

C32

C33

C34

C35

C36

C38

C40

C42

C43

C44

C45

C46

C47

C48

C49

C51

C53

C54

C55

C56

C57

C58

C59

	Un	U	#	PB	FDC	Q
Issues of 1949						
Perf. 10½x11						
C39 6¢ carmine (C33), Jan. 18	.18	.03		.85	1.00	5,070,095,200
C39a Booklet pane of 6	13.50	5.00				
Perf. 11x10½						
C40 6¢ Alexandria 200th Anniv., May 11	.18	.10		.95	1.00	75,085,000
Coil Stamp, Perf. 10 Horizontally						
C41 6¢ carmine (C33), Aug. 25	4.75	.05			1.10	Unlimited
Universal Postal Union Issue, Perf. 11x10½						
C42 10¢ Post Office Dept. Bldg., Nov. 18	.65	.45		4.75	1.25	21,061,300
C43 15¢ Globe and Doves Carrying						
Messages, Oct. 7	.80	.60		3.75	1.50	36,613,100
C44 25¢ Boeing Stratocruiser						
and Globe, Nov. 30	1.20	.85		15.00	1.85	16,217,100
C45 6¢ Wright Brothers, Dec. 17	.20	.10		1.00	2.00	80,405,000
Issue of 1952						
C46 80¢ Diamond Head, Honolulu,						
Hawaii, Mar. 26	15.00	1.50		100.00	12.00	18,876,800
Issue of 1953						
C47 6¢ Powered Flight, May 29	.16	.10		.85	1.25	78,415,000
Issue of 1954						
C48 4¢ Eagle in Flight, Sept. 3	.12	.08		6.00	.75	50,483,600
Issue of 1957						
C49 6¢ Air Force, Aug. 1	.20	.10		1.50	1.25	63,185,000
Issues of 1958						
C50 5¢ rose red (C48), July 31	.22	.15		5.00	.80	72,480,000
Perf. 10½x11						
C51 7¢ Silhouette of Jet Liner, July 31	.22	.03		1.30	.75	532,410,300
C51a Booklet pane of 6	16.50	6.50				1,326,960,000
Coil Stamp, Perf. 10 Horizontally						
C52 7¢ blue (C51)	6.25	.25			.90	157,035,000
Issues of 1959, Perf. 11x10½						
C53 7¢ Alaska Statehood, Jan. 3	.25	.12		1.75	.65	90,055,200
Perf. 11						
C54 7¢ Balloon Jupiter, Aug. 17	.25	.12		1.75	.85	79,290,000
Issued for the 100th anniversary of the carrying of mail by the balloon Jupiter from Lafayette to Crawfordsville, Indiana.						
Perf. 11x10½						
C55 7¢ Hawaii Statehood, Aug. 21	.25	.12		1.75	1.00	84,815,000
Perf. 11						
C56 10¢ Pan American Games, Aug. 27	.50	.40		8.00	.90	38,770,000
Issue of 1959-66						
C57 10¢ Liberty Bell, June 10,1960	3.00	1.00		15.00	1.00	39,960,000
C58 15¢ Statue of Liberty, Jan. 13, 1961	.85	.06		5.00	1.10	Unlimited
C59 25¢ Abraham Lincoln, Apr. 22, 1960	.75	.06		4.00	1.50	Unlimited

		Un	U	#	PB	FDC	Q
	Issue of 1960, Perf. 10½x11						
C60	7¢ Jet Airliner (C51), Aug. 12	.30	.05		1.50	.70	289,460,000
C60a	Booklet pane of 6	22.50	7.00				
	Coil Stamp, Perf. 10 Horizontally						
C61	7¢ carmine (C60), Oct. 22	8.00	.25			1.00	87,140,000
	Issue of 1961, Perf. 11						
C62	13¢ Liberty Bell, June 28,1961	.65	.10		7.00	.80	Unlimited
C63	15¢ Statue of Liberty, Jan. 13, 1961	.40	.08		2.25	1.00	Unlimited
	No. C63 has a gutter between the two parts of the design; No. C58 does not.						
	Issue of 1962, Perf. 10½x11						
C64	8¢ Jetliner over Capitol, Dec. 5	.18	.03		1.10	.60	Unlimited
C64c	Booklet pane of 5 + label	2.25	.50				
	Coil Stamp, Perf. 10 Horizontally						
C65	8¢ carmine (C64), Dec. 5	.60	.08			.80	Unlimited
	Issue of 1963, Perf. 11						
C66	15¢ Montgomery Blair, May 3	1.65	.75		14.00	1.35	42,245,000
	Issues of 1963, Perf. 11x10½						
C67	6¢ Bald Eagle, July 12	.20	.15		5.00	.50	Unlimited
	Perf. 11						
C68	8¢ Amelia Earhart, July 24	.40	.15		5.25	1.85	63,890,000
	Issue of 1964						
C69	8¢ Robert H. Goddard, Oct. 5	1.20	.15		7.50	2.00	65,170,000
	Issues of 1967						
C70	8¢ Alaska Purchase, Mar. 30	.75	.20		10.00	.70	64,710,000
C71	20¢ "Columbia Jays" by Audubon,						
	Apr. 26	1.50	.15		10.00	2.00	165,430,000
	Issues of 1968, Perf. 11x10½						
C72	10¢ 50-Star Runway, Jan. 5	.30	.03		2.25	.60	Unlimited
C72b	Booklet pane of 8	4.00	.75				
C72c	Booklet pane of 5 + label	2.50	.75				
	Coil Stamp, Perf. 10 Vertically						
C73	10¢ carmine (C72)	.75	.04			.60	Unlimited
	Air Mail Service Issue, Perf. 11						
C74	10¢ Curtiss Jenny, May 15	.75	.15		13.50	1.25	74,180,000
C75	20¢ U.S.A. and Jet, Nov. 22	1.00	.06		6.50	1.10	Unlimited
	Issue of 1969						
C76	10¢ Moon Landing, Sept. 9	.35	.15		3.50	1.35	152,364,800
	Issues of 1971-73, Perf. 10½x11, 11x10½						
C77	9¢ Plane, May 15, 1971	.22	.15		3.00	.50	Unlimited
C78	11¢ Silhouette of Jet, May 7, 1971	.25	.03		1.35	.50	Unlimited
C78a	Booklet pane of 4 + 2 labels	1.50	.40				
C79	13¢ Winged Airmail Envelope,						
	Nov. 16, 1973	.32	.10		1.65	.55	Unlimited
C79a	Booklet pane of 5 + label,						
	Dec. 27, 1973	1.35	.70				

C60

C62

C63

C64

C66

C67

C68

C69

C70

C71

C72

C74

C75

C76

C77

C78

C79

C80

C81

C84

C85

C86

C87

C88

C89

C90

C92a

C94a

	Un	U	#	PB	FDC	Q
1971-73 continued						
Perf. 11						
C80	17¢ Statue of Liberty, July 13, 1971	.55	.15		2.75	.60	Unlimited
Perf. 11x10½						
C81	21¢ red, blue and black (C75)						
May 21, 1971	.55	.21		2.75	.75	Unlimited
Coil Stamps, Perf. 10 Vertically						
C82	11¢ Silhouette of Jet, May 7, 1971	.35	.06			.50	Unlimited
C83	13¢ red (C79), Dec. 27, 1973	.40	.10			.50	
Issues of 1972, Perf. 11						
C84	11¢ City of Refuge, May 3	.30	.15		2.75	.65	78,210,000
Perf. 11x10½						
C85	11¢ Skiing and Olympic Rings,						
Aug. 17	.25	.15	(10)	3.50	.50	96,240,000
Issue of 1973						
C86	11¢ De Forest Audions, July 10	.30	.15		1.75	.50	58,705,000
Issues of 1974, Perf. 11						
C87	18¢ Statue of Liberty, Jan. 11	.45	.18		2.50	.65	Unlimited
C88	26¢ Mt. Rushmore National						
Memorial, Jan. 2	.60	.26		2.85	.85	Unlimited
Issue of 1976						
C89	25¢ Plane & Globes, Jan. 2	.50	.25		2.50	.85	
C90	31¢ Plane, Globes & Flag, Jan. 2	.62	.30		3.10	1.10	
Issues of 1978, Wright Brothers Issue, Sept. 23						
C91	31¢ Orville & Wilbur Wright	.62	.30		3.10	1.15	
C92	31¢ Orville & Wilbur Wright	.62	.30		3.10	1.15	
C92a	Pair, #C91-C92	1.25	.65			2.30	
Issues of 1979, Octave Chanute Issue, March 29						
C93	21¢ Octave Chanute	.42	.20		2.10	1.00	
C94	21¢ Octave Chanute	.42	.20		2.10	1.00	
C94a	Pair, #C93-C94	.85				2.00	

BRIEF HISTORY OF AIRMAIL

"The celerity (speed) of the mail should always be equal to the most rapid transition of the traveler." Did Postmaster William T. Barry have any idea, when he uttered these words in 1834, that they might someday refer to Concorde jets and space shuttles?

Chances are he wasn't even dreaming of the simplest forms of airmail—though that service had, in a sense, begun thousands of years earlier, when armies sent messages over long distances by pigeon post.

But let's be fair, and date the history of airmail more reasonably from its inauguration with human carriers. That would be May 15, 1918, when the Post Office Department, with the help of the

May, 1918

Army's Air Service, inaugurated the world's first official airmail service. The route went from Washington to Philadelphia to New York and vice versa—a one-way distance of about 218 miles.

More important than the distance, though, was the reliability of the service. The public, perhaps understandably, was skeptical, and often sent "insurance" copies of their airmail letters by train. But the pilots gradually won their confidence, by demonstrating that no matter what the weather or terrain, the mail could be flown on schedule.

And not only the mail. The public soon realized that people could be transported as swiftly and safely as could their correspondence. At the same time, airmail operators (the service was now in private hands) saw the great potential for profit. By the end of the 1920s, airmail had helped spawn the commercial airline industry.

TWA mail plane.

C97

C98

C96a

C99

C100

CE2

	Un	U	#	PB	FDC	Q
1979 continued						
Wiley Post Issue, Nov. 20						
C95 5¢ Wiley Post	.50	.25		2.50	1.00	
C96 5¢ Wiley Post	.50	.25		2.50	1.00	
C96a Pair, #C95-C96	1.00				2.00	
Olympic Games Issue						
C97 1¢ High Jump	.62	.30			1.15	
Issues of 1980						
C98 0¢ Philip Mazzei, Oct. 13	.80	.40				
C99 8¢ Blanche Stuart Scott, Dec. 30	.56	.28				
C100 5¢ Glenn Curtiss, Dec. 30	.70	.35				
Air Post Special Delivery Stamps						
Issue of 1934, Perf. 11						
CE 6¢ dark blue (CE2)	1.10	.95	(6)	45.00	17.50	
For imperforate variety, see No. 771.						
Issue of 1936						
CE2 6¢ Great Seal of United States	.50	.25		17.50	12.50	

		Un	U	#	PB	FDC	Q
	Special Delivery Stamps.						
	Unwmkd., Issue of 1885, Perf. 12						
E1	10¢ Messenger Running	300.00	30.00	(8)	13,500.00	7,500.00	
	Issue of 1888						
E2	10¢ blue (E3)	300.00	7.50	(8)	13,500.00		
	Issue of 1893						
E3	10¢ Messenger Running	200.00	12.50	(8)	7,500.00		
	Issue of 1894, Line under "Ten Cents"						
E4	10¢ Messenger Running	750.00	17.50	(6)	15,000.00		
	Issue of 1895, Wmkd. (191)						
E5	10¢ blue (E4)	150.00	2.50	(6)	4,500.00		
	Issue of 1902						
E6.	10¢ Messenger on Bicycle	100.00	2.50	(6)	2,750.00		
	Issue of 1908						
E7	10¢ Mercury Helmet and Olive Branch	75.00	27.50	(6)	1,100.00		
	Issue of 1911, Wmkd. (190)						
E8	10¢ ultramarine (E6)	100.00	4.00	(6)	2,750.00		
	Issue of 1914, Perf. 10						
E9	10¢ ultramarine (E6)	235.00	4.25	(6)	5,500.00		
	Unwmkd., Issue of 1916						
E10	10¢ ultramarine (E6)	375.00	17.50	(6)	7,250.00		
	Issue of 1917, Perf. 11						
E11	10¢ ultramarine (E6)	22.50	.30	(6)	375.00		
	Issue of 1922						
E12	10¢ Postman and Motorcycle	40.00	.15	(6)	575.00	500.00	
	Issue of 1925						
E13	15¢ Postman and Motorcycle	27.50	.65	(6)	300.00	225.00	
E14	20¢ Post Office Truck	6.00	1.75	(6)	67.50	125.00	
	Issue of 1927, Perf. 11x10½						
E15	10¢ Postman and Motorcycle	.80	.04		6.50	95.00	
	Issue of 1931						
E16	15¢ orange (E12)	.80	.08		6.50	120.00	
	Issue of 1944						
E17	13¢ Postman and Motorcycle	.65	.06		5.00	10.00	
E18	17¢ Postman and Motorcycle	6.00	2.25		30.00	10.00	
	Issue of 1951						
E19	20¢ black (E14)	2.00	.12		12.00	5.00	
	Issue of 1954-57						
E20	20¢ Delivery of Letter	.70	.08		4.50	3.00	
E21	30¢ Delivery of Letter	1.00	.04		5.25	2.25	
	Issue of 1969-71, Perf. 11						
E22	45¢ Arrows	2.25	.20		14.50	3.50	
E23	60¢ Arrows	1.20	.12		6.00	3.50	

E1

E3

E4

E6

E7

E12

E13

E14

E15

E17

E18

E20

E21

E22

E23

REGISTRATION
AND CERTIFIED MAIL STAMPS
POSTAGE DUE STAMPS

F1

FA1

J2

J19

J25

J33

	Un	U	#	PB	FDC

Registration Stamp

Issued for the prepayment of registry; not usable for postage. Sale discontinued May 28, 1913.

Issue of 1911, Perf. 12, Wmkd. USPS (190)

		Un	U	#	PB	FDC
F1	10¢ Bald Eagle	120.00	4.50	(6)	1,750.00	8,500.00

Certified Mail Stamp

For use on first-class mail for which no indemnity value is claimed, but for which proof of mailing and proof of delivery are available at less cost than registered mail.

Issue of 1955, Perf. 10½x11

		Un	U	#	PB	FDC
FA1	15¢ Letter Carrier	.50	.30		6.25	2.50

Postage Due Stamps

For affixing by a postal clerk to any mail to denote amount to be collected from addressee because of insufficient prepayment of postage.

Printed by American Bank Note Company Issue of 1879, Design of J2, Perf. 12, Unwmd.

		Un	U
J1	1¢ brown	20.00	4.00
J2	2¢ Figure of Value	150.00	4.00
J3	3¢ brown	12.50	2.00
J4	5¢ brown	185.00	17.50
J5	10¢ brown	275.00	7.00
J6	30¢ brown	120.00	15.00
J7	50¢ brown	175.00	30.00

Special Printing

		Un
J8	1¢ deep brown	4,000.00
J9	2¢ deep brown	2,750.00
J10	3¢ deep brown	2,500.00
J11	5¢ deep brown	1,850.00
J12	10¢ deep brown	1,250.00
J13	30¢ deep brown	1,250.00
J14	50¢ deep brown	1,250.00

Regular Issue of 1884-89, Design of J19

		Un	U
J15	1¢ red brown	25.00	2.50
J16	2¢ red brown	27.50	2.50
J17	3¢ red brown	350.00	75.00
J18	5¢ red brown	150.00	7.25
J19	10¢ Figure of Value	125.00	3.50
J20	30¢ red brown	75.00	17.50
J21	50¢ red brown	850.00	110.00

Issue of 1891-93, Design of J25

		Un	U
J22	1¢ bright claret	7.00	.50
J23	2¢ bright claret	9.50	.35
J24	3¢ bright claret	16.00	2.50
J25	5¢ Figure of Value	20.00	2.75
J26	10¢ bright claret	35.00	6.50
J27	30¢ bright claret	175.00	70.00
J28	50¢ bright claret	200.00	75.00

WORLD'S MOST VALUABLE STAMP

In 1856, the postmaster of British Guiana in South America ran out of stamps. To tide the colony over until a fresh supply arrived from London, a local printer produced a few dozen one- and four-cent stamps, each initialed by a postal assistant.

For almost 20 years, all of the one-cent provisionals were lost. But in 1873, a teenager in the colony's capital came across a single one-cent stamp in his attic. He sold it, for about $1.50, to a Scottish collector.

Over the years the stamp passed through the hands of many leading stamp collectors, including Count Phillippe La Renotiere von Ferrary, an Italian-Austrian nobleman who routinely allocated $10,000 a week toward enriching his collection. When the Count died in 1916, Arthur Hind, a New York manufacturer, bought the stamp for about $32,500, reportedly outbidding an agent of King George V of Britain. Rumor has it that when a second Guiana turned up, Hind secretly bought it for more than $60,000, then set it on fire so his stamp would remain unique.

In 1980, this unprepossessing piece of smudged paper fetched a record price of $850,000, the highest price ever paid for a single stamp.

Long-recognized as the most prized of all postage stamps, the British Guiana remains, for its size and weight, the most valuable single object in the world.

GLENN CURTISS

The career of aviation pioneer Glenn Curtiss echoed the history of modern transportation.

Born in 1878, Curtiss started work as a bicycle mechanic, then set up a motorcycle factory and began breaking motorcycle speed records. In 1904, he built a motor for a dirigible, the California Arrow, which in turn led him to experiment with heavier-than-air craft. In 1908, he won a trophy for the first one-mile airplane flight in the U.S.,

C100

and the next year established the country's first flying school. By 1912, he had flown the first successful seaplane and built the first flying boat.

But Curtiss is probably best remembered for one very special plane, the JN series, known affectionately as the "Jenny." These slow, stable two-seaters were developed in 1916 primarily to train prospective U.S. pilots for European duty during World War I. In that capacity they served their country well.

But the Jenny was destined for still greater fame. In 1918, several planes and pilots were loaned by the Army to the Post Office for the initiation of an experimental airmail service. As a result, the Jenny was featured on the first airmail stamp—including the famous sheet with the inverted center! See Scott No. C100.

	Un	U	#	PB	FDC
Printed by the Bureau of Engraving and Printing, Issue of 1894, Design of J33, Perf. 12					
J29	1¢ vermilion	350.00	60.00	(6)	4,500.00
J30	2¢ vermilion	150.00	27.50	(6)	2,000.00
J31	1¢ deep claret	15.00	3.00	(6)	350.00
J32	2¢ deep claret	12.50	1.75	(6)	300.00
J33	3¢ Figure of Value	37.50	13.00	(6)	750.00
J34	5¢ deep claret	42.50	15.00	(6)	850.00
J35	10¢ deep rose	40.00	8.50	(6)	750.00
J36	30¢ deep claret	150.00	40.00		
J37	50¢	300.00	85.00		
Issue of 1895, Design of J33, Wmkd. (191)					
J38	1¢ deep claret	4.00	.30	(6)	175.00
J39	2¢ deep claret	4.00	.20	(6)	175.00
J40	3¢ deep claret	22.50	1.00	(6)	325.00
J41	5¢ deep claret	20.00	1.00	(6)	375.00
J42	10¢ deep claret	25.00	1.75	(6)	450.00
J43	30¢ deep claret	200.00	18.50	(6)	3,000.00
J44	50¢ deep claret	125.00	20.00	(6)	1,750.00
Issue of 1910-12, Design of J33, Wmkd. (190)					
J45	1¢ deep claret	15.00	2.00	(6)	350.00
J46	2¢ deep claret	15.00	.15	(6)	325.00
J47	3¢ deep claret	225.00	10.00	(6)	3,000.00
J48	5¢ deep claret	35.00	2.00	(6)	500.00
J49	10¢ deep claret	40.00	6.00	(6)	1,000.00
J50	50¢ deep claret	450.00	50.00	(6)	5,500.00
Issue of 1914-15, Design of J33, Perf. 10					
J52	1¢ carmine lake	32.50	6.00	(6)	500.00
J53	2¢ carmine lake	15.00	.15	(6)	275.00
J54	3¢ carmine lake	250.00	8.50	(6)	3,500.00
J55	5¢ carmine lake	15.00	1.50	(6)	250.00
J56	10¢ carmine lake	25.00	.85	(6)	500.00
J57	30¢ carmine lake	110.00	12.00	(6)	2,000.00
J58	50¢ carmine lake	4,000.00	285.00	(6)	25,000.00
Issue of 1916, Design of J33, Unwmkd.					
J59	1¢ rose	675.00	120.00	(6)	6,000.00
J60	2¢ rose	55.00	2.50	(6)	650.00
Issue of 1917, Design of J33, Perf. 11					
J61	1¢ carmine rose	1.50	.05	(6)	35.00
J62	2¢ carmine rose	1.25	.04	(6)	30.00
J63	3¢ carmine rose	6.00	.08	(6)	75.00
J64	5¢ carmine	6.00	.08	(6)	75.00
J65	10¢ carmine rose	9.00	.20	(6)	110.00
J66	30¢ carmine rose	40.00	.50	(6)	425.00
J67	50¢ carmine rose	45.00	.12	(6)	450.00

		Un	U	#	PB	FDC
	Issue of 1925, Design of J33					
J68	½¢ dull red	.50	.06	(6)	10.00	
	Issue of 1930-31, Design of J69					
J69	½¢ Figure of Value	3.50	.70	(6)	30.00	
J70	1¢ carmine	2.50	.15	(6)	25.00	
J71	2¢ carmine	3.50	.15	(6)	35.00	
J72	3¢ carmine	17.50	.85	(6)	200.00	
J73	5¢ carmine	17.50	1.50	(6)	175.00	
J74	10¢ carmine	25.00	.50	(6)	300.00	
J75	30¢ carmine	110.00	1.00	(6)	900.00	
J76	50¢ carmine	120.00	.30	(6)	1,000.00	
	Design of J78					
J77	$1 carmine	28.50	.12	(6)	225.00	
J78	$5 "FIVE" on $	45.00	.18	(6)	350.00	
	Issue of 1931-56, Design of J69, Perf. 11x10½					
J79	½¢ dull carmine	1.25	.08		20.00	
J80	1¢ dull carmine	.15	.03		2.00	
J81	2¢ dull carmine	.15	.03		2.00	
J82	3¢ dull carmine	.25	.03		3.00	
J83	5¢ dull carmine	.35	.03		4.00	
J84	10¢ dull carmine	1.00	.03		7.50	
J85	30¢ dull carmine	8.50	.08		40.00	
J86	50¢ dull carmine	9.50	.06		50.00	
	Perf. 10½x11					
J87	$1 scarlet, same design as J78	45.00	.20		300.00	
	Issue of 1959, Perf. 11x10½, Design of J88 and J98					
J88	½¢ Figure of Value	1.00	.70		125.00	
J89	1¢ carmine rose	.04	.04		.50	
J90	2¢ carmine rose	.06	.05		.60	
J91	3¢ carmine rose	.07	.04		.70	
J92	4¢ carmine rose	.08	.04		1.25	
J93	5¢ carmine rose	.10	.04		.75	
J94	6¢ carmine rose	.12	.05		1.40	
J95	7¢ carmine rose	.14	.05		1.60	
J96	8¢ carmine rose	.16	.05		1.75	
J97	10¢ carmine rose	.20	.04		1.25	
J98	30¢ Figure of Value	.70	.05		5.50	
J99	50¢ carmine rose	1.10	.06		6.50	
	Design of J101					
J100	$1 carmine rose	2.00	.06		10.00	
J101	$5 Outline Figure of Value	8.00	.15		40.00	
	Design of J88					
J102	11¢ carmine rose	.22	.04		1.10	
J103	13¢ carmine rose	.26	.04		1.30	

J69

J78

Parcel Post Postage Due Stamps

For affixing by a postal clerk to any parcel post package to denote the amount to be collected from the addressee because of insufficient prepayment of postage.

Beginning July 1, 1913, these stamps were valid for use as regular postage due stamps.

	Issue of 1912, Design of JQ1 and JQ5, Perf. 12		
JQ1	1¢ Figure of Value	8.50	3.00
JQ2	2¢ dark green	75.00	15.00
JQ3	5¢ dark green	9.00	3.50
JQ4	10¢ dark green	135.00	35.00
JQ5	25¢ Figure of Value	65.00	3.50

J88

J98

NEW PLATE SYSTEM

Under a new plate numbering system devised by the U.S. Postal Service and adopted on January 1, 1981, collectors of plate blocks will for the first time be able to track a full, consistent history of all issues, regardless of the format in which they were printed.

Up to now, it was not possible, by looking at a pane of stamps, to determine that pane's place in the manufacture of the issue. The collecting of plate blocks will also be less expensive. Under the new system, the cost (at present postal rates) of a typical, 18¢ stamp, six-color gravure plate block will be 72 cents instead of $2.16.

According to the improved classification, a plate block will consist of four stamps (except in cases where more than four designs appear in the pane), regardless of the number of inks or the type of press used. Offset plate numbers will no longer be trimmed off, but will remain on the selvage of panes; and plate numbers will now be printed on booklet panes and, at intervals, on coil stamps. For a more detailed explanation of the new plate numbering system, write to: Plate Number Information, Philatelic Sales Division, Washington, DC 20265-9997.

J101

JQ1

JQ5

OFFICIAL POSTAGE STAMPS

O7   O14   O18   O34   O44

O52   O57   O76   O91

O71

O93   O95

Official Stamps

The franking privilege having been abolished, as of July 1, 1873, these stamps were provided for each of the departments of Government for the prepayment on official matter.

These stamps were supplanted on May 1, 1879 by penalty envelopes and on July 5, 1884 were declared obsolete.

Designs are as follows: Post Office officials, figures of value and department name; all other departments, various portraits and department names.

Issues of 1873
Printed by the Continental Bank Note Co. Thin Hard Paper
Dept. of Agriculture: Yellow

		Un	U
O1	1¢ Franklin	45.00	25.00
O2	2¢ Jackson	27.50	12.00
O3	3¢ Washington	23.50	3.50
O4	6¢ Lincoln	30.00	11.50
O5	10¢ Jefferson	70.00	42.50
O6	12¢ Clay	115.00	60.00
O7	15¢ Webster	70.00	42.50
O8	24¢ Winfield Scott	85.00	50.00
O9	30¢ Hamilton	120.00	67.50

Executive Dept.

		Un	U
O10	1¢ carmine, Franklin	175.00	85.00
O11	2¢ Jackson	120.00	70.00
O12	3¢ carmine, Washington	135.00	60.00
O13	6¢ carmine, Lincoln	225.00	125.00
O14	10¢ Jefferson	185.00	120.00

Dept. of the Interior: Vermilion

		Un	U
O15	1¢ Franklin	9.00	2.25
O16	2¢ Jackson	8.00	1.50
O17	3¢ Washington	16.50	1.50
O18	6¢ Lincoln	12.50	1.50
O19	10¢ Jefferson	10.00	3.50
O20	12¢ Clay	16.00	2.50
O21	15¢ Webster	32.50	7.25
O22	24¢ W. Scott	25.00	5.50
O23	30¢ Hamilton	25.00	5.75
O24	90¢ Perry	65.00	12.50

Dept. of Justice: Purple

		Un	U
O25	1¢ Franklin	21.00	14.00
O26	2¢ Jackson	45.00	18.50
O27	3¢ Washington	55.00	7.00
O28	6¢ Lincoln	42.50	10.00
O29	10¢ Jefferson	47.50	21.00

		Un	U
O30	12¢ Clay	22.50	10.00
O31	15¢ Webster	75.00	40.00
O32	24¢ W. Scott	235.00	100.00
O33	30¢ Hamilton	200.00	75.00
O34	90¢ Perry	325.00	150.00

Navy Dept.: Ultramarine

		Un	U
O35	1¢ Franklin	25.00	10.00
O36	2¢ Jackson	16.50	8.00
O37	3¢ Washington	17.50	3.00
O38	6¢ Lincoln	14.00	4.50
O39	7¢ Stanton	130.00	50.00
O40	10¢ Jefferson	22.50	10.00
O41	12¢ Clay	32.50	8.25
O42	15¢ Webster	55.00	20.00
O43	24¢ W. Scott	55.00	30.00
O44	30¢ Hamilton	45.00	12.50
O45	90¢ Perry	235.00	80.00

Post Office Dept.: Black

		Un	U
O47	1¢ Figure of Value	7.25	3.00
O48	2¢ Figure of Value	7.00	2.50
O49	3¢ Figure of Value	2.50	.75
O50	6¢ Figure of Value	7.00	1.65
O51	10¢ Figure of Value	32.50	16.50
O52	12¢ Figure of Value	13.50	3.75
O53	15¢ Figure of Value	17.50	6.50
O54	24¢ Figure of Value	21.00	8.25
O55	30¢ Figure of Value	21.00	7.00
O56	90¢ Figure of Value	32.50	9.50

Dept. of State

		Un	U
O57	1¢ dark green Franklin	25.00	9.50
O58	2¢ dark green Jackson	55.00	22.50
O59	3¢ bright green Washington	18.50	7.50
O60	6¢ bright green Lincoln	16.00	7.50
O61	7¢ dark green Stanton	42.50	14.00
O62	10¢ dark green Jefferson	25.00	11.50
O63	12¢ dark green Clay	52.50	27.50
O64	15¢ dark green Webster	37.50	15.00
O65	24¢ dark green W. Scott	130.00	70.00
O66	30¢ Hamilton	110.00	50.00

		Un	U
	1873 continued		
O67	90¢ dark green Perry	250.00	110.00
O68	$2 green and black		
	Seward	475.00	225.00
O69	$5 green and black		
	Seward	3,750.00	2,000.00
O70	$10 green and black		
	Seward	2,350.00	1,300.00
O71	$20 Seward	2,000.00	1,100.00
	Treasury Dept.: Brown		
O72	1¢ Franklin	10.00	1.75
O73	2¢ Jackson	13.50	1.75
O74	3¢ Washington	7.00	1.00
O75	6¢ Lincoln	13.50	1.00
O76	7¢ Stanton	27.50	9.50
O77	10¢ Jefferson	25.00	3.50
O78	12¢ Clay	25.00	1.50
O79	15¢ Webster	28.50	3.25
O80	24¢ W. Scott	130.00	40.00
O81	30¢ Hamilton	35.00	3.25
O82	90¢ Perry	42.50	3.00
	War Dept.: Rose		
O83	1¢ Franklin	40.00	3.25
O84	2¢ Jackson	40.00	5.00
O85	3¢ Washington	37.50	1.00
O86	6¢ Lincoln	135.00	2.50
O87	7¢ Stanton	35.00	20.00
O88	10¢ Jefferson	11.50	3.00
O89	12¢ Clay	37.50	2.00
O90	15¢ Webster	9.00	1.20
O91	24¢ W. Scott	10.00	1.75
O92	30¢ Hamilton	10.00	1.50
O93	90¢ Perry	25.00	10.00
	Issues of 1879 **Printed by the American Bank Note Co. Soft, Porous Paper, Dept. of Agriculture: Yellow**		
O94	1¢ Franklin, issued		
	without gum	1,100.00	
O95	3¢ Washington	130.00	21.00
	Dept. of the Interior: Vermilion		
O96	1¢ Franklin	90.00	55.00
O97	2¢ Jackson	2.50	.75
O98	3¢ Washington	2.00	.60
O99	6¢ Lincoln	3.00	1.00

		Un	U
O100	10¢ Jefferson	25.00	15.00
O101	12¢ Clay	40.00	25.00
O102	15¢ Webster	90.00	55.00
O103	24¢ W. Scott	1,000.00	
	Dept. of Justice: Bluish Purple		
O106	3¢ Washington	35.00	16.50
O107	6¢ Lincoln	85.00	57.50
	Post Office Dept.: Black		
O108	3¢ Figure of Value	4.75	1.40
	Treasury Dept.: Brown		
O109	3¢ Washington	13.50	2.50
O110	6¢ Lincoln	27.50	15.00
O111	10¢ Jefferson	45.00	13.00
O112	30¢ Hamilton	675.00	135.00
O113	90¢ Perry	525.00	125.00
	War Dept.: Rose Red		
O114	1¢ Franklin	1.75	.75
O115	2¢ Jackson	2.25	1.00
O116	3¢ Washington	2.25	.65
O117	6¢ Lincoln	2.00	.70
O118	10¢ Jefferson	12.00	6.00
O119	12¢ Clay	10.00	1.75
O120	30¢ Hamilton	30.00	22.50

Official Postal Savings Mail, Perf. 12
These stamps were used to prepay postage on official correspondence of the Postal Savings Division of the Post Office Department. Discontinued Sept. 23, 1914.

	Issues of 1911, Wmkd. (191)	Un	U
O121	2¢ Official Postal		
	Savings	8.50	1.10
O122	50¢ Official Postal		
	Savings	90.00	32.50
O123	$1 Official Postal		
	Savings	80.00	9.50
	Wmkd. (190)		
O124	1¢ Official Postal		
	Savings	4.00	1.00
O125	2¢ Official Postal		
	Savings	25.00	3.50
O126	10¢ Official Postal		
	Savings	8.50	1.00

O101   O114

O121

FANCY CANCELLATIONS

"The message is the medium" might have been the motto of John Hill, postmaster of Waterbury, Connecticut, about a century ago. Hill was an unusual artist: his "canvas" was the envelope, his medium the cork or wood that served as a cancelling device.

Hill's cancellations and those of his local associates became known as the Waterbury fancy cancels—the most famous of which was Hill's Running Chicken. The design was inspired by a return card of that period which pictured a chicken chasing a grasshopper, and the words, "If you don't catch him in 5 days, return to . . ."

Though it was used for only about three days during November, 1869, the cancellation went through a number of minor changes, including lengthening of the distance between the wings and removal of the rear claw. Only a handful of examples are known to exist, one of them discovered just a few years ago on a revenue stamp. The famous Running Chicken cover, bearing three separate strikes of the cancellation, was auctioned in 1979 for a record $240,000.

NEWSPAPER STAMPS
PARCEL POST STAMPS

PR1   PR2   PR3

PR15   PR18   PR24   PR25   PR26

		Un	U
Newspaper Stamps			
Perf. 12, Issues of 1865			
Printed by the National Bank Note Co.,			
Thin, Hard Paper, No Gum, Unwmkd.,			
Colored Borders			
PR1	5¢ Washington	110.00	
PR2	10¢ Franklin	45.00	
PR3	25¢ Lincoln	50.00	
White Border, Yellowish Paper			
PR4	5¢ light blue (PR1)	22.50	20.00
Reprints of 1875			
Printed by the Continental Bank Note			
Co., Hard, White Paper, No Gum			
PR5	5¢ dull blue (PR1),		
	white border	40.00	
PR6	10¢ dark bluish green,		
	(PR2), colored border	27.50	
PR7	25¢ dark carmine		
	(PR3), colored border	55.00	
Issue of 1880			
Printed by the American Bank Note			
Co., Soft, Porous Paper, White Border			
PR8	5¢ dark blue (PR1)	85.00	

		Un	U
Issue of 1875			
Printed by the Continental Bank Note			
Co., Thin, Hard Paper			
PR9-PR15; "Statue of Freedom" (PR15)			
PR9	2¢ black	6.50	6.50
PR10	3¢ black	8.50	8.50
PR11	4¢ black	7.50	7.50
PR12	6¢ black	9.50	9.50
PR13	8¢ black	14.00	14.00
PR14	9¢ black	24.00	24.00
PR15	10¢ Statue of Freedom	15.00	10.00
PR16-PR23: "Justice" (PR18)			
PR16	12¢ rose	25.00	15.00
PR17	24¢ rose	37.50	25.00
PR22	84¢ rose	115.00	80.00
PR23	96¢ rose	85.00	75.00
PR24	$1.92 Ceres	100.00	75.00
PR25	$3 "Victory"	135.00	100.00
PR26	$6 Clio	265.00	135.00

RAILWAY POST OFFICES

The Railway Post Office system came into existence at a time when postal efficiency was at a low ebb. One western editor was fond of remarking that "our town now has a bi-weekly mail service—the mail goes out one week and tries to come in the next."

Things changed with the inauguration of the RPOs in 1864. The idea of processing the mail on railroad cars got its start on the Hannibal and Saint Joseph Railroad, where the assistant postmaster would often board the train before it reached its destination to get a headstart on sorting the mail. But the first "official" RPO ran between Chicago and Clinton, Iowa. The system was soon regarded as a "wonder of the age" and quickly spread to all the important railroad mail routes.

But the RPO may not have been regarded as a "wonder" by the clerks who rode the trains. With as many as 20 men working in a 60-foot car, conditions were cramped. Rough road beds and high speeds added to the discomfort, and there were the very real threats of train wrecks, derailments and occasional holdups.

The RPO reached its heyday in the 1920s and 30s. But as passenger service diminished, so did the railway post offices, and on June 30, 1977, after 104 years of operation, the last RPO, operating between New York and Washington, D.C., made its final run.

	Un	U
1875 continued		
PR27	$9 Minerva	350.00	165.00
PR28	$12 Vesta	375.00	185.00
PR29	$24 "Peace"	375.00	200.00
PR30	$36 "Commerce"	425.00	250.00
PR31	$48 red brown Hebe		
	(PR78)	575.00	350.00
PR32	$60 violet Indian		
	Maiden (PR79)	575.00	325.00

Special Printing, Hard, White Paper, Without Gum

PR33-PR39: Statue of Freedom (PR15)

PR33	2¢ gray black	50.00	
PR34	3¢ gray black	60.00	
PR35	4¢ gray black	70.00	
PR36	6¢ gray black	85.00	
PR37	8¢ gray black	100.00	
PR38	9¢ gray black	110.00	
PR39	10¢ gray black	125.00	

PR40-PR47: "Justice" (PR18)

PR40	12¢ pale rose	140.00	
PR41	24¢ pale rose	175.00	
PR42	36¢ pale rose	250.00	
PR43	48¢ pale rose	300.00	
PR44	60¢ pale rose	375.00	
PR45	72¢ pale rose	525.00	
PR46	84¢ pale rose	550.00	
PR47	96¢ pale rose	700.00	
PR48	$1.92 dark brown		
	Ceres (PR24)	*2,000.00*	
PR49	$3 vermilion "Victory"		
	(PR25)	*4,500.00*	
PR50	$6 ultra. Clio (PR26)	*5,000.00*	
PR51	$9 yel. Minerva		
	(PR27)	*7,500.00*	
PR52	$12 bl. grn. Vesta		
	(PR28)	*10,000.00*	
PR53	$24 dark gray violet		
	"Peace" (PR29)	____	
PR54	$36 brown rose		
	"Commerce" (PR30)	____	
PR55	$48 red brown Hebe		
	(PR78)	____	

	Un	U
PR56	$60 violet Indian		
	Maiden (PR79)	____	

All values of this issue Nos. PR33 to PR56 exist imperforate but were not regularly issued.

Issue of 1879
Printed by the American Bank Note Co., Soft, Porous Paper

PR57-PR62: Statue of Freedom (PR15)

PR57	2¢ black	4.00	3.50
PR58	3¢ black	5.00	4.50
PR59	4¢ black	5.00	4.50
PR60	6¢ black	10.50	9.00
PR61	8¢ black	10.50	9.00
PR62	10¢ black	10.00	9.00

PR63-PR70: "Justice" (PR18)

PR63	12¢ red	30.00	20.00
PR64	24¢ red	30.00	18.50
PR65	36¢ red	100.00	75.00
PR66	48¢ red	77.50	50.00
PR67	60¢ red	60.00	50.00
PR68	72¢ red	135.00	80.00
PR69	84¢ red	100.00	75.00
PR70	96¢ red	77.50	55.00
PR71	$1.92 pale brown		
	Ceres (PR24)	60.00	50.00
PR72	$3 red vermilion		
	"Victory" (PR25)	60.00	50.00
PR73	$6 blue Clio (PR26)	100.00	65.00
PR74	$9 org. Minerva		
	(PR27)	67.50	45.00
PR75	$12 yellow green		
	Vesta (PR28)	100.00	70.00
PR76	$24 dark violet		
	"Peace" (PR29)	135.00	90.00
PR77	$36 Indian red		
	"Commerce" (PR30)	175.00	110.00
PR78	$48 Hebe	225.00	125.00
PR79	$60 Indian Maiden	250.00	125.00

All values of the 1879 issue except Nos. PR63 to PR66 and PR68 to PR70 exist imperforate but were not regularly issued.

Issue of 1883
Special Printing

PR80	2¢ intense black Statue		
	of Freedom (PR15)	115.00	

PR27

PR28

PR29

PR30

PR78

PR79

HIGHWAY POST OFFICES

On February 10, 1941, a "rolling post office" made its way from Washington, D.C. to Harrisonburg, Virginia—the inaugural route of the Highway Post Office system for carrying cross-country mail.

Orville Liskey, who made the original run, was still riding the "Wash-Harris HPO" 20 years later. "At one time or another," he recalled, "we carried everything that was mailable." Over the years, that included "mail" ranging from Virginia hams to 10,000 chirping chicks, from lizards and queen bees to $800,000 in cash.

One item that the route would not handle, however, was a dead duck. Reportedly, one elderly man persistently tried to mail the mallards, tying address tags to their feet and slapping stamps on their beaks. But the HPO refused to carry them.

Despite the fact that nearly 200 routes were in service by the late 1950s, the HPOs didn't last. The Post Office Department initiated a system of processing mail in stationary offices, and by the late 1960s, almost all the highway routes, including the original one, were eliminated.

GUMMED STAMPS

When the world's first gummed postage stamp was issued in Great Britain in 1840, it met with some opposition. The protestors claimed the glued bits of paper would never work. Servants would pocket the money and send the letters collect, they said. Or the adhesive wouldn't stick, and the stamp would fall off in the mail (which was sometimes true). Or the postmaster would take the money and then fail to put a stamp on the letter.

Despite the doubters, the "One Penny Black" was an instant success. It was not supposed to be used until May 6, 1840, but when the stamp went on sale May 1, the English purchased 1,600,000 immediately. Queen Victoria was so pleased with the design, which featured her picture and the words "Postage" and "One Penny," that the same profile was used until she died in 1901.

The person responsible for the Penny Black was Sir Rowland Hill, who had urged a uniform postal rate so that all letters could be prepaid according to weight. The method of prepayment: "bits of paper just large enough to bear the stamp and covered at the back with a glutinous wash." This and other postal reforms earned Sir Rowland a second "title," that of "father of the postage stamp."

PR90

PR116

PR118

PR119

PR120

PR121

PR122

PR123

PR124

PR125

	Un	U
Regular Issue of 1885		
PR81 1¢ black Statue of		
Freedom (PR15)	3.50	1.75
PR82-PR89: "Justice" (PR18)		
PR82 12¢ carmine	10.50	6.00
PR83 24¢ carmine	12.00	9.00
PR84 36¢ carmine	17.50	11.00
PR85 48¢ carmine	25.00	18.00
PR86 60¢ carmine	37.50	25.00
PR87 72¢ carmine	47.50	30.00
PR88 84¢ carmine	90.00	65.00
PR89 96¢ carmine	72.50	55.00

All values of the 1885 issue exist imperforate but were not regularly issued.

**Issue of 1894
Printed by the Bureau of Engraving and Printing, Soft Wove Paper**

PR90-PR94: Statue of Freedom (PR90)		
PR90 1¢ Statue of Freedom	16.50	
PR91 2¢ intense black	16.50	
PR92 4¢ intense black	22.50	
PR93 6¢ intense black	700.00	
PR94 10¢ intense black	32.50	
PR95-PR99: "Justice" (PR18)		
PR95 12¢ pink	175.00	
PR96 24¢ pink	160.00	
PR97 36¢ pink	1,100.00	
PR98 60¢ pink	1,100.00	
PR99 96¢ pink	1,750.00	
PR100 $3 scarlet "Victory"		
(PR25)	2,750.00	
PR101 $6 pale blue Clio		
(PR26)	3,500.00	

**Issue of 1895, Unwmkd.
PR102-PR105: Statue of Freedom (PR116)**

PR102 1¢ black	14.00	4.00
PR103 2¢ black	16.50	4.50
PR104 5¢ black	21.00	7.00
PR105 10¢ black	42.50	20.00
PR106 25¢ carmine "Justice"		
(PR118)	52.50	20.00

	Un	U
PR107 50¢ carmine "Justice"		
(PR119)	130.00	65.00
PR108 $2 scarlet "Victory"		
(PR120)	160.00	35.00
PR109 $5 ultra Clio (PR121)	260.00	120.00
PR110 $10 green Vesta		
(PR122)	225.00	120.00
PR111 $20 slate "Peace"		
(PR123)	450.00	225.00
PR112 $50 dull rose		
"Commerce" (PR124)	450.00	225.00
PR113 $100 purple Indian		
Maiden (PR125)	500.00	250.00

**Issue of 1895-97
Wmkd. (191), Yellowish Gum**

PR114-PR117: Statue of Freedom (PR116)

PR114 1¢ black	2.50	2.00
PR115 2¢ black	2.50	1.50
PR116 5¢ black	4.00	3.00
PR117 10¢ black	2.50	2.00
PR118 25¢ "Justice"	4.00	3.75
PR119 50¢ "Justice"	4.25	3.50
PR120 $2 "Victory"	7.50	7.50
PR121 $5 Clio	15.00	16.50
PR122 $10 Vesta	11.50	15.00
PR123 $20 "Peace"	12.50	17.50
PR124 $50 "Commerce"	13.50	17.50
PR125 $100 Indian Maiden	17.50	25.00

In 1899, the Government sold 26,989 sets of these stamps, but, as the stock of the high values was not sufficient to make up the required number, the $5, $10, $20, $50 and $100 were reprinted. These are virtually indistinguishable from earlier printings.

Q1

Q2

Q3

Q4

Q5

Q6

Q7

Q8

Q9

Q10

Q11

Q12

QE1

QE2

QE3

QE4

		Un	U

Parcel Post Stamps
Issued for the prepayment of postage on parcel post packages only.

Beginning July 1, 1913, these stamps were valid for all postal purposes.

Issue of 1912-13, Perf. 12

		Un	U
Q1	1¢ Post Office Clerk	4.50	.90
Q2	2¢ City Carrier	4.50	.70
Q3	3¢ Railway Postal Clerk	11.00	5.00
Q4	4¢ Rural Carrier	30.00	2.00
Q5	5¢ Mail Train	27.50	1.25
Q6	10¢ Steamship and Mail Tender	50.00	1.75
Q7	15¢ Automobile Service	70.00	9.00
Q8	20¢ Airplane Carrying Mail	165.00	17.50
Q9	25¢ Manufacturing	65.00	4.50
Q10	50¢ Dairying	275.00	35.00
Q11	75¢ Harvesting	80.00	25.00
Q12	$1 Fruit Growing	475.00	20.00

Special Handling Stamps
For use on parcel post packages to secure the same expeditious handling accorded to first class mail matter.

Issue of 1925-29, Design of QE3, Perf. 11

		Un	U
QE1	10¢ Special Handling	1.75	.75
QE2	15¢ Special Handling	2.00	.75
QE3	20¢ Special Handling	2.25	1.75
QE4	25¢ Special Handling	30.00	7.50

CONFEDERATE STATES OF AMERICA

1

2

3

5

6

8

9

11

13

14

11

	Un	U
General Issues, All Imperf.		
Issue of 1861: Lithographed, Unwatermarked		
1 5¢ Jefferson Davis	100.00	60.00
2 10¢ Thomas Jefferson	125.00	95.00
Issue of 1862		
3 2¢ Andrew Jackson	350.00	450.00
4 5¢ blue J. Davis (6)	60.00	50.00
5 10¢ Thomas Jefferson	600.00	400.00
Typographed		
6 5¢ J. Davis (London print)	6.00	7.00
7 5¢ blue (6) (local print)	10.00	10.00
Issues of 1863, Engraved		
8 2¢ Andrew Jackson	35.00	*150.00*

	Un	U
Thick or Thin Paper		
9 10¢ Jefferson Davis	400.00	275.00
10 10¢ blue (9), (with rectangular frame)	2,250.00	1,250.00
Prices of No. 10 are for copies showing parts of lines on at least two sides of frame.		
11 10¢ Jefferson Davis, die A	7.00	8.00
12 10¢ blue J. Davis, die B (11)	7.50	8.50
Dies A and B differ in that B has an extra line outside its corner ornaments.		
13 20¢ George Washington	22.50	*150.00*
Issue of 1862, Typographed		
14 1¢ John C. Calhoun	75.00	
(This stamp was never put in use.)		

STAMP CLUBS

What Are Benjamin Franklin Stamp Clubs?

The United States Postal Service began a stamp club program in elementary schools in 1974-75. Its purpose was to introduce fourth, fifth, and sixth grade students to the educational and enjoyable hobby of stamp collecting. Various stamp club materials, a monthly newsletter, and special student-involvement projects are distributed to these stamp clubs free-of-charge by the Postal Service. To date, more than 65,000 clubs have been established, offering over 1,500,000 young students an opportunity to learn a fun-filled and educational hobby.

Why Are These Clubs Named After Ben Franklin?

You know all about Ben Franklin's key and kite experiment, his Franklin stove, his bifocals and his Poor Richard's Almanac. But did you know that Franklin was also the Father of the Postal Service? That's why it's his face that appears on the first postage stamp the U.S. ever issued. And that's why, when the Postal Service decided to help establish stamp clubs in schools all over the country, it thought of calling them Benjamin Franklin Stamp Clubs.

How Does A Typical Stamp Club Get Started?

Because the clubs are primarily intended for fourth, fifth, and sixth grade students, the first place to get a club started is in the schools. Some clubs, however, are begun and sponsored by local community and service organizations like the YMCA, Boy Scouts, and Girl Scouts. These clubs also contain elementary school students in the fourth to sixth grades.

If you think you'd like to start a stamp club, your first task is to find members. So publicize your club with announcements on your school's bulletin boards and in the school newsletters . . . with posters in the windows of cooperating stores, banks and restaurants . . . with announcements in local newspapers and over local radio stations, if they're willing to carry club activity news without charge.

J O I N, or D I E.

The first American cartoon was published by Benjamin Franklin in his Pennsylvania Gazette May 9, 1754. The broken parts of the snake are the divided American colonies.

Your announcements should tell when the club will meet, where, and how a prospective member can get additional information.

You'll want a conveniently located place for your meetings, available at no charge to the club. Usually, this means your school classroom, auditorium or other area in your own elementary school. Sometimes, local libraries, churches, museums, community recreation centers, the "Y" or the homes of club members are more convenient locations because of school and bus schedules.

A *club advisor,* usually an interested school teacher or administrative official, will volunteer to help the new club form and conduct its club meetings. A local Postal Service employee in your area will meet with the advisor and typically make a presentation to interested students. That Postal employee will provide the new club with a full supply of organizing materials, including membership cards and certificates, club by-laws and other educational materials. The Postal Service has prepared a lot of other exciting material to help your club get started and to support its activities. These include color movies, film strips, printed brochures, plus stamp albums. Each member also gets a colorful wallet I.D. card, and membership certificate suitable for framing.

The next step is to elect officers. Initially, the club elects only those officers necessary for the club to function properly. Additional officers can be elected as needed, from the club's expanding membership. The rules to govern the club's activities should be developed by the entire membership as early as possible. These rules can be developed using the sample "by-laws" left with the club advisor.

Another of your early club meetings could consist of a field trip to the local post office. Be sure to telephone the Postmaster in advance to see if he can arrange for a guided tour. While at the post office, have the local Postmaster endorse the club charter to make your club official, if this has not already been done.

How Does A Stamp Club Operate?

The entire membership should participate in planning club activities. And planning should start at the very first meeting. Clubs typically keep the business part of each meeting short, and the pleasure part long.

The pleasure part consists of trading, buying, and selling stamps. Other than that, members can exhibit their collections. Guest speakers can be invited to lecture or conduct question and answer sessions. Films can be shown. Stamp auctions can be organized. Group discussions can be set up. Club members also enjoy stamp quiz shows—like the quiz shows on television, but with questions that deal exclusively with stamps and collecting.

But with all that going on, how will members ever remember what's coming up and when? They'll read about it in the club newsletter. Many clubs issue a weekly or monthly bulletin to keep members informed. It doesn't have to be an elaborate publication, and the duplication method used can be the least expensive. A single sheet of paper would do very nicely, with pertinent club information on one side and a calendar of meetings and upcoming events on the other.

Does the idea of starting a stamp club sound a little crazy? It shouldn't—not if you organize well, distribute the work fairly, and take things step by step.

So become a member of a stamp club—whether you join a Benjamin Franklin Stamp Club at school or an ongoing stamp club in your community. The joy of collecting is multiplied many times over when you share it.

U. S. STAMP PRODUCTION

Each year, from the thousands of requests it receives, the Citizens' Stamp Advisory Committee makes recommendations for new stamp and postal stationery issues. The Postmaster General makes the final determinations based on the Committee's recommendations.

The U.S. Postal Service commissions an artist to design the stamp or stationery item. From the artist's design, the Treasury Department's Bureau of Engraving and Printing prepares an actual-size production model. The engraving process or the color separation process begins after the model is approved and ends with either a printing plate or a printing cylinder. Printing plates and cylinders are produced in various ways—depending upon the printing process being used.

Production Techniques and Equipment Used
The Bureau of Engraving and Printing is the main source of supply of U.S. postage stamps. The following kinds of presses print U.S. Postal Service stamps:

Single Color Intaglio Press. These presses are used to print single-color stamps on a continuous web of pregummed paper. Phosphor is applied to the stamps during the printing operation, and stamps may be precancelled at the same time. These presses produce most of our regular postage stamp issues.

Three-color Intaglio Press (sheet fed). This intaglio press prints stamps in up to three colors on sheets of gummed postage stamp paper that passes through the press once only. Phosphor tagging is applied later by a different process. Many colorful commemorative issues are produced on this press, sometimes in combination with offset printing.

Three-color Intaglio Press (web fed). This intaglio press prints stamps in up to three colors on a continuous web of pregummed postage stamp paper that passes through the press once only. Phosphor tagging is applied by a separate unit attached to the press. Many regular booklet and coil postage stamps are produced on this press.

Six-color Gravure Press. This press can print up to six colors and apply phosphor tagging or a seventh color on continuous webs of either gummed or ungummed rolls. It is capable of producing stamps at speeds up to 900 feet-per-minute, and delivering the finished printings in either sheets or rolls.

Eight-color Gravure/Intaglio Press. This press is capable of printing eight colors—five by gravure and three by intaglio—with one pass through the press. When fully employed, the press can print regular, commemorative, or book stamps on a web of pregummed coated paper, phosphor tag them, precancel them, and print on the back if desired. It also perforates, cuts and delivers the stamps in stacks of 100 sheets. This press can be used to produce stamps by gravure alone, intaglio alone or by the two processes in combination.

Offset Presses. The Bureau applies its six offset presses to a variety of tasks, two of them relating to postage stamp production and the rest to other Government printing requirements. Since the United States does not produce postage stamps via the offset method alone, these presses are used to apply colors to stamps that pass also through intaglio presses. The offset presses are used also to apply phosphor to some postage stamps.

Printing of the Space Achievement Issue

The U.S. Space Achievement stamps, issued in May, 1981, were printed in six colors on the gravure press. As the paper went through the press, the **Yellow** ink was applied first, followed by the **Gray** ink. The next color to be applied was **Red.** The fourth plate contained the **Blue. Dark Blue,** the fifth plate, started to bring out greater detail, while the **Black** plate completed the image. Please see the illustrations on page 256 which demonstrate this process.

Yellow

Yellow & **Gray**

Yellow, Gray & **Red**

Yellow, Gray, Red & **Blue**

Yellow, Gray, Red, Blue & **Dark Blue**

Yellow, Gray, Red, Blue, Dark Blue & **Black**

IMPORTANT DATES IN
UNITED STATES POSTAL HISTORY

1639   Ordinance of the general court of Massachusetts designates Richard Fairbanks Tavern as official repository for mail.

1737 – 1753 Benjamin Franklin serves as Postmaster of Philadelphia, PA.

1775   Benjamin Franklin is appointed first Postmaster General by Continental Congress.

1787   The U.S. Constitution authorizes Congress to "establish Post Office."

1789   Congress establishes Post Offices and Office of the Postmaster General; Samuel Osgood appointed first Postmaster under U.S. Constitution.

1842   Postage stamps are introduced in the United States by a private firm, Greig's City Despatch Post of New York.

1845   Some United States Postmasters begin to provide special stamps of local origin to show prepayment of mail. These stamps are called Postmaster's Provisionals and are usually very rare.

1847   The U.S. government issues its first postage stamps (Scott's Nos. 1 and 2).

1855   Prepayment of postage is made compulsory.

1855   Registry service is inaugurated.

1860 – 1861 The Pony Express, a privately operated line which carries letters and special news slips, offers a six-day schedule between San Francisco and St. Joseph, Missouri.

1873   Postal cards first introduced.

1876   The introduction of the first practical canceling machines marks the beginning of a Postal mechanization program that has increased with intensity each year.

1885   Special Delivery service is inaugurated.

1918   Air Mail service is begun. By 1924 the United States has 24-hour transcontinental Air Mail service.

1920   On November 15, the metered mail system is approved and inaugurated.

1969   On July 20, the first postage stamp is cancelled on the moon by Apollo 11 Astronaut Neil Armstrong.

1971   The United States Postal Service is established on the moon by Apollo 15 Astronauts David Scott and James Irwin.

1971   The United States Postal Service, an independent establishment of the Executive Branch of the Government, assumes operation of the United States Post Office Department.

1974   Highway Post Offices are terminated.

1975   America's Postal Service celebrates its 200th anniversary.

1977   Airmail is abolished as a separate rate category.

1977   The Railway Mail service, established in 1864, makes its final run June 30.

1978   Postage stamps and other philatelic items are copyrighted by the U.S. Postal Service.

1978   The U.S. Postal Service awards a contract to a private printing firm for the printing of four commemorative stamps for issuance during 1979 and 1980. These stamps are: John Paul Jones; Benjamin Banneker; Veterans Administration; American Education.

SPECIALTY COLLECTING

Specialty collecting hasn't anything to do with the subject matter of the stamps you collect. It refers strictly to the form in which you collect them.

Blocks of Four A block of four, with two mint stamps above and two below, can come from anywhere on a sheet of stamps. That makes it the most plentiful form of block and the easiest to come by.

Booklet Panes Stamp booklets were first issued in 1898. On the average, two new booklet panes are issued per year. Most philatelists collect entire panes of entire booklets, just as they came from the post office. The first combination pane, consisting of one 9¢ Freedom to Assemble stamp and seven 13¢ Flag stamps was issued March 11, 1977.

Covers Covers (or envelopes) canceled on a postage stamp's first day of issue are collected with tremendous enthusiasm by a large philatelic audience. On page 259 you'll find a more detailed discussion of first day covers.

Plate Blocks The Postal Service adopted a new plate number system effective January 1, 1981. Except in cases where more than four designs appear in a pane of stamps, the new system establishes a plate block as consisting of four stamps regardless of the number of inks or the press used to print the stamps. The new system permits offset plate numbers to remain on the selvage of panes instead of being trimmed off during production and makes possible the printing of plate numbers on booklet panes and the printing at intervals of plate numbers on coil stamps.

Each color plate or cylinder used initially in the production of a stamp will be designated by the number "1", and the numbers for each plate or cylinder will be grouped in the selvage adjacent to a single stamp. Whenever a plate or a cylinder is replaced during the manufacturing process the number "1" will give way to the number "2" in the color of the plate or cylinder replaced.

"Copyright" Blocks The U.S. Postal Service now copyrights all new stamp designs. The copyright "C" in a circle, followed by "United States Postal Service" or "USPS" and the year, appears in the selvage of each pane. The first copyright inscription appeared January 6, 1978, in the margin of sheets of the Carl Sandburg stamp. Most philatelists collect copyrights in blocks of four.

"Mr. ZIP" Blocks The Zoning Improvement Plan—better known as ZIP Code— was devised to increase postal efficiency. And it succeeded dramatically. A "Mr. ZIP" cartoon and slogan were inaugurated January 10, 1964, with the Sam Houston issue. The cartoon and slogan with adjoining block of four immediately became a popular collectible.

Souvenir Cards In 1938 and 1939, the Postal Office Department Philatelic Truck toured the country distributing souvenir sheets that pictured the White House. They were the forerunners of the modern souvenir card. For more detailed information on souvenir cards, see page 262-263.

FIRST DAY COVERS

A first-day cover is an envelope that bears a new stamp cancelled on the first-day of the issue at the post office designated to conduct the first-day ceremonies.

For each new stamp or postal stationery issue, the Postal Service designates one post office where the item is first placed on sale. Usually it's a post office that is in some way related to the subject the stamp commemorates. Other post offices place the stamp on sale the following day.

Here's how you can secure a first-day cover through the Postal Service:

The date and place of issue of new stamps are announced by the Postal Service in the press and on post office bulletin board posters.

When the stamps go on sale at your post office, you can buy them and affix them to your own envelopes. Your stamped and addressed envelopes (peelable labels are permitted) should be mailed inside another envelope to "Customer Affixed Envelopes," care of the Postmaster of the designated first day city. The post office will cancel the envelope and return it to you through the mail. All first-day cover requests must be postmarked no later than 15 days from the date of issuance to qualify for cancellation service.

Or, you can send your pre-addressed envelope to the Name of stamp or postal stationery issue, care of the Postmaster of the designated first day city, and the first-day post office will affix the new stamp. You must include payment to cover the total face value of the stamps that will be affixed. Do not send cash. Payment can be made by check, bank draft, or U.S. Postal money order, payable to the U.S. Postal Service.

The envelope you send for your first-day cover can be plain or cacheted. A cacheted envelope carries a special design at the left. The Postal Service doesn't provide cacheted envelopes, but you can buy them from stamp dealers as well as some department and stationery stores. If you ever receive a damaged first-day cover, though, you can send it right back and it will be replaced.

First-day cover service is one way the Postal Service accommodates collectors, and they spare no effort to get the cover in the mail without delay. But be patient . . . the volume of requests is high and occasionally a post office is completely swamped. The 10¢ Moon Landing Airmail Stamp of 1969, for example, was affixed to 8,700,000 first-day covers.

POSTAL STATIONERY

There are three items in the category of collectibles called postal stationery: (1) embossed stamped envelopes, (2) postal cards and (3) aerogrammes. They're all available at post offices, and the number of Americans who collect them is growing all the time.

Aerogrammes

An aerogramme is a flat sheet of paper that's specially shaped, fold-marked and gummed so that, after the message is written, it can be sealed for privacy in transit. It's letter and envelope in one, it's intended for air mail only, and it carries a message anywhere in the world at a lower postage rate than air mail.

Aerogrammes are produced by the Bureau of Engraving and Printing on a Seven-Color press. It can execute multicolor stamp designs, apply a phosphor tag and gum the sealing flaps.

Just as is the case with stamped envelopes and postal cards, the Postal Service has stepped up its issuance of commemorative aerogrammes in recent years.

Postal Cards

Plain and simple one-color Government postal cards were first issued May 1, 1873. They stayed plain and simple until 1956, when the first U.S. commemorative postal card came out.

"Visit the USA" was the theme of the first pictorial postal card, issued in 1966. Six years later, a series of five picture postal cards hailed "Tourism Year of the Americas." The backs of the cards featured twenty different U.S. scenic attractions.

Postal cards are manufactured at the Government Printing Office in Washington D.C. Regular one-color cards can come off the four high-speed rotary web presses at a rate of 250,000 an hour. The Government Printing Office's two-color sheet-fed offset presses produce the two-color air mail and multi-color com-memorative cards. Some 800 million postal cards are issued each year by the Postal Service, accounting for approximately 2,500 tons of paper annually.

Stamped Envelopes

In the case of stamped envelopes, the stamp is embossed and printed right onto the envelope rather than separately affixed. In recent years the number of com-memorative stamped envelopes issued by the United States has been on the increase. Multicolor was recently introduced to embossed stamp envelopes.

Stamped envelopes are manufactured for the Postal Service under private con-tract. They're issued in a number of sizes and styles, including the window type.

Stamped envelopes were first issued in June, 1853. In 1865 envelopes bearing the purchaser's printed return address were authorized by law. The average annual issues of stamped envelopes today is in excess of 1 billion.

The record for the largest number of stamped envelopes manufactured in a single day goes all the way back to 1932. A new postal rate was going into effect, and an enormous quantity of envelopes was needed to stock the post offices of the nation. To meet the monumental need, the contractor produced, in a single day, a total of 19,168,000 stamped envelopes.

USA
30c

© USPS 1980

Tour The United States

AEROGRAMME · VIA AIR MAIL · PAR AVION

Aerogramme

② Second fold

③ Seal top flap last

③ Seal top flap last

Postal Card

USA IOc

Battle of Cowpens, 1781

15c
USA

AMERICA'S CUP

Stamped Envelope

SOUVENIR CARDS

These cards were issued as souvenirs of the philatelic gatherings at which they were distributed by the United States Postal Service, its predecessor the United States Post Office Department, or the Bureau of Engraving and Printing. They were not valid for postage.

Most of the cards bear reproductions of United States stamps with the design enlarged or altered. The U.S. reproductions are engraved except stamps Nos. 914, 1396, 1460-1462 and C85. The cards are not perforated.

For information regarding current availability of souvenir cards, send postal card following page 256.

A forerunner of the souvenir cards is the 1938 Philatelic Truck souvenir sheet which the Post Office Department issued and distributed in various cities visited by the Philatelic Truck. It shows the White House, printed in blue on white paper. Issued with and without gum. Price, with gum, $115, without gum, $20.

United States Post Office & United States Postal Service

1960 Barcelona, 1st International Philatelic Congress, Mar. 26-Apr. 5. Enlarged vignette, Landing of Columbus from No. 231. Printed in black. 400.00

1968 EFIMEX , International Philatelic Exhibition, Nov. 1-9, Mexico City, Card of 1. No. 292, inscribed in Spanish. 6.00

1970 PHILYMPIA, London International Stamp Exhibition, Sept. 18-26. Card of 3. Nos. 548-550. 4.50

1971 EXFILIMA 71, 3rd Inter-American Philatelic Exhibition, Nov. 6-14, Lima, Peru. Card of 3. Nos. 1111 and 1126, Peru No. 360. Card inscribed in Spanish. 3.50

1972 BELGICA 72, Brussels International Philatelic Exhibition, June 24-July 9. Brussels, Belgium. Card of 3. Nos. 914, 1026 and 1104. Card inscribed in Flemish and French. 3.50
OLYMPIA PHILATELIC MÜNCHEN 72, Aug. 18-Sept. 10, Munich, Germany. Card of 4. Nos. 1460-1462 and C85. Card inscribed in German. 3.75
EXFILBRA 72, 4th Inter-American Philatelic Exhibition, Aug. 26-Sept. 2, Rio de Janeiro, Brazil. Card of 3. No. C14, Brazil Nos. C18-C19. Card inscribed in Portuguese. 3.50
NATIONAL POSTAL FORUM VI, Aug. 28-30, Washington, D.C. Card of 4. No. 1396. 3.50

1973 IBRA 73 Internationale Briefmarken Ausstellung, May 11-20, Munich, Germany. With one No. C13. 4.00
APEX 73, International Airmail Exhibition, July 4-7, Manchester, England. Card of 3. Newfoundland No. C4, U.S. No. C3a and Honduras No. C12. 3.50
POLSKA 73, Swiatowa Wystawa Filatelistyczna, Aug. 19-Sept. 2, Poznan, Poland. Card of 3. No. 1488 and Poland Nos. 1944-1945. Card inscribed in Polish. 4.00
POSTAL PEOPLE CARD, Card of 10 (#1489-1498) distributed to Postal Service employees. Not available to public. 14x11".

1974 HOBBY, The Hobby Industry Association of America Convention and Trade Show, February 3-6, Chicago, Illinois. Card of 4. Nos. 1456-1459. 4.00
INTERNABA, International Philatelic Exhibition, June 7-16, Basel, Switzerland. Card of 8, strip of Nos. 1530-1537. Card inscribed in 4 languages. 4.00
STOCKHOLMIA 74, International frimarksutställning, September 21-29, Stockholm, Sweden. Card of 3. No. 836, Sweden Nos. 300 and 765. Card inscribed in Swedish. 4.50
EXFILMEX 74 UPU, Philatelic Exposition Inter-Americana, October 26-November 3, Mexico City, Mexico. Card of 2. No. 1157 and Mexico No. 910. Card inscribed in Spanish and English. 4.50

1975 ESPANA 75, World Stamp Exhibition, Apr. 4-13, Madrid, Spain. Card of 3. Nos. 233, 1271 and Spain No. 1312. Card inscribed in Spanish. 4.00
ARPHILA 75, June 6-16, Paris, France. Card of 3. Nos. 1187, 1207 and France No. 1117. Card inscribed in French. 3.50

1976 WERABA 76, Third International Space Stamp Exhibition, April 1-4, Zurich, Switzerland. Card of 2. Nos. 1434 and 1435 setenant. 4.00
BICENTENNIAL EXPOSITION on Science and Technology, May 30-Sept. 6, Kennedy Space Center, Fla. Card of 1. No. C76. 5.50
COLORADO STATEHOOD CENTENNIAL, August 1, Card of 3. Nos. 743, 288 and 1670. 5.00
HAFNIA 76, International Stamp Exhibition, Aug. 20-29, Copenhagen, Denmark. Card of 2. No. 5 and Denmark No. 2. Card inscribed in Danish and English. 5.00
ITALIA 76, International Philatelic Exhibition, Oct. 14-24, Milan, Italy. Card of 3. No. 1168 and Italy Nos. 578 and 601. Card inscribed in Italian. 4.00
NORDPOSTA 76, North German Stamp Exhibition, Oct. 30-31, Hamburg, Germany. Card of 3. No. 689 and Germany Nos. B366 and B417. Card inscribed in German. 5.00

1977 AMPHILEX 77, International Philatelic Exhibition, May 26-June 5, Amsterdam, Netherlands. Card of 3. No. 1027 and Netherlands Nos. 41 and 294. Card inscribed in Dutch. 4.50

SAN MARINO 77, International Philatelic Exhibition, Aug. 28-Sept. 4, San Marino. Card of 3. Nos.
1-2 and San Marino No. 1. Card inscribed in
Italian. 5.00

1978 ROCPEX 78, International Philatelic
Exhibition, Mar. 20-29, Taipei, Taiwan. Card of 6.
Nos. 1706-1709 and Taiwan Nos. 1812 and 1816.
Card inscribed in Chinese. 4.00
NAPOSTA 78, Philatelic Exhibition, May 20-25,
Frankfurt, Germany. Card of 3. Nos. 555, 563 and
Germany No. 1216. Card inscribed in German. 4.00

1979 BRASILIANA 79, International Philatelic
Exhibition, Sept. 15-23, Rio de Janeiro, Brazil.
Card of 3. Nos. C 91—C 92 (C 92a) and Brazil
No. A 704. Card inscribed in Portuguese. 3.50
JAPEX 79, International Philatelic Exhibition,
Nov. 2-4, Tokyo, Japan. Card of 2. Nos. 1158 and
Japan No. A 674. Card inscribed in Japanese.
3.50

1980 LONDON 80—IPEX, May 6-14, London,
England. Card of 1. U.S. 2¢ 1907 No. 329. Card
inscribed in English.
NORWEX 80—IPEX, June 13-22, Oslo, Norway.
1975 Norway stamp and two 1925 Nos. 620-621
(Norse-American Issue). Card inscribed in
Norwegian.
ESSEN 80—IPEX, Nov. 15-19, Essen, West
Germany. Card of 2. 1954 West German and No.
1014 Gutenberg Bible. Card inscribed in German.

1981 WIPA 81, May 22-31, Vienna, Austria. Card
of 2. 1967 Austria and No. 1252 American Music.
NSCM, National Stamp Collecting Month, Oct.
1981. Issued to call attention to special month for
stamp collectors. Card of 2. Nos. 245 and 1918.
Card inscribed in English.
PHILATOKYO 81, International Philatelic Exhibition, Oct. 9-18, Tokyo, Japan. Card of 2. Nos. 1531

and Japan No. 800. Card inscribed in Japanese.
NORDPOSTA 81, North German Stamp Exhibition,
Nov. 7-8, Hamburg, Germany. Card of 2. Nos. 923
and Germany 9NB133. Card inscribed in German.

Bureau of Engraving and Printing
1954 POSTAGE STAMP DESIGN EXHIBITION,
National Philatelic Museum, Mar. 13, Philadelphia. Card of 4. Monochrome views of
Washington, D.C. Inscribed: "Souvenir sheet
designed, engraved and printed by members,
Bureau, Engraving and Printing. / Reissued by
popular request". 625.00

1966 SIPEX, 6th International Philatelic Exhibition, May 21-30, Washington, D.C. Card of 3.
Multicolored views of Washington, D.C. Inscribed
"Sixth International Philatelic Exhibition / Washington, D.C. / Designed, Engraved, and Printed
by Union Members of Bureau of Engraving and
Printing". 210.00

1969 SANDIPEX, San Diego Philatelic Exhibition,
July 16-20, San Diego, Cal. Card of 3. Multicolored
views of Washington, D.C. Inscribed: "Sandipex—
San Diego 200th Anniversary—1769-1969". 80.00
A.S.D.A. National Postage Stamp Show, Nov.
21-23, 1969, New York. Card of 4. No. E4. 30.00

1970 INTERPEX, Mar. 13-15, New York. Card of 4.
Nos. 1027, 1035, C35 and C38. 65.00
COMPEX, Combined Philatelic Exhibition of
Chicagoland, May 29-31, Chicago. Card of 4. No.
C18. 20.00
HAPEX, American Philatelic Society Convention,
Nov. 5-8, Honolulu, Hawaii. Card of 3. Nos. 799,
C46 and C55. 25.00

1971 INTERPEX, Mar. 12-14, New York. Card of 4.
No. 1193. Background includes Nos. 1331-1332,
1371 and C76. 5.00

NORWEX 80

Oslo, Norge   13-22. juni 1980

Nybyggere fra Norge kom til
Amerika i 1825 og hjalp til med aa forme
den nye nasjonen.

Dette suvernir-kort er utgitt for aa
hedre den norske internasjonale
frimerkeutstillingen. Det er reproduksjoner
av to amerikanske frimerker utgitt i 1925,
hvorav den ene forestiller sluppen
"Restaurationen," og den andre et
vikingskip og en reproduksjon av
frimerket utgitt i 1975 av det norske
postverket for aa hedre 150 aar jubileumet
for norsk utvandring til Amerika.

W.F. Bolger

William F. Bolger
Postmaster General

ESSEN 80

Aus Anlass der 3. Internationalen Briefmarkenausstellung in Essen geben wir diese philatelistische Erinnerungskarte mit den Gedenkmarken heraus, die die Vereinigten Staaten von Amerika und die Bundesrepublik Deutschland zu Ehren des 500. Jahrestages des Drucks mit beweglichen Lettern herausbrachten.

Johann Gutenberg druckte 1452 in Mainz die Heilige Bibel. Er setzte damit eine Revolution in Gang, die Lesestoff in grossen Mengen verfügbar machte. Hierdurch wurde eine allgemein verbreitete Lesefähigkeit ein erreichbares Ziel.

Diese Briefmarken dokumentieren die internationale Wertschätzung der schöpferischen Leistung Johann Gutenbergs, und sie unterstreichen die Übereinstimmung, die auf den Gebieten der Philatelie und des Postwesens zwischen den beiden Ländern besteht.

W.F. Bolger

William F. Bolger
Postmaster General

WESTPEX, Western Philatelic Exhibition, Apr. 23-25, San Francisco. Card of 4. Nos. 740, 852, 966 and 997. 4.50

NAPEX 71, National Philatelic Exhibition, May 21-23, Washington, D.C. Card of 3. Nos. 990, 991, 992. 4.50

TEXANEX 71, Texas Philatelic Association and American Philatelic Society conventions, Aug. 26-29, San Antonio, Tex. Card of 3. Nos. 938, 1043 and 1242. 4.50

A.S.D.A. National Postage Stamp Show, Nov. 19-21, New York. Card of 3. Nos. C13-C15. 4.50

ANPHILEX '71, Anniversary Philatelic Exhibition, Nov. 26-Dec. 1, New York. Card of 2. Nos. 1-2. 4.50

1972 INTERPEX, Mar. 17-19, New York. Card of 4. No. 1173. Background includes Nos. 976, 1434-1435 and C69. 4.00

NOPEX, Apr. 6-9, New Orleans. Card of 4. No. 1020. Background includes Nos. 323-327. 3.50

SEPAD 72, Oct. 20-22, Philadelpia. Card of 4. No. 1044. 3.50

A.S.D.A. National Postage Stamp Show, Nov. 17-19, New York. Card of 4. Nos. 883, 863, 868 and 888. 3.00

STAMP EXPO, Nov. 24-26, San Francisco. Card of 4. No. C36. 3.00

1973 INTERPEX, March 9-11, New York. Card of 4. No. 976. 4.00

COMPEX 73, May 25-27, Chicago. Card of 4. No. 245. 4.00

NAPEX 73, Sept. 14-16, Washington, D.C. Card of 4. No. C3. Background includes Nos. C4-C6. 3.50

A.S.D.A. National Postage Stamp Show, Nov. 16-18, New York. Card of 4 No. 908. Foreground includes Nos. 1139-1144. 4.00

STAMP EXPO NORTH, Dec. 7-9, San Francisco. Card of 4. No. C20. 4.00

1974 MILCOPEX, March 8-10, Milwaukee, Wisconsin. Card of 4. No. C43. Background depicts U.P.U. monument at Berne, Switzerland. 5.00

1975 NAPEX 75, May 9-11, Washington, D.C. Card of 4. No. 708. 14.00

INTERNATIONAL WOMEN'S YEAR. Card of 3. Nos. 872, 878 and 959. Reproduction of 1886 dollar bill. 35.00

A.S.D.A. National Postage Stamp Show, Nov. 21-23, New York. Bicentennial series. Card of 4. No. 1003. ". . . and maintain the liberty which we have derived from our ancestors." 57.50

1976 INTERPHIL 76, Seventh International Philatelic Exhibition, May 29-June 6, Philadelphia. Bicentennial series. Card of 4. No. 120. "that all men are created equal." 9.50

STAMP EXPO 76, June 11-13, Los Angeles. Bicentennial series. Card of 4. Nos. 1351, 1352, 1345 and 1348 se-tenant vertically. "when we assumed the soldier, we did not lay aside the citizen". 6.50

1977 MILCOPEX, Milwaukee Philatelic Society, Mar. 4-6, Milwaukee. Card of 2. Nos. 733 and 1128. 5.00

ROMPEX 77, Rocky Mountain Philatelic Exhibition, May 20-22, Denver. Card of 4. No. 1001. 4.00

PURIPEX 77, Silver Anniversary Philatelic Exhibit, Sept. 2-5, San Juan, Puerto Rico. Card of 4. No. 801. 5.00

A.S.D.A. National Postage Stamp Show, Nov. 15-20, New York. Card of 4. No. C45. 4.50

1978 CENJEX 78, Federated Stamp Clubs of New Jersey, 30th annual exhibition, June 23-25, Freehold, N.J. Card of 9. Nos. 646, 680, 689, 1086, 1716 and 4 No. 785. 5.00

1981 STAMP EXPO 81, South International Stamp Collectors Society, Mar. 20-22, Anaheim, CA. Card of 4. No. 1287. 5.00

COMMEMORATIVE PANELS

The Postal Service offers American Commemorative Panels for each new commemorative stamp and special Christmas stamps issued. The series first began September 20, 1972 with the issuance of the Wild Life Commemorative Panel. The panels feature stamps in mint condition complemented by reproductions of steel line engravings and stories behind the commemorated subject. For more information about Commemorative Panels, please see postal card following page 256.

 AMERICAN COMMEMORATIVES

50th Anniversary

Solo Transatlantic Flight

79 Lafayette, 22.00
80 Skilled Hands, 22.00
81 Peace Bridge, 22.00
82 Herkimer at
   Oriskany, 22.00
83 Alta, California, 22.00
84 Articles of
   Confederation, 22.00
85 Talking Pictures, 22.00
86 Surrender at Saratoga,
   22.00
87 Energy Conservation
   & Development, 22.00
88 Washington at
   Valley Forge, 25.00
89 Rural Mailbox, 25.00

1978
90 Carl Sandburg, 12.00
91 Captain Cook, 25.00
92 Harriet Tubman, 12.00
93 American Quilts, 20.00
94 American Dance, 15.00
95 French Alliance, 15.00
96 Dr. Papanicolaou, 15.00
97 Jimmie Rodgers, 12.00
98 Photography, 12.00
99 George M. Cohan, 12.00
100 Viking Missions, 25.00
101 American Owls, 22.00
102 American Trees, 22.00
103 Madonna and Child, 15.00
104 Hobby Horse, 15.00

1979
105 Robert F. Kennedy, 15.00
106 Martin Luther King, Jr.,
    15.00
107 Year of the Child, 15.00
108 John Steinbeck, 12.00
109 Albert Einstein, 25.00
110 Pennsylvania Toleware,
    15.00
111 American Architecture,
    15.00
112 Endangered Flora, 15.00
113 Seeing Eye Dogs, 12.00
114 Special Olympics, 12.00
115 John Paul Jones, 25.00
116 15¢ Olympic Games, 20.00
117 Virgin and Child, 15.00
118 Santa Claus, 15.00
119 Will Rogers, 12.00
120 Vietnam Veterans, 12.00
121 10¢, 31¢ Olympic
    Games, 20.00

1980
122 W.C. Fields, 12.00
123 Winter Olympics, 15.00
124 Benjamin Banneker, 12.00
125 Frances Perkins, 12.00
126 Emily Bissell, 12.00
127 Helen Keller/
    Anne Sullivan, 12.00
128 Veterans Administration,
    12.00
129 General Bernardo
    de Galvez, 15.00
130 Coarl Reefs, 15.00
131 Organized Labor, 12.00
132 Edith Wharton, 12.00
133 American Education, 12.00

134 Northwest Indian Masks,
    12.00
135 American Architecture,
    15.00
136 Stained Glass Window,
    15.00
137 Antique Toys, 15.00

1981
138 Everett Dirksen
139 Whitney M. Young
140 Flowers Block (4)
141 American Red Cross
142 Savings & Loan
143 Space Achievement (8)
144 Professional Management
145 Wildlife Habitat (4)
146 International Year Disabled
147 Edna St. Vincent Millay
148 Architecture (4)
149 Jones/Zaharias
150 James Hoban
151 Frederic Remington
152 Yorktown/Virginia Capes
153 Desert Plants (4)
154 Madonna
155 Teddy Bear
156 John Hanson

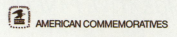

AMERICAN COMMEMORATIVES

Northwest Indian Masks

Tlingit, Bella Coola, Kwak-
iuto, Nezperce. These are but a
few of the strange tribal names of
the earliest inhabitants of the
Pacific Northwest portion of the
American continent.

The remnants of their existence in the area from Yakutat
Bay in southeastern Alaska to
the Columbia River, give evidence of an aesthetic ability that
belies their primitiveness.

Perhaps the most intriguing
aspects of the material culture of
these historic Indian tribes is
their use and design of masks for
religious and social purposes.
While the use of the mask among
American Indians has been
traditional, the tribes of the
Pacific Northwest were among
the first to elevate it to an art
form. From what can be determined, the mask was a fundamental accessory in tribal

dances and religious ceremonies.

The dancing masks, as featured in this commemorative
panel, were most commonly
worn at the "potlatch" — a
lavish festival and feast at which
property was given away or when
dances representing the tradi-
tions of a clan were acted out.
The masks took on a variety of
shapes and forms, often based on
a human or animal creature represented in tribal mythology.

So revered were these pot-
latches, that members went to
great lengths to please and de-
light their hosts by fashioning
the most colorful and realistic
masks possible. A refusal to
attend meant loss of prestige and
rank in a tribal clan.

The endless variation of
motifs and surprising degree of
sophistication found in these
artistic artifacts make them a
hallmark of American Folk Art
in this country today.

These stamps honoring the
artistic achievement of the early
Indian tribes in this country were
designed by Bradbury Thomp-
son, and were issued on September 25, 1980.

Stamps printed by the Bureau of Engraving and Printing, Washington, D.C.

Copyright 1980 United States Postal Service

September 25, 1980 / Printed in U.S.A.

No.134 in a series

SOUVENIR PAGES

The Postal Service offers Souvenir Pages for new stamps. The series began with a page for the Yellowstone Park Centennial stamp issued March 1, 1972. The pages feature one or more stamps tied by the first day cancel, technical data and information on the subject of the issue. More than just collectors' items, Souvenir Pages make wonderful show and conversation pieces. Souvenir Pages are issued in limited editions. For information on becoming a subscriber, see the postal card following page 256.

1972
1 Yellowstone Park, 50.00
2 Cape Hatteras, 50.00
3 Fiorello La Guardia, 50.00
4 City of Refuge, 50.00
5 Wolf Trap Farm, 20.00
6 Colonial Craftsman, 20.00
7 Mount McKinley, 20.00
8 Olympic Games, 15.00
9 Parent Teachers Association, 15.00
10 Wildlife Conservation, 15.00
11 Mail Order, 15.00
12 Osteopathic Medicine, 10.00
13 Tom Sawyer, 10.00
14 Benjamin Franklin, 10.00
15 Christmas, 10.00
16 Pharmacy, 10.00
17 Stamp Collecting, 10.00

1973
18 Eugene O'Neill Coil, 25.00
19 Love, 15.00
20 Pamphleteer, 10.00
21 George Gershwin, 10.00
22 Posting Broadside, 7.00
23 Copernicus, 7.00
24 Postal Service Employees, 10.00
25 Harry S. Truman, 7.00
26 Postrider, 7.00
27 Giannini, 7.00
28 Boston Tea Party, 8.00
29 Progress in Electronics, 7.00
30 Robinson Jeffers, 6.00
31 Lyndon B. Johnson, 6.00
32 Henry O. Tanner, 6.00
33 Willa Cather, 6.00
34 Colonial Drummer, 6.00
35 Angus Cattle, 6.00
36 Christmas, 7.00
37 13¢ Airmail sheet stamp, 5.00
38 10¢ Crossed Flags, 5.00
39 Jefferson Memorial, 5.00
40 13¢ Airmail Coil, 5.00

1974
41 Mount Rushmore, 5.00
42 ZIP Code, 5.00
43 Statue of Liberty, 5.00
44 Elizabeth Blackwell, 5.00
45 Veterans of Foreign Wars, 4.00
46 Robert Frost, 4.00
47 EXPO '74, 4.00
48 Horse Racing, 4.00
49 Skylab, 4.00

50 Universal Postal Union, 6.00
51 Mineral Heritage, 5.00
52 Fort Harrod, 4.00
53 Continental Congress, 5.00
54 Chautauqua, 4.00
55 Kansas Wheat, 4.00
56 Energy Conservation, 4.00
57 6.3¢ Bulk Rate, 4.00
58 Sleepy Hollow, 4.00
59 Retarded Children, 4.00
60 Christmas, two dates, 5.00

1975
61 Benjamin West, 4.00
62 Pioneer, 4.00
63 Collective Bargaining, 4.00
64 Sybil Ludington, 4.00
65 Salem Poor, 4.00
66 Haym Salomon, 4.00
67 Peter Francisco, 4.00
68 Mariner, 4.00
69 Lexington & Concord, both cities, 4.00
70 Paul Laurence Dunbar, 4.00
71 D.W. Griffith, 4.00
72 Bunker Hill, 4.00
73 Military Uniforms, 5.00
74 Apollo Soyuz, 5.00
75 International Women's Year, 4.00
76 Postal Bicentennial, 4.00
77 World Peace Through Law, 5.00
78 Banking & Commerce, 4.00
79 Christmas, 4.00
80 Francis Parkman, 3.00
81 Freedom of the Press, 3.00
82 Old North Church, 3.00
83 Flag & Independence Hall, 3.00
84 Freedom to Assemble, 3.00
85 Liberty Bell Coil, 3.00
86 American Eagle & Shield, 3.00

1976
87 Sprit of '76, 4.00
88 25¢ & 31¢ Airmails, 3.00
89 Interphil, 3.00
90 Fifty State Flag Series, 25.00
91 Freedom to Assemble Coil, 3.00

92 Telephone Centennial, 3.00
93 Commercial Aviation, 3.00
94 Chemistry, 3.00
95 7.9¢ Bulk Rate, 3.00
96 Benjamin Franklin, 3.00
97 Bi Cent SS, 35.00
98 Declaration of Independence, 4.00
99 Olympics, 4.00
100 Clara Maass, 3.00
101 Adolph S. Ochs, 3.00
102 Christmas, 4.00
103 7.7¢ Bulk Rate, 3.00

1977
104 Washington at Princeton, 3.00
105 $1 Vending Machine Booklet Pane, perf. 10, 25.00
106 Sound Recording, 3.00
107 Pueblo Art, 4.00
108 Lindbergh Flight, 3.00
109 Colorado Centennial, 3.00
110 Butterflies, 4.00
111 Lafayette, 3.00
112 Skilled Hands, 4.00
113 Peace Bridge, 3.00
114 Herkimer at Oriskany, 3.00
115 Alta, California, 3.00
116 Articles of Confederation, 3.00
117 Talking Pictures, 3.00
118 Surrender at Saratoga, 3.00
119 Energy, 3.00
120 Christmas, Omaha, 3.00
121 Christmas, Valley Forge, 3.00
122 Petition for Redress Coil, 3.00
123 Petition for Redress sheet stamp, 3.00
124 1¢, 2¢, 3¢, 4¢ Americana, 3.00

1978
125 Carl Sandburg, 3.00
126 Indian Head Penny, 3.00
127 Captain Cook, Anchorage, 3.00
128 Captain Cook, Honolulu, 3.00
129 Harriet Tubman, 3.00
130 American Quilts, 4.00
131 16¢ Statue of Liberty, 3.00

132 Sandy Hook Lighthouse, 3.00
133 American Dance, 4.00
134 French Alliance, 3.00
135 Dr. Papanicolaou, 3.00
136 "A" Stamp, 3.00
137 Jimmie Rodgers, 3.00
138 CAPEX '78, 4.00
139 Oliver Wendell Holmes, 3.00
140 Photography, 3.00
141 Fort McHenry Flag, 3.00
142 George M. Cohan, 3.00
143 Rose Booklet single, 3.00
144 8.4¢ Bulk Rate, 3.00
145 Viking Missions, 3.00
146 Remote Outpost, 3.00
147 American Owls, 4.00
148 Wright Brothers, 3.00
149 American Trees, 4.00
150 Hobby Horse, 3.00
151 Andrea della Robbia, 3.00
152 $2 Kerosene Lamp, 7.00

1979
153 Robert F. Kennedy, 3.00
154 Martin Luther King, Jr., 3.00
155 International Year of the Child, 3.00
156 John Steinbeck, 3.00
157 Albert Einstein, 3.00
158 Octave Chanute, 4.00
159 Pennsylvania Toleware, 4.00
160 American Architecture, 4.00
161 Endangered Flora, 4.00
162 Seeing Eye Dogs, 3.00
163 $1 Americana, 5.00

164 Special Olympics, 3.00
165 $5 Americana, 10.00
166 30¢ Americana, 4.00
167 50¢ Americana, 4.00
168 Olympics, 3.00
169 John Paul Jones, 3.00
170 15¢ Olympic, 4.00
171 Gerard David Madonna, 3.00
172 Santa Claus, 3.00
173 3.1¢ Coil, 3.00
174 31¢ Olympic, 4.00
175 Will Rogers, 3.00
176 Vietnam Veterans, 3.00
177 Wiley Post, 4.00

1980
178 W. C. Fields, 3.00
179 Winter Olympics, 4.00
180 Windmills Booklet, 4.00
181 Benjamin Banneker, 2.00
182 Letter Writing, 3.00
183 1¢ Quill Pen Coil, 2.00
184 Frances Perkins, 2.00
185 Dolley Madison, 2.00
186 Emily Bissell, 2.00
187 3.5¢ Non-Profit Bulk Rate Coil, 2.00
188 Helen Keller/Anne Sullivan, 2.00
189 Veterans Administration, 2.00
190 General Bernardo de Galvez, 2.00
191 Coral Reefs, 3.00
192 Organized Labor, 2.00
193 Edith Wharton, 2.00
194 American Education, 2.00
195 Northwest Indian Masks, 3.00
196 Architecture, 3.00
197 Phillip Mazzei, 2.50

198 Stained Glass Window, 2.00
199 Antique Toys, 2.00
200 19¢ Sequoyah, 2.00
201 28¢ Scott A/M, 2.50
202 35¢ Curtiss A/M, 2.50

1981
203 Everett Dirksen, 2.00
204 Whitney M. Young, 2.00
205 "B" Sheet & Coil, 3.00
206 "B" Booklet Pane, 4.00
207 18¢ Flag Sheet & Coil, 3.00
208 18¢ Flag Booklet Pane, 4.00
209 12¢ Americana S & C, 3.00
210 Flowers Block (4), 4.00
211 American Red Cross, 2.00
212 George Mason, 2.00
213 Savings & Loan, 2.00
214 Animals Booklet Pane, 4.50
215 18¢ Surrey Coil, 2.50
216 Space Achievement (8), 4.00
217 17¢ Rachel Carson, 2.00
218 35¢ Dr. Charles Drew, 2.50
219 Professional Management, 2.00
220 17¢ Electric Car Coil, 2.50
221 Wildlife Habitat (4), 3.00
222 International Year Disabled, 2.00
223 Edna St. Vincent Millay, 2.00
224 Alcoholism, 2.00
225 Architecture (4), 3.00
226 Jones/Zaharis, 2.00
227 James Hoban, 2.00
228 Frederic Remington, 2.00
229 Yorktown/Virginia Capes, 2.00
230 Desert Plants (4), 3.00
231 Madonna, 2.00
232 Teddy Bear, 2.00
233 John Hanson, 2.00

Issue Date: April 23, 1981
First Day City: Fort Valley, Georgia
Designer: Lowell Nesbit
        New York City, New York
Modeler: Frank J. Waslick
Press: Gravure
Color: Pink, yellow, light red, light blue, dark blue and dark red
Image Area: 1.075 x 1.075 inches or 27.30 x 27.30 millimeters
Plate Number: One
Stamps to Pane: 48
Selvage: © U. S. Postal Service
        ® Use Correct ZIP Code
        ® Mr. ZIP

Flower Commemorative Stamps

A block of four 18-cent commemorative stamps featuring flowers will be issued April 23 in Fort Valley, Georgia. The flower stamps will be the first commemoratives to be issued reflecting the new First-Class postage rate of 18 cents which became effective March 22.

Magnificent bearers of color, flowers decorate our world. They are nature's way of dazzling the human eye. Lowell Nesbit of New York City captured this feeling in the original paintings he executed for these stamp designs. Mr. Nesbit specializes in large-scale paintings of flowers. His work is widely exhibited in both Europe and South America. The paintings he rendered feature popular large flowers cultivated in the United States: the camellia, the lily, the dahlia and the rose. They reflect interpretations of several of his previous paintings; however, they do not represent any specific species of flowers. These are Mr. Nesbit's first stamp designs.

Each of the full-color vignettes in the designs appears on a light pink background. The vignettes dominate the center of each design and, beneath each one, in one line of blue type, is the name of the flower and "USA 18¢."

STAMP COLLECTING KITS

U.S. Postal Service Stamp Collecting Kits are an easy, fun introduction to the fascinating world of stamps. Besides getting you over the hurdle of "where to start," USPS Kits are one of the best values available to the beginning collector. And they're a perfect way to expand into a topical collection.

Your local post office may have additional Collecting Kits beyond those featured here. Since availability may vary, you may wish to check more than one post office. **The American Revolution Kit,** introduced during 1980, contains a vivid selection of stamps (both U.S. and foreign) depicting one of the most famous struggles in history. Watch for kits of new topics coming to your local post office in early 1982.

Every USPS Collecting Kit contains four basic collecting tools: a 20-page, color-illustrated album with background information and display space for each stamp; a selection of genuine, colorful stamps ready for mounting; a convenient packet of mounting hinges; and The Introduction to Stamp Collecting, a 24-page booklet containing all the guidelines you need to start your own collection.

To request additional information, use the postal card following page 256.

COMMEMORATIVE MINT SETS

For the beginning and experienced collector alike, Commemorative Mint Sets a
a fascinating and convenient way to capture the spirit and history of this country
Each year the U.S. Postal Service issues a new Commemorative Mint Set that
includes all the commemorative stamps and Christmas stamps issued for that
year, along with a handy album for displaying them. Inside each colorfully illustrated album is a display area supplied with acetate strips to keep your stamps
mint fresh. There's also an interesting background story for each stamp and its
subject.

Commemorative Mint Sets are a good way to start a commemorative collection.
Or, if you've missed certain issues when they were available through your post
office, you can fill the gap in your collection with a Mint Set.

979   1980   1981

The **1981 Mint Set** contains 20 issues with a total of 40 individual stamps.
n addition to two colorful Christmas stamps which feature both contemporary
and traditional designs, this year's set includes the spectacular Space Achievement block of eight along with four stamp blocks of Flowers, Wildlife Habitats,
American Architecture, and Desert Plants. $8.25

The **1980 Mint Set** of Commemorative and Special Stamps contains sixteen
commemoratives. In addition to colorful, four-stamp blocks of Coral Reefs,
American Architecture, Northwest Indian Masks, and Winter Olympics, this set
includes two Christmas stamps in both contemporary and traditional designs.
$5.00

The **1979 Mint Set** contains a total of twenty-nine commemoratives, including
he exciting 1980 Olympics Set, and handsome blocks of four on Endangered
Flora, Pennsylvania Toleware, and American Architecture. $5.25

1980 DEFINITIVE MINT SET

For the first time, the U.S. Postal Service is offering a 1980 mint set of definitive stamps and postal stationery. Designed as a companion piece to the 1980 Commemorative Mint Set, it is similar in design and features an interesting narrative on each issue. The eight-page booklet contains three insert pages, complete with plastic strips, for mounting the stamps and stationery items.

Issued in a limited edition of 400,000 (compared with the annual commemorative mint set production of 1.2 million), each Definitive Set contains one of each of the 20 regular stamps, five postal cards, four embossed envelopes and one aerogramme. Paired with the 1980 commemorative mint set, it will provide collectors with one of every postal item issued by the Postal Service in 1980.

Definitive Mint Sets may be purchased at more than 13,000 Stamp Collecting Centers or by mail order from the Postal Service's Philatelic Sales Division, Washington, DC, 20265-9997. Retail price for the set is $6.50*(plus 50¢ postage and handling when ordered from the Sales Division). For additional information, send postal card following page 256.

PHILATELIC CENTERS AND PRODUCTS

In addition to the 13,000 Stamp Collecting Centers at post offices, the U.S. Postal Service also maintains more than 300 Philatelic Centers located in major population centers throughout the country. Each of these Centers carries an extensive range of stamps, stationery and collateral materials issued by the Postal Service.

Philatelic Centers have been developed to serve the collector and make it convenient for you to acquire the U.S. Postal Service philatelic products you require. Please check locally for the nearest Philatelic Center in your area.

Philatelic Centers offer the postal materials shown on these pages, as well as a number of other collector-oriented products.

Space Achievement Folder. A colorful booklet featuring a mint block of Space Achievement commemorative stamps is available at post office Stamp Collecting Centers. Spectacular NASA photographs taken from outer space accompany lively text.

Stamp Collecting Kits. U.S. Postal Service Stamp Collecting Kits are a quick introduction to the world of stamps. Check with your local post office to see which kits are currently available.

Souvenir Cards.
Souvenir Cards are issued to commemorate philatelic gatherings. To secure more information about Souvenir Cards, please send the card following Page 256.

Mint Sets.
Each year, the Postal Service issues a new Commemorative Mint Set. During 1981, the Postal Service also offered a special mint set folder containing all 1980 definitive stamps and postal stationery. Stop in at your local post office or Philatelic Center to secure these sets.

Women's Mint Set.
The Women's Mint Set honors 34 extraordinary women who have been recognized over the years on U.S. postage stamps. Sets can be purchased at your post office Stamp Collecting Center or at Philatelic Centers.

AMERICAN COMMEMORATIVE PANEL SERIES

The next time you come across a special occasion, why not mark it with an exceptional gift from the U.S. Postal Service?

Since 1972, we've annually offered limited edition Commemorative Panels to honor each new commemorative issue for that year, including specials like Christmas stamps. The Wildlife Commemorative Panel was the first issue, and the enthusiasm it received set a pace for all those that have followed.

When you select your first Commemorative Panel, we think you'll understand that enthusiasm. Each consists of a beautifully designed, 8½ x 11¼" page that features four or more newly-issued commemorative stamps in mint condition. Handsome intaglio-printed reproductions of fine, steel line engravings (many over a century old) complement the stamps, and thoughtful stories accompany each commemorative subject. The result is a fascinating display that quickly gets even the casual participant totally involved.

Commemorative Panels combine the finest examples of stamp art with quality reproductions of the engraver's craft. As gifts, awards or just a gesture to a friend or relative, they're simply wonderful. And they're collector's items in themselves. Why not share one with someone? Or, if you already have, treat yourself! Cost is $4 per panel plus 50¢ postage and handling fee. Yearly subsriptions are available at $64 (which includes each panel issued throughout the year).

For additional information, send postal card following page 256.

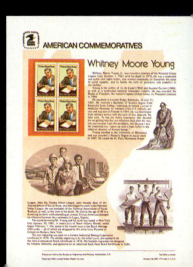

MAJOR U.S. PHILATELIC SOCIETIES AND PUBLICATIONS

Philatelic Societies

American Air Mail Society
102 Arbor Rd.
Cinnaminson, NJ 08077

American First Day Cover Society
Mrs. Monte Eiserman
Membership Chairman
14359 Chadbourne
Houston, TX 77079

American Philatelic Society
Box 800
State College, PA 16801
   A full complement of services and resources for the philatelist. Membership offers: American Philatelic Research Library; expertizing service; estate advisory service; translation services; a stamp theft committee which functions as a clearing house for stamp theft information; and a speakers' bureau.

American Stamp Dealer's Association
840 Willis Ave.
Albertson, NY 11507

American Topical Association
3308-W North 50th Street
Milwaukee, WI 53216
   Concentrates on the specialty of topical collecting. Offers handbooks on specific topics; an exhibition award; a slide and film loan service; information and translation services; and an heirs' and estate service.

Bureau Issues Association
19 Maple Street
Arlington, MA 02174

Collectors Club, Inc.
22 East 35th Street
New York, NY 10016
   Regular services include library and reading rooms, a publication and lectures on philatelic subjects. The group also honors a great American collector annually and actively supports national and international exhibitions.

Council of Philatelic Organizations
2918 Michele Dr.
Norristown, PA 19403
   An organization comprised of 175 member philatelic groups. Objectives include: to educate the general public to the many benefits and pleasures of collecting stamps.

Junior Philatelists of America
Box 195
Minetto, NY 13115
   Provides an auction department, library service, tape and slide service, stamp identification and translation services.

National Association of Precancel Collectors
5121 Park Blvd.
Wildwood, NJ 08260

The Perfins Club
10550 Western Ave.
Stanton, CA 90680

Philatelic Foundation
270 Madison Ave.
New York, NY 10016
   Known for their expertization service, the Foundation also maintains an Expert Committee and publishes educational information.

Plate Block Collector Club
Box 937
Homestead, FL 33030

Plate Number Society
9600 Colesville Rd.
Silver Springs, MD 20901

Postal History Society
Box 20
Bayside, NY 11361

Post Mark Collectors Club
Bernice White
3487 Firstenberger Rd.
Marion, OH 43302

Society of Philatelic Americans
Box 9041
Wilmington, DE 19809
   Monthly journal, sales circuits, exchange department, expertization and insurance.

United Postal Stationery Society
Mrs. J. Thomas
Box 48
Redlands, CA 92373

The United States Possessions Philatelic Society
141 Lyford Drive
Tiburon, CA 94920

The Universal Ship Cancellation Society
P.O. Box 13
New Britain, CT 06050

Brookman Price List of U.S. Stamps
Minneapolis, MN

Catalogue of United States Souvenir Cards
The Washington Press
Florham Park, NJ 07932

First Day Cover Catalogue (U.S.-U.N.)
Washington Press
Florham Park, NJ 07932

Souvenir Pages Price List
Charles D. Simmons
P.O. Box 6238
Buena Park, CA 90622

Commemorative Panel Price List
Frank Riolo
P.O. Box 1540
Delray Beach, FL 33444

Fleetwoods Standard First Day Cover Catalog
Unicover Corporation
Cheyenne, WY 82001

Harris Illustrated Postage Stamp Catalog
Boston, MA 02117

Minkus New World Wide Stamp Catalogue
NY

American Air Mail Catalogue
American Air Mail Society
Cinnaminson, NJ 08077

Scott Standard Postage Stamp Catalogue
NY

Magazines and Newspapers

Canadian Stamp News
1567 Sedlescomb Drive
Mississauga, Ont. L4X1M5

Linn's Stamp News
Box 29
Sidney, OH 45367

Mekeel's Weekly Stamp News
Box 1660
Portland, ME 04104

Minkus Stamp Journal
116 West 32nd Street
New York, NY 10001

Scott's Monthly Stamp Journal
3 East 57th St.
New York, NY 10022

Stamps
153 Waverly Place
New York, NY 10014

Stamp Collector
Box 10
Albany, OR 97321

Stamp Show News & Philatelic Review
1839 Palmer Ave.
Larchmont, NY 10538

Stamp World
Box 29
Sidney, OH 45367
Monthly publication directed to informational and feature articles on stamp subjects, stamp designs and other general topics.

Philatelic Literature

Brookman, Lester G. *The 19th Century Postage Stamps of the United States* (3 volumes). NY, 1968.

Chase, Carroll C. *The 3¢ Stamps of the United States, 1942.*

Johl, Max G. *The United States Commemorative Stamps of the Twentieth Century, 1947.*

Linn's World Stamp Almanac, Sidney, OH, 1978.

Mueller, Barbara R. *United States Postage Stamps, 1958.*

Patrick, Douglas and Mary. *The Musson Stamp Dictionary, 1972.*

D.G. Phillips Publ. Co. *The American Stampless Cover Catalog, 1978.*

Scheele, Carl H. *A Short History of the Mail Service, 1970.*

Scott's New Handbook for Philatelists. NY, 1967.

Thorp, Prescott H. *Stamped Envelopes and Wrappers of the United States.* Netcong, NJ, 1954.

United Postal Stationery Society. *United States Postal Card Catalog.* Albany, OR, 1975.

United States Postal Service *United States Postage Stamp, Pub. 9.* Washington, DC, 1970 as revised.
A compendium of philatelic information on U.S. stamps. Updated periodically. Available through the Government Printing Office.

INDEX OF COMMEMORATIVE STAMPS & STORIES

278